JOURNEY INTO ISLAM

Akbar Ahmed speaking at one of the main mosques in Deoband, India, the most orthodox center of Islam in South Asia. On the left is the head cleric, while team member Hailey Woldt sits on the right.

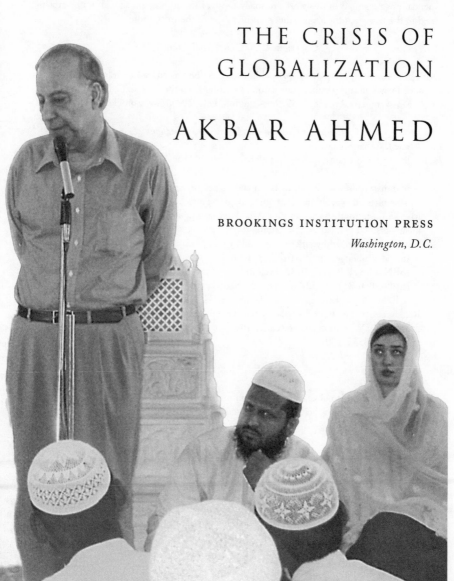

JOURNEY INTO ISLAM

THE CRISIS OF GLOBALIZATION

AKBAR AHMED

BROOKINGS INSTITUTION PRESS

Washington, D.C.

Copyright © 2007 by Akbar Ahmed

Library of Congress Cataloging-in-Publication data
Ahmed, Akbar S.
    Journey into Islam : the crisis of globalization / Akbar Ahmed.
        p.   cm.
    Summary: "Presents a tour of Islam and its peoples as it follows author's anthropological expedition to the three major regions of the Muslim world—the Middle East, South Asia, and East Asia. Reveals unique information on large, often misunderstood populations, describing the experiences and perceptions of ordinary Muslims, women, and youth"—Provided by publisher.
    Includes bibliographical references and index.
    ISBN-13: 978-0-8157-0132-3 (cloth : alk. paper)
    ISBN-10: 0-8157-0132-2 (cloth : alk. paper)
    1. Religious awakening—Islam. 2. Islam—21st century. 3. Globalization—Religious aspects—Islam. 4. Islamic renewal—Islamic countries. 5. Islamic countries—Description and travel. I. Title.
    BP163.A3535 2007
    297.09'0511—dc22   2007010770

                                 3 5 7 9 8 6 4 2

The paper used in this publication meets minimum requirements of theAmerican National Standard for Information Sciences—Permanence of Paper for Printed Library Materials: ANSI Z39.48-1992.

Typeset in Adobe Caslon

Composition by Cynthia Stock
Silver Spring, Maryland

Printed by R. R. Donnelley
Harrisonburg, Virginia

CONTENTS

ACKNOWLEDGMENTS

THIS BOOK IS the product of a journey to the Muslim world with a team of assistants dedicated to unraveling the complexities of Islam. Keenly aware of the need to see into Muslim societies, I initiated a project that would allow me to experience them firsthand. Along the way, I benefited immensely from the collective wisdom, insights, and support of many people, including generous hosts in the field, too numerous to name but all of invaluable assistance.

This project would not have been possible without the extraordinary support of Interim President Cornelius Kerwin and Dean Louis Goodman of American University, Stephen Cohen and Peter Singer of the Brookings Institution, and Luis Lugo and Tim Shah of the Pew Forum on Religion and Public Life. I am particularly indebted to Dean Goodman for his friendship and support before, during, and after the project. Most encouraging, I was appointed principal investigator for the project "Islam in the Age of Globalization" along with another Muslim as my research assistant at a time of growing Islamophobia. This seemed a sign of American willingness to understand the Muslim world on its own terms.

I am also extremely grateful for the friendship and support of Jean and Steve Case of the Case Foundation, Ambassador Doug Holladay and Robert Woody of the Buxton Initiative, Lachlan and Martha Reed, John Goodman, Nasser Kazeminy, Millicent and Robert Monks, Seeme and Malik Hasan of the Hasan Family Foundation to Promote Understanding between the United States and the Muslim World, and Haruhisa Handa of the International Shinto Foundation.

A marvelous team worked with me on this project from start to finish with unfailing belief in and commitment to its objectives. I deeply appreciate what they did to help me survive the physically exhausting and emotionally challenging journey, not to mention the intensive phase of writing this book. They filled me with optimism and hope for the future. Each participated and contributed in different ways, playing an integral role in the whole. Undaunted by schedule changes or even illness, they pressed on with collecting data or conducting interviews, their desire to learn and enthusiasm a constant source of inspiration. The team was with me when I interviewed presidents and princes, toured universities and madrassahs, spoke at international centers, and visited synagogues, churches, mosques, and even Hindu and Sikh temples. I learned so much from them that our roles often became reversed, the students becoming the teachers.

Hadia Mubarak, my officially designated research assistant during and after the field trip, is an Arab-American Muslim with an abiding interest in the subject and its possible implications for the Muslim community in the United States. Hailey Woldt and Frankie Martin, two of my star students in an honors program I taught at American University, overcame several obstacles to accompany me. Tridivesh Singh Maini, another student, accompanied me in India and put together an excellent program there. Jonathan Hayden, my office assistant, joined me during the last stages of the journey. I was delighted to see Zeenat, my wife, and Nafees, my daughter, who met us in Pakistan, and Amineh, my oldest daughter, fresh from obtaining a Ph.D. in anthropology at Cambridge University, also joined us during the last stages of the journey, and I benefited from her presence and anthropological insights. In addition, Jerusha Ghazanfari and Aishah Ma'ruf assisted me in Washington, D.C., Talha Kose in Istanbul, and Krystle Kaul in Cairo. Mela Norman and Marta Zoladz helped sort the data and chart the findings upon our return.

Those who would complain of the lack of discipline and commitment among the young should look to the team's accomplishments in the summer of 2006, on our return from the Muslim world. Between mid-April and August of that year, we codified the questionnaires, wrote up the interviews, and held a seminar to discuss our findings, and my book based on the journey was completed—all this under very trying conditions: Hadia's mother was hospitalized at this time, Jonathan had suffered a broken hand, Frankie often worked well into the early hours researching some fact for the book, and Hailey toiled week after week, even on Saturdays and Sundays, after already taking an entire term off from university to go on the field trip. She was the only one of the team to accompany me from start to finish, and largely because of her untiring commitment, energy, and insights, I was able to complete the first draft of this book in three months. Also, almost all the photographs in the book were taken either by Hailey or with her camera. Her parting words to me and my family at the end of that grueling summer captured her enthusiasm: "I will remember this time as some of the happiest months of my life, learning . . . and truly living as you all have shown me how to."

Throughout the journey, I was invited to lecture at various institutions and events: the U.S.–Islamic World Forum at Doha, the Islamic Research Center in Istanbul, a Friday sermon in a Damascus mosque, the Royal Institute for Interfaith Studies and the Princess Sumaya University for Technology in Amman, the Sindh Club in Karachi, the National Institute of Historical and Cultural Research in Islamabad, Hamdard and Jamia Millia Islamia universities in New Delhi, a Soka Gakkai event in Kuala Lumpur, the International Institute of Islamic Thought and Civilization and International Islamic University of Malaysia in Kuala Lumpur, the University Tun Abdul Razak in Petaling Jaya near Kuala Lumpur, and the State Islamic University in Jakarta. I would like to thank these institutions for their gracious hospitality in welcoming me and my team.

I am grateful to the following for their comments on different drafts of the manuscript: Roger Boase, Rajmohan Gandhi, Anthony Giddens, Hillel Levine, Judea Pearl, Lawrence Rosen, Sir Jonathan Sacks, Tamara Sonn, and Elie Wiesel.

My sincere thanks also go to all those at Brookings who helped to steer this book into print, especially Steve Grand. I am particularly grateful to Bob Faherty of the Brookings Institution Press for his enthusiasm for the project and to those who worked ably and diligently on the book's production: Larry Converse, Vicky Macintyre, Janet Walker, and Susan Woollen.

Finally, I owe more than words can convey to my loving and wonderful family, each one contributing so much to the understanding of Islam around us: Zeenat, Amineh, Arsallah, Babar, Fatima, Umar, Melody, and Nafees. I would like to single out Zeenat, who brought sagacity and understanding to the complex issues raised by the project and was wholeheartedly involved in completing it. The range and depth of her contribution were extraordinary: she contributed to and understood the central ideas, participated in the interviews, and helped complete the various drafts in spite of the time when she was ill or when she was exhausted from her work at the office and running the house. I thank her for her devotion to the project and can only marvel at her steadfastness, companionship, and friendship with love in my heart and gratitude in my soul. This book could not have been completed without her, and therefore I wish to dedicate it to Zeenat with love.

AKBAR AHMED
April 2007

JOURNEY
INTO ISLAM

ONE

An Anthropological Excursion into the Muslim World

"The actions of Osama bin Laden, Hezbollah, Hamas, and the Taliban, *even if* they kill women and children, are perfectly justified in Islam." These chilling words, presaging more murder and mayhem, were casually uttered on a sunny day under a blue Indian sky by the politest of young men. The speaker was our host, Aijaz Qasmi, always smiling faintly behind his thick glasses and beard, and dressed in traditional South Asian Muslim attire, white linen pants with a long coat and small white skullcap. He was escorting me and my companions to an important stop on our journey into Islam: Deoband, the preeminent *madrassah*, or religious educational center, of South Asian Islam. Aijaz was one of its chief ideologues.

Deoband has given its name to a school of thought within Islam. Like the better-known Wahhabi movement in the Arab world, it stands for assertive action in defending, preserving, and transmitting Islamic tradition and identity. And like the Muslim Brotherhood in the Middle East, Deoband is a beacon of Islamic identity to many Muslims. To many in the West, Deoband and its spokespersons such as Aijaz would be the "enemy."

As we neared our destination, the landscape grew desolate; there were no road signs in any language, no gas stations, not even tea stalls. With lofty hopes of learning something about the state and mood of Islam in the age of globalization, I began my journey on this isolated narrow road several hours from Delhi. If we were taken hostage or chopped up into little

1

bits, I whispered to my young American team, "no one will know about it for at least two weeks."

This was an attempt at levity to keep our travels from becoming too daunting for my companions—my students, Hailey Woldt and Frankie Martin—eager to venture into the world with the boldness that only comes with youth. Since I was an "honored" guest and said that Hailey was like my "daughter" and Frankie like my "son," I was certain we would be perfectly safe. Although these students had read E. M. Forster's classic depiction of Islam in *A Passage to India,* they had also been brought up on *Indiana Jones and the Temple of Doom.* They were accompanying me on this journey with total confidence, trusting their professor to bring them back safely. Like Professor Jones, I had to keep them out of harm's way yet enable them to participate fully in the study.

Neither of them had been to the Muslim world before, now a particularly troubled one. Undeterred by this or the concerns of their family and friends, they took time off from their academic year, paid for the travel themselves, and placed their trust in me. No teacher can expect a higher reward, and I hope the reader will appreciate why they became such a special part of the project for me. I know they reciprocated.[1]

During our conversation in the van, Aijaz, who was sitting in the front seat and looking back, seemed to brush off any of Hailey's questions and direct the conversation to me. As a Muslim, I understood that for him this was orthodox behavior. He was honoring Hailey's status as a woman by not looking at her. To do so would be considered a sign of disrespect. He would have noted with appreciation that she was dressed in impeccable Muslim clothes, which she had gotten from Pakistan: a white, loose *shalwar kameez* and a white veil to cover her head in the mosque, as is customary.

He won't look at me, she scribbled on a note in obvious indignation and passed it to me discreetly. Although I could see Hailey emerging as a perceptive observer of culture and custom in the tradition of the great Western female travelers to the Muslim world of the twentieth century, her American sense of impatience was never too far beneath the surface. I signaled to her to calm down. This was neither the time nor the place to escalate a clash of cultures.

One question she had posed was whether attacks against innocent people were justified in the Quran. We were talking of *jihad,* which derives from an Arabic word meaning "to strive" but which people in the West have come to associate with aggressive military action. For the Prophet, the term had two connotations: the "greatest jihad," the struggle to elevate oneself spiritually and morally, which has nothing to do with violence, least of all against innocent women and children; and the "lesser jihad," the defense of one's family and community in the face of attack. In this case, too, there is no mention of aggression. According to Aijaz, Muslim attacks on Americans and Israelis, which he considered one entity, were actually acts of self-defense; furthermore, American and Israeli women and children were not necessarily innocent, as was clear from their support of the military committing atrocities in Afghanistan, Iraq, and Palestine. Aijaz believed that Americans backed by Israelis even encouraged torture in places like Abu Ghraib and Guantánamo Bay. Since the American and Israeli people could stop these crimes but were not doing so, they were theoretically guilty of the same atrocities.

Aijaz had made these arguments in a recent bestseller written in Urdu, *Jihad and Terrorism*.[2] Then in its seventh edition, the book reflected Muslim outrage because Muslims were under attack and being killed throughout the world. So-called Islamic violence, wrote Aijaz, was a justifiable defense against "American" and "Israeli barbarism." Aijaz felt his way of life, his culture, and his religion were facing an onslaught. These "barbarians," said Aijaz, were even assailing the holy Prophet of Islam, "peace be upon him." Hence every Muslim was morally obligated to join the jihad, that is, the defense of the great faith of Islam and their "brothers" all over the world. Speaking passionately now, Aijaz told us that Muslims will never give up their faith, will defend Islam to the death, and will triumph in the U.S. war on Islam. For Aijaz, the true champions of Islam were the Taliban—and Osama bin Laden, to whose name he added the reverential title of *sheikh*. This attitude, I thought, was going to complicate matters for Muslims like me, who wished to promote Islam's authentic teachings of compassion and peace.

To see whether he tolerated more moderate Muslim views, I asked his opinion of Mohammed Ali Jinnah, the founder of Pakistan and a leader who promoted women's rights, human rights, and respect for the law. To my surprise, he did not condemn Jinnah as a godless secularist but thought him a great political leader, though not a great *Muslim* leader. This meant he was not necessarily a role model for Muslims and was thus irrelevant for Islam. Jinnah could be acknowledged for parochial reasons, to be sure. A redeeming feature, for Aijaz, was that one of Jinnah's close supporters was a well-known Deoband religious figure. For Aijaz, the crux of every argument was the Deoband connection. Aijaz's own surname—Qasmi—was inspired by Maulana Qasim Nanouwoti, the founding father of Deoband.

When I sought his views about the mystical side of Islam, Aijaz became circumspect. I mentioned Moin-uddin Chisti, the famous Sufi mystic (1141–1230 C.E.) who promoted a compassionate form of Islam and who is buried in Ajmer, in the heart of Rajasthan deep in rural India. Aijaz said he had never visited Ajmer, looked away in silence, and left the matter there. Perhaps Ajmer was a dark and dangerous avenue for him to explore.

On the subject of technology, Aijaz's answers were again surprising. Instead of condemning modern technology as an extension of the West, which I thought he might do, he proudly pulled out his business card bearing the title "Web Editor" for the Deoband website. In this capacity, Aijaz explained, he was able to address, guide, and instruct thousands of young Muslims throughout South Asia. He saw no contradiction in using Western technology to disseminate the Islamic message.

This and other of Aijaz's remarks made all too clear the enormity of the gap between the United States and the Muslim world. Frankie's sober comment captured it simply and precisely: "I thought things were bad while I was in D.C., but it's even worse." On that day, these young Americans came face to face with their nation's greatest challenge in the twenty-first century: the crisis with the Muslim world.

Aijaz's Vision of Globalization

Aijaz was in fact commenting on globalization without once using the word. In his mind, globalization was synonymous with the greed of multinational corporations that exploited the natural resources of Muslim countries, the anger vented by the United States in the bombing of Afghanistan and then Iraq after September 11, 2001, and the ignorance displayed in the Western media about Aijaz's religion, culture, and traditions. Aijaz also associated it with a culture of gratuitous sex and violence, glorified by Hollywood. Americans, he added, constitute only 6 percent of the world's population yet consume 60 percent of the world's natural resources, as confirmed by the epidemic of obesity throughout the country and the extravagance of even the middle class.

Aijaz had unwittingly equated the actions of the United States—and, correspondingly, the forces of globalization—with the "three poisons" that the Buddha had warned could destroy individuals and even societies: greed, anger, and ignorance. In Islamic theology the "cure" for precisely these vices is *adl* (justice), *ihsan* (compassion/goodness), and *ilm* (knowledge). The antidote for greed is justice for others; anger can only be controlled by compassion; and ignorance dispelled by knowledge.

I dwell on Aijaz's impassioned arguments at the outset of this discussion because they epitomize the crisis that globalization has wrought on the Muslim world and that is essential for Western minds to grasp. Contrary to the concepts of adl and ihsan, television screens are showing Muslims that CEOs of multinational corporations can amass tremendous wealth while other people in their own countries and elsewhere are starving, that thousands of innocent people can be killed in Afghanistan and Iraq, that the Palestinians in the heartland of the Muslim world can be oppressed without receiving any help or hope from the West, that hundreds of millions of Muslims can live under harsh governments with little hope of justice. Muslims feel they have no voice in these circumstances and are not invited to participate in many of the global events that concern them. To add insult to injury, American culture has invaded their society through the media and the deluge of Western products. The Muslim reaction to all this is colored with passion and anger. To cope with what is perceived as an out-of-control world and preserve their sense of security, Muslims are returning to their roots.

These overwhelming circumstances have encouraged some Muslim communities to cloak themselves with a defensive, militant, and strained attitude toward the West. This outlook, promulgated by influential leaders of these communities, threatens and unsettles human discourse globally, because it values indifference and cruelty, permits men like bin Laden to become heroes, and goes against the grain of notions of justice, compassion, and wisdom common to all religious traditions.

Since the "war on terror" was launched, communities in Iraq, and to some degree Afghanistan, have descended into anarchy, allowing ancient religious, tribal, and sectarian rivalries to surface once again. In the absence of daily calm, people begin to look at the dictatorship of Saddam Hussein, for example, with something close to nostalgia. People live in a perpetual state of uncertainty: not knowing whether their homes are safe day or night, whether they will arrive at work, or whether their children will return home from school. Even worse, the killers remain unknown and at large. Some blame American soldiers, others the shadowy insurgents, and still others elements within the Iraqi government forces. The war on terror is degenerating into a war of all against all. Taking a page from English philosopher Thomas Hobbes, Muslim jurists have historically considered tyranny preferable to anarchy, and this was reiterated in our conversations across the Muslim world. Over a millennium ago, Imam Malik, a highly influential jurist and founder of one of the four primary legal schools in Islam, stated: "One hour of anarchy is worse than sixty years of tyranny."[3]

While no one denies the great benefits of globalization—economic development policies like microfinancing have lifted millions out of poverty in India and Bangladesh, and new technologies have permitted the swift distribution of medical and relief aid to Pakistan's earthquake victims and to the survivors of Indonesia's tsunami—many of the world's citizens associate globalization with a lack of compassion. In better times, compassion could have prevented the savage cruelties of the past few years, such as the shooting of an entire Haditha family by American soldiers and the beheading of Nick Berg in Iraq and of Daniel Pearl in Pakistan. Since the war on terror began, neither side has regained its sense of balance, compassion, and wisdom that it once held so dear.

Throughout our journey, each and every discussion led directly or indirectly to events that took place far away in America on September 11, 2001, and to the passions generated by that day. The United States and the Muslim world had become irreversibly connected in an adversarial relationship, and henceforth every action taken by one side would elicit a reaction from the other. September 11 changed and challenged both worlds in unexpected ways.

September 11, 2001

On September 11, 2001, a few minutes before 9 a.m., I walked into a classroom at American University in Washington, D.C., having joined the teaching staff only a few days earlier. I was about to hold my second class on the subject of Islam, which at that point seemed of remote interest to the young Americans seated before me. I wondered whether I would ever get their attention.

I had hardly begun explaining that Islam can only be understood in the complex framework of theology, sociology, and international affairs, that its story centers on a major traditional civilization confronting the forces of globalization, when two students abruptly left the class, only to return a few minutes later looking dazed and agitated. A ripple of hushed murmurs spread throughout the room. The only words I could make out were, "Something terrible has happened." A few more students walked out of the class, their cell phones in hand. Muslims had flown a plane into a building in New York, someone whispered. An ashen-faced student said a plane full of passengers had also smashed into the Pentagon, only a few miles away from our campus. This was beginning to sound like an implausible Hollywood film.

As I tried to continue my discussion of U.S.-Muslim relations, little did I realize that the most climactic moment of American history in the twenty-first century was taking place right outside our walls and a few hundred miles to the north. It did not take long for the enormity of the morning's events to sink in. Whatever had happened and whoever was responsible, Muslims everywhere would be tainted by the tragedies in New York, Washington, and Pennsylvania. The world would never be the same again.

What was transpiring was a massive Muslim failure. Not only were the perpetrators Muslims, but they had committed an act forbidden in Islam, namely the killing of innocent people. On a deeper level, Muslim leaders had failed to adapt to the rules of the modern world, and Muslim scholars had failed to disseminate their wisdom throughout their societies. Equally important, the world at large had neglected to understand Islam and accommodate one of its great and widespread religions.

Before arriving in Washington, I had spent many years explaining the complexities of Islam to a variety of people in different forums. At times I spoke to Muslim audiences to help them understand their world. As someone who had lived and worked in both Muslim and Western nations, I suspected that a storm of unimaginable ferocity was brewing, and when it finally did arrive on September 11, the need for understanding had become more urgent than ever before.

I was confident, however, that Americans would react with common sense, compassion, and wisdom. Such a response would not only show moral strength but also set the planet on a sound course for the future.

Little did I suspect that the response would come so swiftly and consist of unalloyed anger.

As a scholar teaching Islam and a Muslim living in the United States, I saw that I was facing the greatest challenge of my life. I resolved to put to good use my education, my friendships, and experiences in different Muslim communities: I would redouble my efforts to help non-Muslims and Muslims alike appreciate the true features of Islam and thereby forge a bond between them. Without that common understanding, the entire world would sink deeper into conflict.

Since then, not a day has passed that I have not spent time talking about Islam—in the media, on campus, or with colleagues committed to interfaith dialogue. This book, which is the result of research conducted in nine Muslim countries and among Muslims living in the West, is part of that effort. The book is about that terrible day in September, the events leading up to it, the subsequent developments, and their implications for the immediate future and beyond. It is about the clash between Western nations and Islam—perhaps the most misunderstood of all religions—in an age of startling interconnectedness, when events in one part of the world make an almost instant impact on another part, drawing distant societies into immediate contact. It is, in essence, an attempt to identify the global problems societies face, to suggest solutions, and above all, to appeal to the powerful and prosperous to join in creating wider understanding and friendship between different communities through compassion, wisdom, and restraint.

When Worlds Collide

The events of the past few years have cast an ominous shadow over our planet. They have unleashed what President George W. Bush has termed a global "war on terror." It is like no other war in the past. There is neither a visible nor identifiable enemy, and there is no end in sight. It is not really about religions or civilizations, yet both are involved. Islam is not the central issue, yet it is widely believed to be inextricably linked with the widespread violence and insecurity. The cause is not globalization—the transformations taking place in technology, transport, economic development, media communications, and the conduct of international politics—yet because of the war, the pressures of change are advancing on traditional societies such as Islamic ones. Never before in history has it been more urgent to define elusive terms like "war" and "religion," to exercise wisdom in human relations, to recognize superficial opinions (in the media, these may be little more than prejudices related in thirty-second sound bites yet they are readily accepted as fact), or to decry cruelty and indifference to human suffering.

This global war is not about the end of time, yet presidents around the globe—both Muslim and non-Muslim—behave as if they are recklessly marching toward Armageddon. To many, the apocalyptic view is confirmed because of the widespread violence, anarchy, and the lack of justice—signs that the end of time is at hand. While Christian Evangelists talk fervently of the Second Coming of Jesus and the final battle between good and evil (in which it is implied that Muslims will be cast as the anti-Christ), most Muslim Shia await the return of the Hidden Imam who will lead them in a similar conflict. To complicate matters, Muslims believe Jesus will be on their side in the battle against evil and that they will triumph. President Bush's policies, now known as the Bush Doctrine, which is based on notions such as "preemptive strike" and "regime change," and Mahmoud Ahmadinejad's statements calling for the eradication of Israel thus become the logical first steps toward the realization of this prophecy of confrontation between good and evil. Never has there been such a need for those rarely, if ever, mentioned words—"compassion" and "love."

September 11, 2001, marked the collision of two civilizations: that of the West, led and represented by the United States, and that composed of Muslim societies, all followers of Islam. In Samuel Huntington's thesis, this is part of an ongoing historic clash between Western and non-Western civilizations, which American commentators have further reduced to a confrontation between the United States and Islam. As if to drive home the point, the publishers of the first paperback edition of Huntington's book on the clash had two flags juxtaposed on the cover, one representing the stars and stripes of the United States and the other a white crescent and star against a green background.[4] The matter is somewhat more complex.

Both civilizations were ethnically diverse, populated by communities with different historical backgrounds, and they were already in a tense relationship. The United States, freshly triumphant from the collapse of its old adversary, the Soviet Union, was psychologically ready to stand up to another global threat. The provocative rhetoric of some Muslims, such as Osama bin Laden, and the bombings of the American embassies in Africa and of the U.S.S. *Cole,* had been the initial justification for targeting the Muslim world. Muslims were equally frustrated by a number of concerns: American impotence in resolving the Palestinian and Kashmir problem, the abandonment of Afghanistan after its population was decimated in fighting the Soviet Union, and the stationing of American troops in Saudi Arabia, home to Islam's holiest sites.

Even so, the wreckage, blood, and confusion of September 11 shocked the vast majority of the Muslim world, which sympathized with the grieving Americans. Public gatherings of support and prayers for the departed were held in Cairo, Tehran, and Islamabad. This goodwill did not last. Sorrow and sympathy turned into anger when the United States vented its fury on Afghanistan and, later, Iraq. As the United States continued its seemingly blind pursuit of the elusive goals of democracy and security, the relationship between the two worlds descended into conflict, and they appeared to move farther and farther apart.

I had known a different United States. Two decades ago I was a visiting professor at the Institute for Advanced Study at Princeton, fresh from the rugged and isolated hills and mountains of Waziristan in Pakistan, now known as the place where bin Laden may be hiding. I was enchanted by the serene lakes, forests, and walks of the institute and dazzled by my distinguished colleagues, some Nobel Prize winners. The Americans I met were warm, open, and welcoming. Although I recognized this community did not fully represent American society, it left a lasting impression of American generosity, respect for learning, and openness to new ideas. When deciding in the summer of 2000 where to live, I easily chose the United States. That is how I found myself in Washington on September 11, 2001, when Islam made a direct, dramatic, and indelible entry onto the world stage.

The nineteen hijackers were Muslim. They had destroyed key financial symbols of globalization in New York and attacked the foremost military symbol of the United States. They had also killed 2,973 innocent civilians, with another 24 missing and presumed dead. The United States, the very embodiment of the concept and practice of globalization, was struck at its heart. These dire acts were also a serious blow to the values of justice, compassion, and knowledge that I admired in both civilizations.

The United States, the sole superpower of the world and the only one with the capacity to lead the way in meeting global challenges, instead paid court to anger, its energies and resources focused on exacting revenge. With Muslim anger and frustration mounting as well, both civilizations let hatred and prejudice dominate the new chapter in globalization. Since 9/11 both have turned their backs on other global crises of serious proportions, none of which will be resolved until the world of Islam is brought into a mutually respectful partnership with the rest of the world.

This will not be easy. If anything, 9/11 underlined the deep philosophic and historical divisions between the West and the Muslim world. The perception of Islam as out of step with the West is at the heart of Western self-definition. The West believes it has successfully come to terms with and has balanced faith and reason, whereas Islam has not. It is this contradiction between the West, supposedly dominated by secularist and rational thought, and traditional Muslim society that is seen as the basis for friction and misunderstanding. Is it to be assumed then that Islam, as some of its critics claim, is incompatible with reason?

Until half a millennium ago—in what Europe calls the Middle Ages—faith and reason did exist in comfortable harmony and accommodation in Islam. Scholars argued that faith enhanced understanding of the secular and material world and therefore deepened faith itself. As a consequence, the sacred text was reinterpreted. Many Muslim thinkers argued that if the Quran appeared to contradict what reason states God should be like, then the text needed to be reexamined and even reinterpreted in the light of contemporary perceptions. God, they said, has given humans not only the Word but also reason, which serves as a guide to the text.

About three centuries ago, reason began overtaking faith in Christian societies, necessitating the separation of church and state, and promoting rationalism, logic, and science, along with industrial progress. Material improvement soon became the primary goal of human society and in its highest form precluded religion, which, it was said, clung to outdated traditions. The Industrial Revolution and subsequent influence of capitalist thinking and practices were evidence of this new emphasis.

From the nineteenth century onward, European nations following this path expanded their power in the world, colonizing and exploiting less developed societies and bringing much of the Muslim world directly under the sway of European imperialism. By the middle of the twentieth century, these Muslim lands began reemerging in different political forms as a result of diverse "independence" struggles. Some aspired to establish democracies, others were satisfied to embrace royal dynasties propped up by Western powers, and still others looked to socialist models, which were then fashionable and supported by Moscow.

Since the late twentieth century, the Muslim world has plunged into the age of globalization, which to many of its people resembles a new form of Western imperialism. Its emphasis is on producing the most goods at the lowest cost, along the way accumulating wealth for some and higher standards of living regardless of the cost to society. Neither faith, in its pure spiritual sense, nor reason, based in classical notions of justice and logic, appears to figure prominently in the philosophy of globalization. The absence of faith and reason along with the events of 9/11 have further distorted the West's approach to Islam.

Journey to the Muslim World

All these factors have created a great deal of consternation in the Muslim world. As a result, the voices claiming to speak on behalf of Islam since 9/11 have been divergent and conflicting. Struck by this turmoil and the West's poor understanding of it, I decided to return to the Muslim world to hear what Muslims were actually saying and experiencing without the filter of CNN or BBC news and to assess how they were responding to globalization. Too often, visiting scholars become immersed in their own theories and neglect to look outside at the real Muslim world. I wished to avoid this mistake by observing, talking to, and listening to Muslims. When I discussed the idea of a long fieldwork journey of this nature with American University, the Brookings Institution, and the Pew Forum on Religion and Public Life, they all gave it their support.

One obvious way to better understand Muslim society, it seemed, was to find out who has inspired its members and shaped their values from the past to the present. To this end, it was important to learn which books they are reading, how the Internet and international media are affecting their lives, and ultimately whether the Muslim psyche can be defined and how it relates to Islam. This was not going to be a typical "think tank" study consisting of interviews with like-minded counterparts in comfortable surroundings. Rather, it would be a genuine attempt to delve into Muslim society and document the experiences and perceptions of ordinary Muslims across a broad geographical spectrum.

The regions we visited—the Middle East, South Asia, and Far East Asia—differ in several important respects. A distinguishing feature of the Middle East is that it has a common language, Arabic, which is also the language in which the Quran was revealed to the Prophet; furthermore, the Prophet himself was an Arab. Because the Quran and the life of the Prophet form the foundation of Islamic ideology and identity, Arabs have a proprietary sense of spirituality and advantage over other Muslims. Some Arab nations are rich in oil and some are directly affected by the conflicts in Israel and Iraq because of their geographic proximity. A striking feature of the next region, South Asia, is its Indic populations. Here Hindu yogis and Muslim Sufis have interacted to find mutual ways to understand the divine across the gap of different religions. This area still exudes the vitality that gave rise to the Mughals and other powerful Muslim empires, which rivaled those of the Arab region. The third region, Far East Asia, including Malaysia and Indonesia, is neither Arabic-speaking nor has been part of any great Muslim empire. Islam arrived there gently and slowly, through traders and Sufis, and has adjusted to and blended with different religions, notably Hinduism, Buddhism, and Christianity.

Our approach, by necessity, was multidisciplinary: we sought to draw from the best insights of political science, sociology, theology, and above all, anthropology. I believe anthropology presents as accurate a picture as possible of an *entire* society through its holistic and universal methodologies.[5] Anthropologists live among and interact with the people they study, collecting information on distinctive patterns of behavior through "participant observation," as well as questionnaires and interviews. These patterns—in our case, patterns relating to leadership, the impact of foreign ideas on society, the role of women, and tribal codes of behavior at a time of change and widespread unrest and even violence—can provide clues to a society's defining features and are what one of anthropology's founding fathers, Bronislaw Malinowski, called "the imponderabilia of native life and of typical behavior."[6] As another of the discipline's senior figures has rightly pointed out, "anthropology provides a scientific basis for dealing with the crucial dilemma of the world today: how can peoples of different appearances, mutually unintelligible languages, and dissimilar ways of life get along peaceably together?"[7]

Even some of the books written by anthropologists a generation ago are worth reading for their perceptiveness, in contrast to the dismal state of contemporary commentary. Clifford Geertz's *Islam Observed* and Ernest Gellner's *Muslim Society,* for example, present a masterly analysis of Muslim communities from Morocco to Indonesia and constantly surprise the reader with fresh insights.[8]

When I worked on my Ph.D. at London University's School of Oriental and African Studies three decades ago and studied the Pukhtun tribes, called by the British the Pathans and who lived along the Pakistan-Afghanistan border, the social scientist, in the ideal, would spend a year preparing for fieldwork, then a year conducting research in the field, and a final year writing up the findings. Developments in information technology, communications, and travel since then have altered the conditions of traditional anthropological fieldwork, making even remote societies more accessible, but also inducing some changes in them. As a result, we found that an intensive few months in the field were sufficient to achieve our objectives. This, then, was not a traditional anthropological study but an anthropological excursion.

Research Method

Our own questionnaires were designed to gain insight into contemporary Muslim society through real people's emotions and opinions on world affairs. They were administered to about 120 persons at various sites (universities, hotels, cafes, madrassahs, mosques, and private homes) in each country visited and included queries about what respondents read, what changes they had noted in their societies, the nature of their daily interaction with technology and the news, and, most important, their personal views on contemporary and historical role models (see the appendix).

The personal interview technique, however, proved especially valuable because respondents felt less inhibited in one-on-one conversations. In the repressive atmosphere of many Muslim nations where intelligence agencies are ever vigilant, individuals are reluctant to commit their true political opinions in writing. Often people would be frank in private conversations and guarded in their formal written answers. Many teachers, for example, told me that students had a much greater fascination with bin Laden than they had revealed to us in their classroom settings. Because of this, we did not see our questionnaires as a standard statistical instrument, but rather as a supplemental source of information for "testing the waters" of each country rather than taking their accurate temperature.

Our overall approach was closer to a personal account and assessment of what has been happening in the Muslim world since 9/11. Interestingly, the Pew Global Attitudes Project, conducted at the same time on a large scale throughout the Muslim world, Europe, and the United States, broadly supports our findings and our conclusions.[9]

Though the questions appeared deceptively simple, they yielded important and relevant information. For instance, the first question of the list asks for five contemporary role models among Muslims (if the respondent had none, examples from outside Muslim society could be given). If the mystic poet Maulana Rumi was named here, we knew the respondent was more likely to be tolerant of others; if Pervez Musharraf was named, then the respondent might favor economic and political cooperation with the West. And if Osama bin Laden or Mahmoud Ahmadinejad were named, then the respondent probably preferred a role model that would "stand up to the West." Personal conversations and responses to questionnaires alike indicated no clear-cut contemporary role models for Muslims in the Middle East and South Asia. Perhaps our respondents were being politically correct. But Indonesia, the largest Muslim nation in the world, did show a clear—and radical—trend. Bin Laden was the second most popular role model there, and Saddam Hussein and Yasser Arafat competed for fourth place, with almost 20 percent of the vote. We surmised that respondents who selected figures representing Islamic modernity, such as M. Syafi'i Anwar—and Ismail Noor in Malaysia—must have felt isolated and persecuted in their society. A similar radical trend may well have existed in other Muslim societies we visited but was not expressed to us quite so openly. What was clear was that the sleeping giant of the East was stirring. The world needed to take notice.

Role models from the past also reveal a great deal about contemporary society. In Damascus, the two names at the top of the list of most of those we questioned were Umar, the caliph of Islam from the seventh century, and Saladin (Sultan Salahaddin) from the twelfth century—ahead of even the Prophet, who would be the expected top choice for most Muslims. But these answers contained a subtext: both Umar and Saladin conquered Jerusalem for the Muslims, both were magnanimous and pious Muslim rulers, and, most important, both were victorious on the battlefield. With Jerusalem only a short drive away from Damascus and no longer under Muslim rule, Muslims are looking desperately for a modern Umar or Saladin.

Our informal surveys provided the beginning of what we anticipated learning more about—that while Muslims were aware of the processes of globalization and many wished to participate in them, they felt they were being denied access to its benefits. In their disappointment, they turned in anger to role models who promised them some hope of redeeming their honor and dignity. That is why so many young Muslims in the age of globalization prefer bin Laden to Bill Gates.

While our base of operations for the trip might often be a large hotel, we also visited places far from its confines. By visiting markets or remote towns or just taking taxis, for instance, we were able to converse with ordinary Muslims, usually wary of political conversations with strangers but more forthright when they came to know I was a Muslim. We thus saw a side of Muslim society that is not often on public display.

In addition, interviews with important Muslim figures provided a glimpse into their inner thoughts about not only their role models but also their vision of the future of the *ummah*, the global body of Muslims. Some of their responses were indeed unexpected. President Pervez Musharraf sat up excitedly as he described the successful military campaigns of his hero, Napoleon Bonaparte (Austerlitz was his favorite Napoleon victory). Mustafa Ceric, the Grand Mufti of Bosnia, whom we interviewed in Doha, named Imam Abu Hamid Muhammad al-Ghazzali, the renowned philosopher and scholar, as his role model. Benazir Bhutto spoke poignantly of her role model, Fatima, the daughter of the Prophet, with whom she identified closely because both had lost their beloved fathers at a crucial time in their lives. Not surprisingly, the premier role model from the past for each of these Muslim world figures was the Prophet of Islam.

These Muslim leaders were reflecting a larger sentiment in the Muslim world. The Prophet was the ultimate role model for the vast majority of Muslims, irrespective of gender, age, ethnicity, or nationality. I was not surprised therefore to find that the distorted perception of Islam in the West—which includes the attacks on the Prophet—was uppermost in the minds of Muslims when asked what they thought was the most important problem facing Islam. The expected answers—Israel, the plight of the Palestinians, the situation in Iraq—were all overshadowed by the idea that Islam was being maligned in the West. Those planning a strategy in the

Surrounded by portraits of Mughal emperors, the former prime minister of Pakistan, Chaudhry Shujat Hussain, second from left, and the chief minister of Punjab, the largest province of Pakistan, Parvez Elahi, far right, host a lunch at Elahi's office in Lahore for the team, including Akbar Ahmed on the far left and Hailey Woldt.

capitals of the West to win the hearts and minds of the Muslim world need to keep this reality in mind.

My team and I were fully aware of the cultural context of our survey. Because I was traveling as a Muslim, we all had extraordinary access to people throughout our journey. Many invited us to their homes for meals and informal gatherings, where we learned a great deal about the workings of their societies: among those extending such hospitality were friends in Istanbul, Sheikh Farfour in Damascus, friends and family in Karachi and Islamabad, and the head cleric in Deoband. Even well-known political figures invited us to lunch and dinner and shared their ideas about Islam and experiences in Muslim society. In Pakistan, for example, our hosts included Muhammad Mian Soomro, chairman of the Senate of Pakistan; senator Mushahid Hussain; former minister Shafqat Shah Jamote; Asad Shah; Sadrudin Hashwani; and Ghazanfar Mehdi.

Chaudhry Shujat Hussain, the former prime minister of Pakistan, and Parvez Elahi, the chief minister of Punjab, Pakistan's largest province, sent a police convoy to the airport in Lahore to escort us to lunch before we departed for Delhi. They not only received us warmly but also gave each of us a colorful Pakistani rug as a token of our visit. Hussain was a friendly and gracious host, even when he jokingly complained that I was "as bad as Bush" after learning that I intended to spend double the amount of time in India as I did in Pakistan. He was referring to President Bush's recent one-day visit to Pakistan, which created a storm of criticism in the media because he had spent almost a week in India. The image of young Americans lunching with the former prime minister of Pakistan in the grand private dining room of the chief minister of the Punjab, with its portraits of the Mughal emperors, was a testimony to the inherent hospitality of the people we visited and the range of our study. Throughout the journey we also received similar welcomes from the American embassies, usually guarded like high-security prisons, and the Pakistani embassies, and we gained further insights from the viewpoints and experiences of the diplomats.

Real and immediate dangers did not stop us from venturing beyond the high walls and security guards of the hotels and embassies. I gave public lectures in mosques and madrassahs, in addition to other forums. At each venue I faced a barrage of anti-Americanism and equally strong anti-Semitism (the latter becoming comparatively more nuanced, yet still passionate, as we moved out of the Arab world). I would respond that neither America nor the Jewish community is a monolith, pointing out that it is a mistake for Muslims as much as Americans to see the other in monolithic garb. I noted that a bishop and a rabbi, as well as others, had quite consciously reached out to me in Washington in the dark days after 9/11 and made me feel welcome, and mentioned especially the Christmas greeting sent by one—Bishop John Chane of the National Cathedral—which moved me greatly with its Abrahamic message of compassion, understanding, and above all, unity: "The Angel Gabriel was sent by God to reveal the Law to Moses," it read, and to "reveal the sacred Quran to the Prophet Muhammad." The greeting, with its acknowledgment of the Quran as "sacred" and Muhammad as "Prophet" was enough of a theological earthquake in my mind, but in the context of the general hostility toward Muslims after 9/11, the bishop's words displayed extraordinary courage, imagination, and compassion.

On the Muslim side, the Syrian minister of expatriates, Bouthaina Shaaban, and many other Muslims throughout our travels expressed similar sentiments of communal spirituality. Shaaban told us that "from 627 to 647 C.E., Muslims and Christians were praying together in the Umayyad

Inside the Umayyad Mosque in Damascus, Muslims pray at the shrine of St. John the Baptist, known as the Prophet Yahya in Islam. Saladin, the great Muslim ruler, is buried within the mosque precincts.

Mosque until they decided to build a church. We shouldn't think of East and West. You can't be a Muslim until you believe in Abraham and Christ. The oldest synagogue in the world is in Damascus. The oldest church in the world is in Damascus."

Bouthaina Shaaban is right. Islamic history reflects a cultural richness and complexity that affirms Islam's capacity to accommodate different traditions. This was confirmed for us by a visit to the Grand Mosque in Damascus, built by the Umayyads, the first great Muslim dynasty. When it was erected in the seventh century, the mosque shared space with a preexisting church, and Muslims and Christians worshipped together. In the eighth century, however, the caliph of Islam ordered a full-fledged mosque built in its place in order to symbolize the growing importance of Damascus as the capital of the Muslim world. The largest and most impressive of its time, the Grand Mosque is said to have contained the largest golden mosaic in the world until a fire in 1893 damaged the mosaic and almost destroyed the mosque.

The architecture of the Grand Mosque dramatically illustrates Byzantine, Roman, and Arabic influences, although the overall plan is based on the Prophet's house in Medina. The mosque holds a shrine dedicated to the head of John the Baptist, who is revered in Islam as Yahya the Prophet; another shrine for the head of Hussein, the grandson of the Prophet of Islam and the son of Ali, who is especially venerated by the Shia; and, just outside the mosque's walls, a simple and small grave for Saladin, one of the greatest rulers of Islam. Pope John Paul II visited the relics of John the Baptist in 2001, thus becoming the first pope ever to visit a mosque. On my visit, I saw all manner of pilgrims at each of these historical sites: Christians and Muslims praying at John's shrine, Shia women dressed in black who were from Iran and still mourning the death of Hussein, and scholars and tourists paying quiet tribute to the great Saladin.

Many Muslims on the journey mentioned that Jews and Christians were the "People of the Book" whom God holds in the highest esteem and with whom Muslims share common bonds. This was a message that I had been endeavoring to spread in the United States. During my talks before Muslim audiences, I would also mention that I was personally inspired by the example of my friend Judea Pearl, who had lost his only son, Danny, in a brutal and senseless killing in Karachi. As a father, I knew how deep the wound was for Judea and his wife, Ruth. Having gotten to know him as a friend over the years through our dialogues conducted nationally and internationally in promoting Jewish-Muslim understanding, I have seen him heroically transform this personal tragedy into a bridge to reach out to and understand the very civilization that produced the killers of his son. I would also explain that friendships such as these have helped transform the relationships among Muslims, Jews, and Christians in the United States.

Danny Pearl was killed by hatred, and the problem with hatred is that it thrives on falsehood. I was shocked to discover the extent to which fictitious literature such as *The Protocols of the Elders of Zion* was being used to propagate hatred against Jewish communities. Films made recently in the Middle East are based on this fiction, and millions appear to accept the *Protocols* as the truth. In this climate, statements questioning the Holocaust and encouraging the extermination of entire peoples are accommodated, although many Muslims such as myself find them unacceptable and tasteless and have said so in public. At the same time, similar lies about Muslims being "Satan worshippers" and followers of a man who was a "terrorist" are being circulated and accepted as truth. Such stereotypes encourage further falsehoods and create an atmosphere that can lend itself to violence.

To check the spread of such misperceptions requires more than polite manners. The idea that the Jews somehow directly or indirectly "control" the world through different forms of conspiracies permeates discussion in the Muslim world on many levels, from passionate expressions of an ideological worldview to idle chatter in the bazaar. Even high-profile politicians may make lighthearted references to it, as I discovered in my personal conversation with Benazir Bhutto in Doha in February 2006. Benazir, who in spite of being prime minister of Pakistan twice—a tough job that had led her father to the gallows—still retains a youthful sense of humor. When we met, she coyly said, with a twinkle in her eye, "So, you are now working for the *Sabaaan* Center?" Even if she had not elongated the vowel, I would have understood the innuendo linking my association as a fellow at the Brookings center with the patron after which it was named, a prominent Jewish philanthropist. I smiled, thinking of the irony: we were both guests at the conference organized by the very same center and dedicated to promoting understanding between the United States and the Muslim world.

Because of the high levels of anti-Americanism and anti-Semitism we encountered on our journey, many people were inclined to blame non-Muslims for various conspiracies against Islam. Many told our team that the violence on September 11, and, later, the London bombings on July 7, 2005, was not committed by Muslims but by people who wish to defame Islam. This clear state of denial was distressing to people like me who condemned the violence and accepted the overwhelming and widely available evidence—including interviews on television. Equally distressing, Muslims seemed unable to accept the fact that Muslims were responsible for the bloody clashes between Shia and Sunni in the mosques of Pakistan or the suburbs of Iraq, or the brutal deaths of Daniel Pearl, Margaret Hassan, and Nicholas Berg. In forum after forum, I spoke out against such violence and the need to emphasize to Muslim youth that this does not comport with the true nature of Islam.

In its ideal teachings, Islam has always given priority in human affairs to learning and the use of the mind rather than emotion and anger. As I would remind my Muslim audiences, the Prophet said, "The ink of the scholar is more sacred than the blood of the martyr." This saying is of immense significance and has ramifications for the contemporary situation in the Muslim world. Too many young Muslims are being encouraged to reverse the saying of the Prophet and are being instructed to emphasize sacrifice and blood over scholarship and reason. I would want every Muslim teacher and leader to use it as their motto; I would want every non-Muslim to understand the true nature of Islam through it.

Even more startling than the skepticism expressed by Muslims about events surrounding 9/11 was the change in American attitudes toward the events of that day: by 2006 one-third of Americans were expressing doubts, and a growing literature was putting forward different controversial theories.[10] People were, slowly at first, challenging the administration's policies not only on the war on terror, but also on Iraq and even its strategy for security.

In response to the high levels of anti-Americanism and anti-Semitism on our trip, I could not resist giving in to my professorial instincts and suggesting some relevant reading material to my audiences, whether in mosques or madrassahs. The first book was *The Dignity of Difference* by Jonathan Sacks, the chief rabbi of the United Kingdom.[11] A powerful plea for Abrahamic understanding in the age of globalization, it underlines the need for compassion in all areas of global interaction, including the distribution of wealth. This was probably one of the few times that a Muslim recommended a Jewish author, a rabbi at that, in a mosque in Damascus, the Royal Institute in Amman, and in the madrassahs of Delhi—much to the surprise of the audience, I am sure.

I also recommended Karen Armstrong's *The Battle for God*, which describes the intense internal debate taking place in Judaism, Christianity, and Islam between the fundamentalists and their more moderate or liberal coreligionists.[12] *Islam under Siege*, my own book, would be the third recommendation. It argues that the societies of today are all feeling under siege.[13] After 9/11 Americans felt continually under attack; indeed, the news was broadcast on TV as "America under Siege." Israelis have always felt embattled, surrounded by millions of neighbors who would like the state to disappear from the map. Muslims, with many grievances, feel very much under siege. When societies feel hemmed in, they tend to become defensive, and there is little room for wisdom or compassion.

In addition, when I introduced the Americans who had accompanied me on my travels, I reminded audiences that it was unfair for Muslims to dismiss all Americans in monolithic terms as haters of Muslims. After all, here were these idealistic young students traveling to the heart of the Muslim world in friendship and with a desire to improve understanding. By creating goodwill and exemplifying public diplomacy at its best, these young Americans were true ambassadors of their society because they had taken the trouble to visit Muslim lands, were committed to building bridges, and were raising the right questions, as shown by Jonathan Hayden's comments in the field:

> In Jakarta, Indonesia, I handed out a questionnaire to a class of fifty college students at an Islamic University. The questionnaire was designed to reveal their feelings toward the West, globalization, and changes within Islam. The class was about 70 percent women, aged nineteen to twenty-three. Their *hijab* [or head covering] was mandatory, but if the women were to take it off, they would've looked like any college class in America.
>
> They were sweet, funny kids who wanted to take pictures afterward and ask questions about the U.S. Why, then, did roughly 75 percent of them list as their role models people like Osama bin Laden, Saddam Hussein, Ayatollah Khomeini, Yousef al-Qaradawi (of Al-Jazeera), Yasser Arafat, and Iranian President Mahmoud Ahmadinejad? We obviously have a problem. If these young students are choosing as heroes people who are hostile to the U.S., what can we do to change this? What has led to this? Who can help us? And where are the moderate Muslims? We must try to answer these questions if we are to build bridges with countries with a largely Muslim population and avert the "clash of civilizations."
>
> The answers obviously do not come easily and will take much time to work out. But one of the things I noticed in Malaysia and Indonesia is the vital role that moderate Muslims will play. I hesitate to use the word "moderate" because of its negative connotations. From what I've gathered, moderates are viewed as people who are unwilling to stand up for anything.
>
> But the people that I am talking about when I use the term "moderate Muslim" are those who are standing up for the true identity of Islam while actively living in this "age of globalization." From what I've learned on this trip, moderate Muslims are practicing the compassionate and just Islam that is taught in the Quran without rejecting modernity and the West. They are, as I learned, hardly weak.[14]

The power and effects of the global media also became clear during our travels. The global media have fed into the feeling of urgency and terror associated with Islam. While in Amman, we heard reports of an explosion that had killed an American diplomat and several Pakistanis yards from the Marriott Hotel in Karachi adjacent to the American consulate, just days before we were due to arrive; another recent explosion hit the Marriott in Jakarta where we had stayed; and explosions shook Istanbul, Delhi, and Islamabad just after our visits. It felt like Russian roulette—how long could we escape the fatal hit?

Our own trip had not escaped media attention. It was faithfully recorded as a "travelogue" on Beliefnet.com, where I gave updates and insights into the countries we were visiting, and Hailey, Frankie, Jonathan, and Amineh Hoti provided their own articles.[15] I was interviewed at length by some of the leading national newspapers, such as the *Nation* in Pakistan and the *Indian Express* and *Hindustan Times* in India. I also appeared on Al-Jazeera in Qatar and Doordarshan in India, which broadcast the interview in prime time to an estimated audience of 500 million people in South Asia. My team took a tour of the Al-Jazeera studios and watched the filming of the nightly news. We found Muslims everywhere well informed about world events because of the media. The imam of Delhi's Jama Masjid Madrassah told us that he knew exactly where Secretary of State Condoleezza Rice was traveling at all times.

As I approach the twilight of my life, this journey had a final great-adventure quality for me. My last long excursion through the length and breadth of the Muslim world had taken place for the BBC television series "Living Islam," broadcast in 1993, but developments in politics, economics, the media, and information technology since then had moved at a rapid pace. On this trip, everywhere I went someone had either read something by me on the Internet or seen me on television.[16] In Istanbul, as I sat having lunch with the head of a leading think tank early in the tour, a large man with a thick and somewhat unruly beard aggressively strode up to our table and stood towering over us. "You are Akbar Ahmed, are you not?" he said soberly. I nodded my head and smiled slowly, trying to ascertain which way the conversation was going to go. "I am a Muslim convert from Chile, and I saw you explaining Islam on the Oprah show," he continued. "Thank you for your work."

Throughout the journey I was struck both by the global reach of the U.S. media and the global spirit of the Muslim population. The world had

At a mosque and madrassah complex in Delhi, a crowd of youngsters gathers with the team, seen in the back, for a Friday night lecture. The location is near the great mosque built by the Emperor Shah Jehan.

come closer in a way I could not have imagined on my last long trip, and much had also changed. I quickly became aware that the problem of understanding and dealing with global Islam is far larger than I had anticipated. Even so, I returned with a fresh sense of hope after seeing concerned and kind-natured individuals from all races and religions on every leg of my journey. Their vitality and passion demonstrate that a common ground for dialogue exists. Therefore the book documents the several layers of our journey: it describes an extended field trip to the Muslim world by a professor and a young, curious, and energetic team; by a social scientist seeking a theoretical understanding of the impact of globalization and the challenges posed to traditional societies; by a revenant Muslim scholar attempting to comprehend his community with a view to helping it find its way; by a Pakistani visiting home after several years in the West; and by an optimist seeking to promote dialogue and understanding between two increasingly hostile civilizations by making both aware of the global dangers facing everyone.

Islam in the Age of Globalization

Unlike other discussions of Islam, this one will not treat Islam as an isolated case in diagnosing its ailments. To the precepts of my earlier book, *Islam under Siege*, in which I argued that all societies today feel under physical threat, I would now like to add that all—perhaps with the exception of American society—also feel threatened culturally by the tidal wave of globalization. Islam is of particular interest because of its close negative and positive relationship to the United States, but also because its followers now number 1.4 billion and span five continents, which makes it the perfect subject for a case study of a traditional civilization undergoing change in the age of globalization.

The scale of the problems posed by globalization has been widely discussed, but with few suggestions as to how they might be solved. Thomas Friedman of the *New York Times*, one of the best-known commentators on the subject, takes a benign view, equating globalization with "Americanization" and the spread of democracy and American values.[17] Although Friedman is aware that India and China are vigorously challenging the United States for primacy, he remains optimistic about the spirit and age of globalization. Ideally, it is expected to create conditions that will connect the different nations of the world and thereby establish a mutually beneficial "global village."

Other views are darker. Standard textbooks point to the massive social, economic, and technological transformations now under way because of globalization, with consequences that are difficult to predict.[18] Rapid and far-reaching social, economic, and technological changes in its wake are forcing people around the world to adjust their lives. Faced with so much change, many individuals are uncertain and anxious about the future, which scholars label "panic culture" or "risk society."[19] For Anthony Giddens, a leading social scientist, globalization "creates a world of winners and losers, a few on the fast track to prosperity, the majority condemned to a life of misery and despair."[20] Thus he sees globalization as little more than "global pillage."[21]

Borrowing a phrase from anthropologist Edmund Leach, Giddens argues that globalization is creating a "runaway world."[22] Leach had used the phrase in the title of a lecture series, punctuating it with a question mark, but, says Giddens, developments over the past few decades indicate that now it *is* a runaway world: "This is not—at least at the moment—a global order driven by collective human will. Instead, it is emerging in an anarchic, haphazard, fashion. . . . It is not settled or secure, but fraught with anxieties as well as scarred by deep divisions. Many of us feel in the grip of forces over which we have no power."[23]

Although both Friedman and Giddens recognize globalization's economic successes and failures, they fall short of raising the greater moral issues, particularly the fact that globalization lacks a moral core. This is precisely the reason that greed, anger, and ignorance—Buddha's three poisons—are able to flourish without restraint and define the present age.[24] Although these three negative qualities have always been part of the human fabric, they have been kept in check by traditional ideas of faith and codes of behavior, which embody justice, compassion, and knowledge. These concepts, respectively, are the antidotes to the poisons and can be found in all great faiths: Judaism, Christianity, Islam—and indeed Hinduism, which gave birth to Buddhism.[25] Each religion believes it best equips individuals to deal with the poisons, however different the method of tackling them.

The Abrahamic approach—which is to balance living in this world with an eye on the next—an idea that is more developed in Christianity and Islam than in Judaism—is radically rejected by the Indic religions. In Hinduism, which provides the template for the Indic faiths, death, the climactic and final event in the life of the Abrahamic believer, is but the start of yet another cycle of birth and rebirth. The approach to material life is thus less urgent and compelling. Traditional Hinduism divides an individual's life into four stages, each spanning about two decades: student, householder, ascetic, and, finally, the seeker. The last two stages are sometimes merged, and in them a man, accompanied by his wife, is expected to leave all his material possessions and withdraw from the world to live in forests and mountains searching for truth. The poisons are no longer a threat now because at the moment of renouncing the world, the individual discovers the antidote. The Indic approach is not only philosophically attractive but empirically known to be effective in the lives of individuals. Perhaps the Abrahamic faiths need to learn from it by looking more closely at their own rich spiritual and mystical legacy.

For the purposes of the present argument, however, one needs to point out that globalization is a juggernaut, and that no society, Abrahamic or Indic, can escape its embrace.

Hindu and Buddhist societies face much the same challenges as other societies, as is evident from the Hindu majority's violence against the Muslims in India and the Buddhist majority's treatment of Hindus in Sri Lanka. They too are still grappling with the poisons, despite the Indic philosophy of withdrawal and nonviolence. The scale and intensity of the riots there took the people of Indic faiths by complete surprise, for they never imagined that such violence was possible. This violence between religious groups is fueled by the technology, international media images, and global networks available to local groups, which are part of the process of globalization. In addition, there are other aspects of globalization that affect societies influenced by the Indic religions, such as the weakening of the central state structures and the excessive harshness of their response to what they see as signs of dissent among the minority community; both the majority and minority communities are also now too quick to use the lethal weapons so easily available to them on civilian or military targets. Thus, the ethnic and religious bloodshed is both a cause and a symptom of the anger, hatred, and ignorance of societies in our age of globalization.

More modern philosophies, such as nationalism, socialism, and fascism, which tend to dismiss traditional religions as backward and outdated, have not managed to check the poisons either. If anything, under them the spread has accelerated through the power and use of technology. Even those who reject religion altogether often bear prejudices such as racism, which provide rich soil for the spread of the poisons. There is ample evidence of so-called Western liberal and humanist commentators parading their anger, hatred, and ignorance of Islam after 9/11.

Over the past half century, globalization has produced physical as well as moral consequences. Perhaps most serious, rampant industrialization and consumerism have abetted global warming. The frequency of cyclones and tornadoes, record temperatures, excessive rains, and severe droughts, as well as the more rapid melting of glaciers, are all symptoms of the problem.[26] Even so all countries continue to follow in the footsteps of Western nations, with Asian industrial giants like China more interested in becoming part of the globalized economy than protecting the environment.

Another consequence of globalization can be seen in the economic sphere, in the greatly increasing asymmetry in living conditions. Poverty kills thousands of people annually through the lack of health care and food; about one billion people earn less than a dollar a day; and, as if to mock these figures, 358 individuals own more financial wealth than half of the world's population collectively.[27] The statistics of despair, like the figures of disparity between the rich and the poor, are widely available (for example, see United Nations reports). To add to the problem, the world's population jumped from 2.5 billion half a century ago to 6.5 billion today and will be about 11 billion by the middle of the century.[28] These demographic trends cannot be ignored. The planet's natural resources will be unable to sustain human life without some drastic measures to control population, either through human efforts or those of Mother Nature.

Globalization has also brought increasing access to tools of violence, from homemade bombs to biological weapons. Anyone, anywhere, and at anytime, could fall prey to religious or ethnic hatred. Admittedly, societies have faced such hatred before, not to mention the problems cited earlier— the exploitation of natural resources, excessive interest in amassing material wealth, the pressures of large populations—and have often gone to war over them. It is the scale and scope of globalization today that, without restraint or balance, places humankind at a dangerous point in its history. Disillusioned with the promise of globalization and alarmed by the nature and extent of the violence in its wake, concerned intellectuals are writing books with titles such as *World on Fire* and *Savage Century: Back to Barbarism.*[29]

All religions and societies are responding to the problems culminating in the crisis of globalization in different ways, some even ignoring them. As in the Islamic world, backlashes against globalization can be seen in Latin America, for example, where Leftist governments have swept into power in Venezuela, Bolivia, and Ecuador, and in China—with an estimated Muslim population of anywhere between the official figure of 20 million to perhaps as many as 100 million—where widespread economic inequality and privatization policies have led to tens of thousands of protests, riots, and other instances of social instability in recent years.[30] Islam, the focus of this study, provides fertile ground for examining the impact of and response to global forces in a largely traditional context. Its followers are spread across the world and in markedly different ethnic settings. Their behavior can shed greater light on traditional societies that can help improve relations between them and industrialized societies. Perhaps most important, it will help others better understand Islam, which has now attained global significance.

New and Old Patterns in Muslim Society

Before setting out on our journey, I expected to rely on Max Weber's classic categories of leadership—charismatic, traditional, and rational-legal authority—to define styles of leadership in the Muslim world. Charismatic leadership is rooted in personality traits that attract followers yet need not be a permanent part of an individual's character. Indeed, charisma actually resides in the mesmerized eyes of the follower. Charisma is thus an evanescent quality and its assessment subjective, as one man's charismatic leader may be another's villain. What is clear is that a correlation exists between success and high levels of charisma, on the one hand, and between failure and plummeting charisma, on the other. By contrast, the next two categories of leadership have little to do with individual qualities. Traditional authority is a product of lineage and birth. An individual in a certain kind of society may assume a leadership role because he is the elder son or has inherited his father's estate or legacy. Rational-legal authority is a social construct that evolved in Europe as a result of society's need to impose rules and regulations to control elected officials governing the population. This is considered the best form of authority as it is bureaucratic and regulated and therefore "controlled."

The Weberian categories were excellent as background theory. Once in the Muslim world, however, I realized that relations between it and the United States, the still unfolding events since 9/11 and the processes of globalization, have affected the forms of Muslim leadership so drastically that the Weberian categories would prove inadequate. The shadowy "insurgent" is but one example that does not fit neatly into the Weber scheme. Having no concrete or tangible identity, this individual falls outside all three categories. In any case, too many Muslim leaders straddle two or three of the Weberian categories and therefore make it difficult to explain Muslim leadership through this conceptual frame. The late King Hussein of Jordan, for example, can be classified as a charismatic, traditional, or even rational-legal leader; he inspired his people, was descended from the Prophet's lineage, and worked with a parliament that ratified the monarchy.

Apart from Weber, I build on and extend the arguments of other transcendental figures of the social sciences, such as Ibn Khaldun and the more contemporary Emile Durkheim. Ibn Khaldun's theory posits that the rise and fall of dynasties has more to do with the loss of social vitality and social cohesion than with the moods of God. Durkheim explains the levels of suicide in society, for example, as a reflection of social breakdown rather than divine wrath or moral turpitude. Weber's discussion of the Protestant work ethic illuminates how religious behavior can affect the spirit of capitalism and consequently improve economic growth. The accumulated work of these thinkers leads to the broad conclusion that one cannot understand how humans see and relate to the divine without understanding society itself. Sociology, then, determines the kind of theology a society will formulate and practice.

Durkheim and Weber are giants among the preeminent European social scientists of the nineteenth and twentieth centuries. This was a time of intellectual effervescence that produced in one spectacular burst figures like Marx, Freud, Tolstoy, H. G. Wells, and Einstein. By contrast, Ibn Khaldun is unique in that he seems to appear from nowhere in a dusty and obscure North African town and leaves behind no local schools of thought or army of disciples. He is a true one-off, a one-man intellectual powerhouse whose ideas continue to dazzle scholars all over the world, even today.

For several years I have been studying—and writing about—leadership models in Muslim society so as to suggest how to change and direct it toward a better future. In *Islam under Siege,* I explored two categories: inclusivists and exclusivists.[31] Jinnah, the founder of Pakistan, typified the former, and the Taliban of Afghanistan the latter. Earlier, I had identified two enduring strains in Muslim society: the first, mystic and universalist, and the second, orthodox and literalist.[32] Dara Shikoh, the elder son of Shah Jehan, the Mughal emperor of India, personified the former, and his younger brother, Aurangzeb, the latter. In this book I develop these ideas further.

The primary purpose of this study is to determine how Muslims are constructing their religious identities—and therefore a whole range of actions and strategies—as a result of their current situation. Today, every violent action in one part of the world is capable of provoking an equally violent reaction in another. The chief catalyst is the transmission of television images and those on the Internet that create a heightened sense of tension. The rapidity of the responses and the publicity they are given in the media ensure that every society is kept in a state of high anxiety as ordinary people become caught up in this rapid series of actions and reactions through their television sets. Certain kinds of leaders have emerged to represent the current mood, whereas others have been marginalized. Style of leadership is clearly related to the rapidity with which actions and reactions can be presented.

All world religions seek to discover the best path to understanding the divine in order to lead a fulfilling life on earth. In this search, some people try to look for parallels and analogies outside their own tradition; others try to incorporate principles from life around them to strengthen their own beliefs; and still others focus on preserving their own legacy as much as possible. These different approaches give rise to internal contradictions and dilemmas within the major world faiths, and they also affect relations with other religions. Take, for example, Judaism, the oldest Abrahamic faith. Judaism has resolved its inner tensions to some extent by demarcating and identifying its different perspectives within three branches: Reform, Orthodox, and Conservative. Of course, other interpretations are offered by smaller branches such as Hassidism and Reconstructivism. Members of each persuasion believe they are interpreting Judaism with integrity.[33]

Similarly, Islam attempts to differentiate its various approaches or worldviews, some of which overlap while some are in opposition. These approaches can best be summarized as "accepting," "preserving," and "synthesizing." Those who believe in acceptance approach the divine through universal mysticism; those who believe in preserving opt for straightforward orthodoxy or a literal interpretation of the faith; and the synthesizers seek to interact with modernism and the ideas it values, such as democracy, women's rights, and human rights. Again, each perspective is considered the truest form of the faith and a means of counteracting the three poisons. Each is affected by globalization, and each causes internal tensions within Islamic society. Hence Islam's response to the forces of globalization also takes at least three distinct forms: mystics reach out to other faiths, traditionalists want to preserve the purity of Islam, and modernists attempt to synthesize society with other non-Muslim systems. Because most people in the West do not understand the complexity of Muslim society through models such as ours, they reduce understanding of U.S. relations with the Muslim world to good versus evil, and divide Muslims crudely into moderates versus extremists.

The Three Muslim Models in Play Today

Three towns in India serve as metaphors for these worldviews: Ajmer, Deoband, and Aligarh, respectively. Just as Waterloo has come to mean more than a geographical location in Europe, so these three names represent different interpretations of Islam in the minds of local people associated with a particular Muslim perspective. The fact that all three towns are situated in South Asia—and, as it happens, in India—is merely a neat coincidence of history and geography. The important point is that the models named after them can be recognized universally in Muslim societies, although sometimes disguised under different labels and forms.

Although the word "model" is somewhat amorphous for this context, it does capture the sense of a "system," or way of thinking. If there is a mystic model of human thought and practice in Islam, it is Sufism. Thus, those who love Moin-uddin Chisti, the founder of the Chisti order whose shrine is in Ajmer, would also find Rumi, who is buried in Konya in Turkey, an inspiring and beloved Sufi master. All Sufis are passionately inspired directly by the Prophet of Islam, whom they see through a mystic lens:

> It is said that when God existed alone, the silent totality resonating in the darkness before light, the immersion of all that was to be in the solitary, unique One, after a period of timelessness which cannot be described or reckoned, something happened, something changed or shifted and a stunning, luminous presence emerged from all that was contained. In amazement God contemplated this light, radiating His consciousness as perception and awareness, asking it to identify itself, and the *nur* replied to our God that it was a light which had been with Him and had come from Him, a light which was the expression of His grace, His plentitude, His totality. God, who was delighted with the response, gave this extraordinary light the name *Nur Muhammad,* declaring then He would make all that would be created with this *nur*, this *Nur Muhammad.*[34]

The Prophet radiates and has come to embody *nur,* or light: "Nur Muhammad." It is what characterizes human beings since Adam: "Finally, He created Adam, man, the most exalted of His creation, pressing the light of *Nur Muhammad* on his forehead, announcing that human beings would know what even the angels would not know."[35] For a Sufi, the Prophet, Islam, and Sufism are fused into one with the goodness and compassion that radiates from God. This is how a leading contemporary Sufi defines Sufism:

> Sufism and Islam cannot be separated in the same way that higher consciousness or awakening cannot be separated from Islam. Islam is not an historical phenomenon that began 1,400 years ago. It is the timeless art of awakening by means of submission. Sufism is the *heart* of Islam. It is as ancient as the rise of human consciousness. . . . Genuine Sufis are essentially similar wherever they come from, in that they share an inner light and awakening and an outer courtesy and service to humanity. Apparent differences between Sufis tend to relate to matters concerning spiritual practices or prescriptions for the purification of hearts. The sweet fruit of Sufism is the same. It is only the trees which may look different and which may flower in different seasons.[36]

Those who adhere to this model range from austere puritanical mystics to those who take drugs and even alcohol, which are prohibited in Islam: "Also, as with other spiritual movements and revivals, we find instances of some Sufis taking things to extremes and even distorting the multi-dimensions of Islam. Excess esotericism or the rejection of the bounds of outer behavior or the balanced prophetic way, are examples of this phenomenon, although they are the exception rather than the rule."[37]

During World War II, local Sufi groups in the Balkans saved Jewish lives from Nazi persecution. Norman Gershman, an American who plans to write about this little-known period in history, was told that this was "a religious act of faith" for the Muslim Bektashi sect headquartered in Albania.[38] In an interview with Gershman, the world head of this sect explained: "We Bektashi see God everywhere, in everyone. God is in every pore and every cell. Therefore all are God's children. There cannot be infidels. There cannot be Discrimination. If one sees a good face one is seeing the face of God. 'God is beauty. Beauty is God. There is no God but God.'"

Throughout this book, I use the word "Ajmer" to refer to all those Muslims inspired by the Sufi and mystical tradition within Islam. I use "Deoband" to refer to all mainstream Islamic movements—whether the

Wahhabis in Saudi Arabia or the Muslim Brotherhood and Hamas in the Middle East—that have a deep affinity with its position. In other words, Deoband is a generic term for Islamic movements based in orthodox Islam that consciously trace their worldview to mainstream Islamic tradition and thought. These movements also identify themselves through their association with some key figures in Islam—for example, the scholar Ibn Taymiyya from the past, and, more recently, Syed Qutb from the Arab world, and Maulana Maududi from South Asia. Many of the Deoband persuasion would consider Aurangzeb, Mughal emperor in India, the ideal Muslim ruler.

Ibn Taymiyya, one of the most influential Deoband thinkers, lived and wrote in the fourteenth century, when the Muslim heartland was reeling from the Mongol invasions from the east and earlier attacks by the Crusaders from the west. The uncertainty and violence in the wake of these invasions made an impression on Taymiyya's thinking, which therefore needs to be understood in the context of his times. Gone was the easy, open acceptance of non-Muslims, especially Jews and Christians, of Ibn Rushd or even Rumi. However distrustful of non-Muslims, Taymiyya remained an Islamic scholar who insisted on religious freedom and security for Jews and Christians in accordance with the Quran.

Ibn Taymiyya's significance today is that he introduced two themes into Islamic discourse of lasting influence in Muslim societies. First, he stoutly rejected fatalism or passivity in the face of injustice and its reliance on the intercession of saints, instead emphasizing personal responsibility for one's own life. Second, he stressed the need to keep Islamic law as flexible as possible within the concept of *ijtihad* (independent reasoning based on the Quran or scholarly texts). Islamic law, he argued, was open to reinterpretation and needed to take into account the context in which society functioned. Ijtihad must remain active, he said, for otherwise Islamic law itself would become ossified and irrelevant. He vigorously opposed the widespread idea—which is still mentioned in ultraconservative circles—that the gates of ijtihad were closed forever by the four great jurists of Sunni Islam. In Taymiyya's view, Muslims in every generation must constantly revert to the original seventh-century sources rather than mindlessly apply the teachings of the scholars, however noteworthy and pious. The failure of ijtihad, Ibn Taymiyya argued, meant the loss of vitality in Muslim society and therefore set the course for its downfall.

The call for ijtihad was echoed in the eighteenth century by Muhammad Abdul Wahhab, the founder of what in time would be called the Wahhabi movement. Abdul Wahhab interpreted Taymiyya in an even more literalist manner than Taymiyya himself may have wished. Wahhabis, taking their cue from Abdul Wahhab, have been particularly dismissive of Sufi thinking and practice and in favor of the aggressive identification of what was pure in Islam from the seventh century. Some orthodox scholars argue—despite a clear injunction in the Quran against suicide—that suicide bombings that kill innocent civilians are justified, because Muslims are in the middle of an all-out and total war against their faith in which their own innocent people are being killed. This kind of reasoning is ijtihad.

Taymiyya is the inspiration for a wide range of Muslim scholars such as Syed Qutb and Maulana Maududi, schools of thought such as Deoband, and activists like bin Laden and the leaders of the Muslim Brotherhood. Today, Taymiyya's message has been reduced to two precepts: the need to actively defend Islam and, simultaneously, to strive to re-create the purity of early Muslim society. This is the interpretation of Islam that Western commentators characterize as "radical Islam," "political Islam," "jihadist," or the recently coined term, "Islamofascist." Taymiyya's complex ideas have been reduced to a bare shibboleth, a rallying slogan, a battle cry that is the charter of action for millions of Muslims across the world.

Not everyone adhering to the Deoband model would agree with or accept the methods of bin Laden, however. Most of its followers simply wish to retain their ideals and practices with integrity and without external interference, especially by the West, but do not necessarily support violence. There is clearly a range of opinions and methods on how best to defend tradition in the Deoband model. In this discussion, then, the term "Deoband model" conveys a range of Muslim responses that are broadly similar in their purpose and content, despite variations due to culture, region, and personal convictions.

Like Ajmer and Deoband, "Aligarh" in this book conveys a broad but distinct modernist Muslim response to the world. This branch began in the nineteenth century as a direct consequence of Western imperialism. Its followers range from Sir Sayyed Ahmad Khan in India and Muhammad Abduh in Egypt in the nineteenth century to socialist leaders of the Middle East, the modernizing Mohammad Reza Pahlavi, shah of Iran, and the democratic leaders of Malaysia in the twentieth century. Leaders of this persuasion include genuine democrats and military dictators—all espousing democracy. Whether they are devout or more secular Muslims, followers of Aligarh share the desire to engage with modern ideas while preserving what to them is essential to Islam.

A Muslim must balance the need to strive for the next world while living in this one—it is well to recall the classic definition of ideal Islam as achieving perfect equilibrium between these worlds, *deen* and *dunya,* respectively, or between spirituality and worldliness. Each of the models just defined attempts to achieve precisely this, although by means of manifestly different strategies. In each case, Muslims work to find a happy medium between the pull of the market and the mosque. The problem, as will become clear, is that each lays greater emphasis on one or the other, which upsets the delicate balance that Islam once struggled so assiduously to maintain. So while Ajmer followers may spend more time thinking of the hereafter and ignoring this world, those favoring the Aligarh model may be doing the opposite. Confident that it is the guardian of the faith, Deoband believes that it has struck the right balance between deen and dunya.

The models just described also provide some perspective on the broad Muslim responses to one another. That is one of the advantages of reducing large and complex populations to models and categories. Ajmer followers, for example, think Deobandis are too critical of other faiths and too preoccupied with opposing mysticism, while they find Aligarh followers too concerned with the material world. For their part, the followers of Deoband would consider those of Ajmer guilty of innovation and close to heresy and those of Aligarh far too secular and too influenced by the West. The Aligarh group would perceive Ajmer as backward and would dismiss Deoband as little more than a rabble of ignorant clerics, country bumpkins, and benighted rustics. President Ayub Khan of Pakistan, who had studied at Aligarh and came to power through a military coup, would publicly refer to the latter as "those damn mullahs." Jinnah, although he had not studied at Aligarh himself, saw its students as "the arsenal" of the Muslims in his campaign for a modern Muslim homeland to be called Pakistan and himself was constantly attacked by clerics as a "nonbeliever."

However, these are not watertight models but "ideal types" that only approximate reality, and this is one of the drawbacks of categorizing people into special groups. The categories are not a substitute for reality. At times the models overlap, and at others individuals move from one to another. Furthermore, some Muslim thinkers have sought to reconcile the three models. Back in the eleventh century, Ghazzali, when a university instructor in Baghdad, studied Sufi mystic thought, orthodox Islam, and Greek philosophy—from which the Ajmer, Deoband, and Aligarh models are descended. Something of a celebrity in scholarly circles, Ghazzali withdrew from society to grapple with the main intellectual trends of his time and reemerged with a series of influential works offering a balance between mysticism, faith, and rationality. Over the centuries, Muslim intellectuals have turned to Ghazzali's work to find inspiration and help them meet the challenges of life. Not surprisingly, throughout our trip leading Muslims regularly named Ghazzali as a role model. Yet because of the ambitious sophistication of his thought, he is consistently misunderstood and misquoted.

Another individual whose work synthesizes the different and often contradictory views that the three models represent is the poet and philosopher Allama Iqbal, who touched a vast number of ordinary people. In his unrestrained admiration for the thirteenth-century poet and mystic Rumi, he appears to advocate the Ajmer model, yet his most popular poems, the "Shikwa," or "Complaint" (of Muslims to God for their plight), and the "Jawab-i-Shikwa," or "Reply to Complaint" (God's answer), embody the Deoband worldview. Letters written during the last months of his life to Jinnah, who best symbolizes the Aligarh model, developed the idea of a modern Muslim nation to be called Pakistan, meaning the "land of the pure." To Muslims, Iqbal's verses are not contradictory but a manifestation of the struggle of ideas in human society. Iqbal's universal popularity was confirmed for me as people throughout our journey referred to him as a worthy role model. A poet's capacity to cross linguistic, cultural, and international borders was illustrated during our stop in Damascus, at a farewell dinner given in our honor by the Pakistan ambassador: one of our Syrian hosts, Muhammad Habash, recited an Arabic version of Iqbal's two poems. His enthusiasm was as apparent as the delight of the audience.

Contradictory as it may seem, all three models draw their inspiration from the one name that provides unity to the diverse global Muslim community: the Prophet Muhammad. He is so greatly respected that traditional

Muslims will invariably say "Peace be upon him" whenever his name is mentioned. In the Iqbal poems just mentioned, God advises Muslims:

If you are faithful to Muhammad, then I am yours.
Why do you want this universe?
I will give you the key to knowledge itself.

Muslims everywhere, regardless of race, age, social class, gender, or sect, relate to him in a special way. They see in the Prophet an inspiration for their own lives.

The Prophet's popularity reflects both the paradox and strength of Islam: the Ajmer mystics will sing songs of love for the Prophet and trace their spiritual lineage directly to him; the orthodox Deoband will hold him up as their ultimate exemplar, imitating him down to style of beard and length of trousers; and the Aligarh modernist will cite him proudly as the original revolutionary of history, who gave rights to women, minorities, and the disenfranchised. All agree that the Prophet is the best interpreter of the Quran and accordingly Islam. His powerful words provide the unity that binds the diverse cultural and political branches of Islam, especially when faced with a common threat.

Many Western commentators consider Ajmer and Aligarh followers to be "with us" and the Deoband "against us." Yet if the often repeated question "Where are the moderates?" is any indication, they appear to think the former have disappeared from the radar. By showing the complexity and nuances of the Muslim world, I hope to suggest ways for the West to understand Muslim society.

Moreover, these models shed light on the "them" in the war on terror, making clear that Muslim countries do not neatly fit one model or another. Afghanistan, where the Taliban have reemerged and where the insurgents are fighting on behalf of the Pukhtun tribes against U.S. soldiers and the northern tribes, provides a prime example of the three models in concert. The Afghans have a known love for mystic literature—this is the land that gave birth to Rumi—but they also supported the Deoband model during the rule of the Taliban, especially in Kandahar and Kabul. The present presidential form of government with a new national army and police structure leans more toward the Aligarh model. These are still early days for the Aligarh model, and there is evidence that the Deoband model remains strong. A similar interplay between the three models can also be seen in other Muslim societies such as in Somalia. It is essential not only to identify these models but also to relate them to each other and to larger theoretical discussions about leadership. Their relevance is not only historical and theoretical but of direct sociological concern to any discussion of contemporary Islam.

With the aid of these models, one can also better appreciate how mainstream Muslims view themselves. Structurally, ideologically, and philosophically, the Ajmer model is antithetical to the strongly material and consumerist philosophies behind globalization. Sufis—who are to be found among both Shia and Sunni—emphasize concern for common humanity, poverty, and the imperative for compassion. Sufi thought urges people to constantly contemplate the afterlife and not concentrate so much on wealth or material gain in this life. Hence the Sufis are almost invisible in the age of globalization, yet not inactive. They are neither consumers nor aggressive advocates of their way of thinking but offer a genuine and long-term solution to some of the problems facing all of human civilization. The Ajmer model, which embodies pluralism and acceptance of others, is perhaps the only one that can lead Muslims out of the ethnic, religious, and political conflicts that globalization has thrust on them and that they continue to ignore at their peril.

For Deoband, faith and reason cannot be separated. Many verses in the Quran, Deoband followers would point out, emphasize the use of the mind and reason. The word for knowledge is the second most prevalent word in the Quran after that for God. God, they would say, has stated there is no greater quality than the intellect. One cannot fully worship God unless one does so intelligently and puts to full use one's capacity to reason. According to Deobandis, the great days of Islam were a consequence of the fusion of faith and reason. That was when Islamic scholars shone and their knowledge stood at the cutting edge of intellectual development. The general collapse of political power and influence over the past two centuries can be overcome, Deoband supporters would argue, by reviving the purity of Islam through the earliest model, which led to the triumph of the Muslims in the first place.

Because Deoband maintained its "purity" by drawing boundaries around itself, it is able to protect itself best from the tidal waves of globalization. With logic and consistency, Deoband can point to and resist the hollowness of globalization, its crass materialism, and images of moral laxity depicted on television. It therefore emphasizes the moral superiority of Islam and seeks to create a sense of pride based on Muslim identity. In the Deoband view, the West is not only morally bankrupt but also violent and sadistic, especially since 9/11. The scandals of Abu Ghraib attest to this and confirm the prediction of Muslim sages and saints that Islam will ultimately triumph. Far from being apologetic, Deoband is riding a crest in the Muslim world, although it may take very different forms and reactions, ranging from suicide bombings to participating in local elections and processions in the streets. Globalization appears to be stimulating the Deoband model more than the other two models and pushing it to take a more active role in Muslim society.

On the surface, the Aligarh model seems more in tune with the West's modern terminology and concepts such as democracy, reason, progress, and science than the other models. According to quintessential figures in this model, such as Sir Sayyed Ahmad Khan in South Asia and Muhammad Abduh in the Middle East, Islam by definition means the balance between faith and reason. They hoped Muslim society would achieve a synthesis between Islamic tradition and Western modernity. Some Muslims advocated the complete separation of church and state, as in Turkey under Kemal Ataturk. Indeed, Turkey had even gone to the extreme of beginning to reject Islam in many of its forms. But the promises of nationalist achievement, genuine democracy, and economic progress for all never really materialized. Most Muslim countries have not embraced genuine democracy or widespread and permanent economic progress. Instead, experiments with this model are beset by regimes of the strongman type or, as in Afghanistan and Iraq, are plunged into turmoil and anarchy and are considered shoddy imitations of the West that have failed to deliver. Muslims in this model face the danger of compromising faith without acquiring reason.

Our travels in the Muslim world confirmed that Muslims align themselves according to these models. Those we encountered who believe in the Ajmer model had deep faith in their own position but appeared on the defensive, not only because they were under attack by the more orthodox Muslims—especially some groups of the Deoband model—but also because it was difficult to survive in the age of globalization and make their voices heard. Those of the Aligarh model appeared in disarray and saw the future in uncertain terms. Confidence, aggression, and a sense of triumph marked those of the Deoband model. History had finally turned their way.

Not surprisingly, then, members of my team elicited a wide range of reactions in the communities we visited on our journey. They were observing us just as much as we were observing them. I have used some of this material in the text. Muslim reactions to our female companions, Hailey and Hadia, provided a telling contrast, allowing us to observe firsthand how these reactions worked within our three Muslim models and to comment on their authenticity and integrity. Blond with blue eyes, Hailey represented the typical American female with European ancestry. With her brown eyes and olive complexion, Hadia symbolized a new kind of American of Arab and Muslim parentage, and she wore the *hijab* over her hair. The mystics of the Ajmer model accepted Hailey with the same easy hospitality they extended to the entire team, while those of the orthodox Deoband model, with impeccable propriety, extended her hospitality only within their women's gatherings, all the while pretending she did not exist. It was left to the modern young Muslim male, whether in Istanbul or Amman, to see her as a stereotype—the waiting-to-be-seduced Western female. Their attitude toward Hailey rather neatly summed up the predicament of the Aligarh model. They had abandoned traditional Muslim behavior and had not quite made the transition to Western social behavior, education, and culture and were therefore inclined to easily misread signs and situations. Thus they ended up being neither of the past nor really of the present.

Matters for Hailey quickly improved when she learned how to read signals in Muslim societies, even in the greeting of people. A handshake between a male and female is not encouraged in traditional society, as it would violate established social norms. A young Muslim male being offered a hand to shake by a young American female could well read something more into it than a social greeting. Clothing also had significance. When Hailey began to dress in more traditional outfits, such as long skirts, loose shirts, and an occasional headscarf, particularly in houses of worship, she found herself no longer attracting unwelcome male attention. In Karachi she refused to enter Jinnah's mausoleum until she found a headscarf to show respect for the memory of the father of the Pakistani nation, and when I mentioned this to a large audience at a public event in Islamabad, just after she had spoken, people were impressed. The next day the

Hadia Mubarak answers questions in a madrassah in Delhi about her experiences as an American Muslim. Questions about American Muslims and the negative image of Islam in the West were frequent on the trip.

national press noted her gesture of respect with appreciation. At the end of a long day at the university at Deoband in India, a senior member of the faculty who had been escorting us around expressed his gratitude for our visit in a classroom full of bearded young men. So impressed was he with the deportment and dress of Hailey that he addressed her as "holy Hailey." At a time of high levels of anti-Americanism in the region, a student had won friends for the United States by showing cultural sensitivity.

Hadia was another matter. She was accepted by the mystics at Ajmer and welcomed with admiration by Deoband followers. The latter saw her as proudly representing Islam in the United States and were grateful. Even the orthodox madrassahs, normally an all-male preserve, invited her to speak to a gathering of several hundred young male students, who were enthralled by what she had to say in Arabic. Whether in Istanbul or Aligarh itself, those of the Aligarh model once again had problems. In Istanbul, they even tried to prevent Hadia from entering the premises of a university campus because of her hijab. In Aligarh, an angry mob of students assailed her with a barrage of hostile questions about American foreign policy. While not making any improper sexual suggestions, they nonetheless expressed an undefined anger when dealing with her. Perhaps they considered her hijab a symbol of their own predicament: they were constantly on the defensive because Islam has been criticized for being a backward religion.

Differences between the Shia and Sunni Sects

To add to its complexity, Islam is composed of two major sects, the Sunni and the Shia, each of which has been influenced by the worldviews of our three models in varying ways. Today, roughly 85–90 percent of the Muslim world is Sunni and the rest mainly Shia. On a theological level, the two sects show virtually no differences—both believe in the same God, Prophet, Quran, and the values that are inherent in Islam. There are distinct differences on a political and sociological level, however, and they date back to the death of the Prophet in 632 C.E.

Shia belief and identity originate in the question of who should have been the first political successor to the Prophet of God and borne the title of first caliph, or head of the Islamic community he had established. Shia believe that the Prophet's son-in-law, Ali, was the rightful successor. Ali was not only an extraordinary figure—a wise scholar and brave warrior—but also the first male to declare his belief in the message of Islam. Ali did become the ruler of Islam, but only after Abu Bakr, Umar, and Uthman—all three highly revered figures in Sunni Islam—had held the position. Ali is also the father of the prominent Shia figure Hussein, who would be martyred at Karbala, in modern-day Iraq—a seminal event in Shia history and marked by massive pilgrimages to Karbala today.

This initial difference over the succession developed into a sectarian schism under Umar's rule, when what was then the Persian Empire converted to Islam. The Persians brought with them—as did people in other parts of the Muslim world—many of their customs and sense of national pride. They had just suffered defeat at the hands of the Arabs, whom they despised as backward tribesmen lacking in culture and intellect. It seemed logical for them to identify with Ali in their new religion because this affiliation enabled them to retain a sense of superiority while seeing themselves as a persecuted minority within the world body of Muslims dominated by the Sunni. Over time, sociological differences seeped into religious observance, which affected rituals. The respect and status that Shia clerics enjoy in society is unmatched in the Sunni sect, whose religious scholars have to compete with traditional leaders and with other leaders for a voice. Furthermore, Shia identify with Ali so intensely that Sunni often accuse them of paying more respect to Ali than to the Prophet himself in the Islamic cosmos. Paradoxically, both Sunni and Shia revere and are inspired by the same historical figures—the Prophet, his daughter, Fatima, her husband, Ali, and their son, Hussein.

Umar, the second ruler of Islam after the Prophet's death, is a particular flashpoint between the two communities. Sunni consider him a role model, as responses to our questionnaires indicated, whereas Shia have mixed feelings about him: he is one of those who usurped Ali's rightful place as successor to the Prophet but also the ruler who ordered the successful invasion and conquest of Persia that brought the Persians into Islam. Sunni elders oftentimes whisper that in the old days, when Shia warriors went hunting, they would pull back the bow with the arrow in position and whisper a prayer that it might find its true mark in the heart of Umar.

Ayatollah Ruhollah Khomeini, who led the Islamic revolution in Iran against the shah, came to represent everything that was opposed to Western modernity in the view of people in the West and even the modernists among the Shia who believed in their own version of the Aligarh model. Khomeini did reach out to the Sunni, however, arguing that there was no theological difference between the two sects. His slogan was "neither east nor west, Islam is best," but in the end, the politics of Iran engulfed him. His country plunged into a long and bloody war with Iraq, and the Iranian revolution ran out of steam.

The animus between Shia and Sunni has often sparked rioting in areas where Shia are in the minority, such as Saudi Arabia and Pakistan. In Iran, on the other hand, the Sunni minorities, especially tribal groups such as the Kurds on the western borders and the Baluch on the eastern, have historically been persecuted by the Shia. As Khomeini pointed out, this friction between Sunni and Shia has little to do with substantial or irreconcilable theological differences. Rather, the blame lies with ethnic, sociological, and psychological factors.

Currently, the bonds and relationships between Shia and Sunni are collapsing into sectarian violence in Shia-dominated Iraq, Sunni-dominated

Pakistan, and in Lebanon where both are balanced in strength. Friends and neighbors are inflicting extreme pain on each other, knowing as they do their mutual weaknesses and sensitivities. Dark and deep irrational impulses prompted by malice are being expressed through the most vicious acts of cruelty. The intensity and widespread nature of the current violence within Islam confirm that something is amiss in the human condition today.

Sociologically, Shia communities exhibit many Ajmer tendencies, since the Sufi component of Ajmer has contributed richly to Shia culture. At the same time, religious Shia clerics who feel particularly strongly that they are defenders of the faith appear to be more in line with the Deoband model, and until recently the Shia response to modernity has seemed closer to the Aligarh model. Recall that Persia (Iran), a Shia stronghold, was never colonized by the West—there was no Aligarh university and therefore no Sir Sayyed Ahmad Khan, Allama Iqbal, or Jinnah. For the Shia, modernity meant rejecting both the Shia equivalent of the Ajmer and Deoband models—that is, any form of traditional religion—and being blindly infatuated with the West. From the 1950s until he was overthrown, the shah of Iran came to embody this embrace of the West and rejection of traditional values and was alienated from his people. Shia Islam does have a few modernist figures, however, such as the Iranian sociologist Ali Shariati, trained in France. But none of them has ever been in power. Today, the Shia equivalent of Deoband dominates Iran. The country's present drive to build a nuclear program that could provoke another world crisis needs to be seen in the context of the Shia sense of persecution and the Iranian Shia position within the ideology of Islam.[39]

At the Crossroads

What lies at the core of all great world faiths is clearly missing in today's world: a sense of justice, compassion, and knowledge. The tidal wave of globalization has swept over the world with economic and financial might, fomenting anger, greed, and ignorance. In such an environment, feelings of compassion and understanding for others become irrelevant—human beings and human relationships do not appear to matter. This characteristic of globalization has been accelerated since 9/11. Learned professors of law—those who should know better—have justified the use of torture in its most degrading forms in secret prison camps.[40] The U.S. war on terror has become a distorted symbol of globalization associated with torture and the suspension of human rights to millions of the poor and dispossessed and those who feel for them. This challenges the naïve, ethnocentric assumption of Western intellectuals that globalization promotes "cosmopolitan tolerance" and that this is a characteristic of Western culture that can now be transmitted to the rest of the world.[41] The human race is at the point of losing what makes it human: compassion. It needs to rediscover compassion for every one of its social units, from immediate kin to the larger societies that share this planet.

Governments therefore need to be encouraged to conduct serious dialogue and make efforts at understanding even those they strongly oppose, instead of isolating and alienating them. A rejection of the Deoband model in the Middle East, for example, not only further radicalized its supporters but in the end broadened its base in society. The tactic of neither recognizing nor talking to Deoband supporters has palpably failed. Governments also need to help revive the models of Ajmer and Aligarh marginalized at present. Compassion for and understanding of other societies is the only way to resolve the serious problems civilization now faces. In Muslim society alone, those problems are multifold: illiteracy, lack of health care, poverty, and legitimate political grievances relating to Palestinians, Kashmiris, Muslims in the Balkans, and Chechens. To add to this complexity, Muslims form a traditional yet global community committed to their faith. The future of the human race depends on international dialogue with these and other populations.

That means doing something that has never been done before in human history: jointly applying the moral codes universal to all faiths and great legal systems. Time is of the essence here. The poisons are spreading so rapidly that without immediate remedial action, no antidote may ever be found.

This book represents a crucial first step in that direction: it explains why defining the problem of Islam's relations with the West is not just a routine exercise of an academic nature but, because incorrect assumptions will invariably lead to flawed conclusions, vital to the process of true understanding. Labeling Islam with newer and ever more widely extravagant titles, such as "Islamofascism," may create more problems than can be imagined. We have therefore probed deeply into how Islam is being defined in our time, who is doing the defining, and why. We have suggested alternative ways of looking at the same problems.

The book also proposes how to achieve dialogue and understanding between societies through practical examples from the field. It not only raises theoretical questions but recounts actual cases describing real people. From the bazaars of the Middle East, the mosques and temples of South Asia, and the college campuses of the Far East we hear voices—Muslim and non-Muslim—that are seldom if ever heard. The book echoes their faith and message of hope.

Unfortunately, American thinkers and policymakers appear to be as transfixed with negative energy about Islam as Muslims are about American culture and its policies. Neither is showing the wisdom, courage, and commitment needed to make the world a better—and definitely safer—place. This will require a change of mind and, more important, a change of heart.

TWO

The Struggle within Islam

AUGUST 29, 1659, was a hot and humid day in Delhi, the capital of the mighty Mughal Empire. Large throngs lined the main streets to catch a glimpse of their favorite prince, Dara Shikoh, heir apparent to Shah Jehan, who had built the celebrated Taj Mahal. But this was not a happy occasion. Dara was on his way to be executed.[1] As the crowd caught sight of him, a gasp went up. Pale, drawn, and clothed in filthy rags, Dara looked down from a ragged elephant covered in dirt. Aware that every attempt was being made to publicly humiliate him, he sat with characteristic dignity and poise, his bewildered fifteen-year-old son beside him. Both knew that this was their last journey.

Malik Jiwan, an Afghan nobleman, then appeared, and the crowds booed and hissed. Some pelted him with cow dung in contempt of his betrayal of their Dara, who had once saved Malik from a similar fate. The nobleman had returned the favor by betraying Dara to Aurangzeb, Dara's younger brother and tormentor, who had usurped the throne and now ruled in Delhi. When Shah Jehan fell ill, Aurangzeb, a battle-hardened veteran and commander of the imperial army, imprisoned his father and challenged Dara in battle, easily defeating him.

That victory sealed Dara's fate. He was tried, found guilty of apostasy, and sentenced to death. When Dara's severed head was brought before him, Aurangzeb exclaimed, "As I did not look at this infidel's face during his lifetime, I have no wish to do so now."[2] He had the head placed in a box and sent to Shah Jehan in his prison cell. Ill and dejected at the cruel fate of his favorite son, the father sadly remembered visiting the tomb of the great Sufi saint at Ajmer before Dara's birth and praying for a son and heir. Upon the birth of his son, Shah Jehan honored the saint for successfully interceding with God on the emperor's behalf by ordering a grand celebration that included fireworks exploding across the night sky in a thousand patterns and alms to the poor. Shah Jehan would spend the rest of his days looking at the Taj Mahal in the distance through a slit in his cell, pining for his beloved wife buried therein, and mourning the loss of his dearest son, Dara.

Despite Aurangzeb's victory on the battlefield, Dara's ideals were not so easily vanquished. Though a scholar of the Islamic tradition, the charismatic and sophisticated Dara had been widely popular with all religions, having reached out to Hindus and Sikhs in genuine friendship, and was instrumental in translating into Persian for the first time the great Hindu holy texts, the *Upanishads* and the *Bhagavad Gita*. It would be from these translations, often called the *Sirr-i-Akbar* (The Greatest Mystery), that Europe would discover the classic Hindu texts several centuries later.

In several major works, Dara disputed the view that Hinduism was a religion of idol worshippers, calling it the original monotheistic faith because its idea of Brahman, the God of infinite being in Hinduism, predated even the Abrahamic faiths. Perhaps his best-known work is the *Majma al-Bahrain* (The Mingling of the Two Oceans), which attempts to establish the unity of the Abrahamic and the Indic religions through the compassionate mysticism taught in Sufism and Hinduism, both of which, argued Dara, see *ishq,* or "love," in the most ideal sense at the core of the divine. From love was born the Great Soul, known as the soul of Muhammad the Prophet of Islam, and from love was also born Mahatman, the Great Soul of Hinduism. A ring worn by Dara reflected the ultimate unity of divinity, with "Prabhu" on one side and "Allah" on the other—the names of the divine in Hinduism and Islam, respectively. "Mysticism is equality," wrote Dara. "If I know that an infidel, immersed in sin, is singing the note of monotheism, I go to him, hear him, and am grateful to him."[3]

Notwithstanding his love of mystics of all faiths, Dara had little time for Islam's religious clerics: "Paradise is there, where there is no mullah."[4] In the end, it would be these very clerics who would decide his fate and declare him an apostate. Yet he was attracted to Islam's mystical and universalist message and drew inspiration directly from the Prophet of Islam. At the same time, as the elder son of the emperor of India, a land with a majority Hindu population, he was aware of the predicament of the small Muslim elite ruling over vast numbers of a different faith. His thoughts naturally turned to discovering the common bond between Islam and the Indic religions. He was also inspired by the example of his great-grandfather, Emperor Akbar, who "insisted in the 1590s on the need for free and open dialogue and free choice, and also arranged recurrent discussions involving not only mainstream Muslim and Hindu thinkers, but also Christians, Jews, Parsees, Jains, and even atheists."[5]

Among those attracted to Dara's circle of varied friends and admirers was Sarmad, an Armenian Jew from Persia, who was both a merchant and a mystic. Though a convert to Islam, Sarmad suffused his poetry with universal mysticism. He reveled in the thought of Dara as the next emperor, who would usher in a reign of peace and spiritual enlightenment. Like Dara, Sarmad suffered an untimely death under Aurangzeb, whose interpretation of Islam eventually triumphed over Dara's visionary attempt to unite the great traditions of the Islamic and Indic faiths.

An austere man, Aurangzeb disliked music, instituted Islamic law, patronized Islamic education, and imposed a tax on his non-Muslim subjects. He laboriously made copies of the Quran, then sold them and distributed the money to the needy. In contrast to the Taj Mahal, where his parents lie buried, his grave is a simple one in the orthodox Islamic tradition. Stanley Wolpert, one of the most noted historians of India, describes Aurangzeb as "at once the most pious and the most ruthless of the Great Mughals. . . . He was hailed by Sunni Islam as India's only caliph and reviled by Hindudom even more than the Ghaznavids and Ghurs [former Muslim dynasties] had been for the suffering he self-righteously inflicted on non-Muslim subjects in peacetime as well as in war."[6]

It was no surprise for me to find Mughal emperor Aurangzeb's handwritten Quran in the library of Deoband. To many Muslims throughout South Asia, Aurangzeb's name has come to symbolize a strong and assertive orthodox Islam. When referring to him, his admirers use his official title "Alamgir," or "the world conqueror," and others add to his name *Waliullah*—meaning "the friend of God." In E. M. Forster's *A Passage to India*, the Muslim hero, Dr. Aziz, dreams of following Aurangzeb into battle, his ideal champion of Islam. The same Muslims who admired Aurangzeb reviled Dara as someone who had lost his path.

By the time of his death in 1707, Emperor Aurangzeb had extended the boundaries of the Mughal Empire to include much of today's Afghanistan, Pakistan, India, and Bangladesh—whose collective population now constitutes about one-fourth of the world community. So grand and powerful was the impression Mughal emperors made on Europeans that the very word Mughal entered the English language, and its derivative, "mogul," is used to refer to powerful Hollywood tycoons.[7]

But at the end of Aurangzeb's reign, the Muslim empire was drawing ever tighter boundaries around itself in the face of several emerging forces, particularly a Hindu and Sikh backlash against the legacy of Aurangzeb's rule. In addition, the British, who had arrived in the seventeenth century, were expanding their influence—and continued to do so until they had India colonized in the nineteenth century.

In 1857 India was rocked by uprisings, called the "Great Indian Mutiny" by the British and the "First War of Independence" by the Indians. Although many groups participated in the fighting, the British blamed the Muslims. The Mughal Empire was terminated, the emperor exiled to Rangoon, and the remaining heirs to the dynasty put to death. Persian was banned as the official language and replaced by English. A new social hierarchy and new values adverse to Islamic practices were instituted. Contemporary accounts describe Mughal noblemen bereft of their wealth starving to death and princesses becoming prostitutes in order to survive.[8] With the way of life they had known for centuries fast disappearing, India's Muslims recognized the time had come to respond to their rapidly declining position. By the mid-nineteenth century, Dara's vision of a mystical Islam had faded and Aurangzeb's orthodox traditionalism was being reinforced. In the highly charged environment of this period, some Muslims fell back to the Ajmer model embodied by Dara Shikoh, but others followed a more aggressive jihad against the British, as advocated by Deoband, in an effort to protect their beliefs and way of life. Neither model fully served the needs of the community, however. The times called for an altogether different Muslim response that engaged directly with the emerging and dominant Western world. A "modernist" response was not long in coming. It would originate in a college newly established in the town of Aligarh in India.

"Peace with All"

My namesake, Akbar the Great, walked barefoot for days through the hot deserts of Rajasthan to pray at the shrine of Moin-uddin Chisti at Ajmer. Although one of the most powerful and richest rulers in Asia—perhaps in the world at that time—Akbar deliberately humbled himself in public to beg the saint to intercede with God on his behalf for a son. He thus set an example for his descendants much as Shah Jehan had done. The saint's reputation as the spiritually powerful and mysterious Gharib-Nawaz (Blesser of the Poor) was further enhanced with the birth of Akbar's heir. Over the centuries, stories of improbable miracles as a result of praying at Ajmer became legend, and supplicants seeking God's blessings thus assumed the role of "beggars"—whether it was a Mughal emperor praying for a son or simply an individual like myself seeking to promote peace and understanding. Indeed, being a supplicant is the most effective way to check what modern society calls the ego. In its various guises, especially excessive power and riches, this is precisely what the mystics wished to control through *fana,* or annihilation, because they saw it as an obstacle to spiritual enlightenment and personal development.

This spirit suffused Akbar's rule and helped him unite the different races and religions of his vast empire. His governors were ordered to spend their spare time reading the mystic verses of Maulana Rumi. Attracted to Akbar's humanism, no doubt, my father named me after the emperor.

In March 2006, I found myself once again a "beggar" in Ajmer. For me, there is no place on earth quite like it. The very air is heavy with spirituality. Every visit revives my spirit and reconfirms for me the ultimate blessings of a caring, compassionate, and universal God. Dusk was falling and the first stars already twinkling as I entered the shrine, greeted by the sweet sounds of sacred devotional music. All around me, young and old, men and women, rich and poor milled about with an air of contentment. From the great variety of nationalities, races, and religions, it seemed all of humanity was there.

As is customary before entering the shrine, my team and I took off our shoes. My students, I noticed, had discreetly rid themselves of their cell phones and iPods, the appurtenances of globalization they usually carried around as part of their identity. They, too, were entering into the spirit of the shrine and putting aside the most conspicuous signs of their egos. All

Hailey Woldt, Frankie Martin, and Akbar Ahmed listen to devotional music late at night in the courtyard of the Sufi shrine in Ajmer, India. The message, "Peace with all," of the well-loved Sufi mystic who is buried here, Moin-uddin Chisti, attracts thousands of pilgrims from all faiths annually.

of us also covered our heads as a sign of respect. Frankie and I were given a bright pink cloth to wrap around our heads like turbans. Hadia was already wearing the hijab so was correctly dressed, and Hailey had worn traditional Muslim dress with her hair covered. Tridivesh Singh, a Sikh and our guide in India, already wore a turban.

We were accompanied by Muqaddas Moini, a direct descendant of the saint and a keeper of the shrine, who had been my host on an earlier visit to film *Living Islam* for the BBC. Moini produced a flat basket containing red rose petals mixed with white flowers arranged in circles with all circles leading back to one center and thereby representing the oneness of God. He pointedly asked Hailey to place the basket on her head so that she could perform the ritual of showering the saint's grave with the flowers. From my last visit, I knew that this was a special honor, and everyone in my team was aware of the symbolism that it represented: a young Christian female being selected to honor a Muslim saint. This was the Ajmer model in action.

We filed into the innermost sanctum of the shrine behind Hailey, shuffling slowly amid the jostling visitors moving closer to the grave. A haze of incense enveloped the worshippers as they respectfully threw the bright red and white petals on the grave and tied brightly colored strings to the metal gates protecting it. After filing out, the team remained within the shrine to offer a silent prayer. Everyone sat lost in thought, many moved to tears of joy and serenity, as if time had evaporated. Our Muslim, Christian, and Sikh identities, though still intact, had expanded and merged in the magical air of Ajmer. We were simply pilgrims united as one and sharing a sense of a common divinity.

For Hailey, balancing the basket of flowers upon her head had been "an electrifying experience": "I could feel the pulses and energy of everyone in the shrine. I felt connected through my energy to all of humanity, through the rose petals which I threw on the saint's grave to the stars in the sky and the sand on the beaches. The shrine, my body, the colors all dissolved into the universe and into a blissful feeling of nothing; my identity did not matter here. I felt close to my God, the only God, as the other worshippers felt close to Him." She felt the saint had indeed "invited" her to his shrine, referring to the popular saying in Ajmer that unless the saint invites the visitor, the pilgrimage will not be a success.

As the sweet music from the courtyard drifted our way, we moved outside to sit on simple rugs under a sweet-smelling tree, and the lights and colors of the night began washing over us as in a dream. The music and the words praising the mercy and glory of God expressed the human yearning for spiritual union with the divine and again brought tears of joy to those around us as they swayed to the rhythm. Frankie described the experience as "a retreat from the world I had been a part of only seconds earlier. The music and sounds of the mosque bound me to that reality, but my thoughts began to drift elsewhere, as if carried by the music to pure feeling, a feeling of calmness and peace. I had one foot in the 'real' world, and one someplace else. I held on to this, whatever it was, for about fifteen minutes before I opened my eyes, and I and the rest of the team sat near the musicians in the courtyard for a while, talking among ourselves and trying to put into words what was almost impossible to communicate." I quietly asked my team whether they felt any sense of unease in the midst of this large crowd of strangers so late at night and in the middle of Rajasthan. Hadia remarked that "many of the women would look at us and politely nod their head. We nodded back." Far more than words, such gestures conveyed "the idea that even though your religion, culture, language, and dress may differ from mine, even though I may never come across you again throughout my lifetime, I acknowledge and understand the commonality of our existence, the oneness of our origin and our shared destiny. That gesture meant to me, 'I can connect with you because you are a human being to me before anything else.'"

Back in the twelfth century, when Moin-uddin Chisti had made a pilgrimage to the tomb of the Prophet in Medina to reflect on the nature of God in one of Islam's holiest places, the Prophet appeared to him in a vision urging him "to go to Hindustan (India) to spread the word of Islam" and handed him a pomegranate revealing the chosen destination, Ajmer. Chisti left on his mission immediately and in time came to be known as the "deputy of the Prophet in India." He introduced Islam without alienating the other religions there, converting Hindus not through the sword but through peace and love. The saint's philosophy was summed up in his motto, *sulh-i-kul,* or "peace with all."

Our trip to Ajmer and reception there were a testament to Chisti's philosophy, reputation, and power, particularly the acceptance that is at the heart of the Ajmer model—which inspired Dara Shikoh and Akbar. Acceptance and tolerance were in evidence again the next day, when Tridivesh arranged for us to visit the famous Hindu and Sikh temples at nearby Pushkar, a picturesque whitewashed town with a "holy" lake at its center. At the Hindu temple, we watched as women swam in the lake to purify themselves and cows wandered through the streets. At the Sikh temple, called Gurdwara Singh Sabha, we sat on the floor alongside other visitors and shared in a communal meal given by the priests.

Afterward, the priests kindly granted Hadia permission to pray in the courtyard, although it was unusual for a Muslim to be praying in a Sikh temple. Tridivesh stood close by, watching over her. That experience, her friendship with Tridivesh and Sucha, our driver, and the entire trip to India transformed her view of Sikhs. Hadia said: "As a young girl, I thought that Sikhs hated Muslims. However, after interacting with many Sikhs during this trip and enjoying the hospitality of Tridivesh's mother and father, I learned to admire and respect their commitment to their religion, which actually bears much resemblance to Islam." Hadia was very perceptive in

Akbar Ahmed was welcomed warmly to India by his former Sikh student, Tridivesh Singh, on the left. The friendship reflects the common bonds between different faiths in spite of the conflict between Sikhs and Muslims and gives hope for the future. Sucha Singh, the team's driver, is on the right.

her comment, especially considering she had never been to this part of the world before.

Tridivesh would say, for all to hear, that he was my "nephew" to express his affection for me from the time he was my student in Washington, D.C. He discusses the Sufi bonds with the origins of the Sikh faith in his recently published book in which he inscribed the following words for me: "My dear Sir/Chacha and family [*chacha* is widely understood as "father's brother" in South Asia]. It is thanks to your inspiration/support/encouragement that I thought of writing this book."[9] The creation of what anthropologists call a "fictitious lineage" allowed Tridivesh to make this bold statement and thus transcend race and religion. In an environment where relations between Sikhs and Muslims have traditionally been as acrimonious as those between the Palestinians and Israelis, and Sikhs in my own youth were considered the enemies of Islam, this was as significant a statement as one can wish for in the quest for understanding.

Tridivesh and his parents had welcomed us to India in the true spirit of sulh-i-kul. The impulse of Sufism and its mystic roots of universal acceptance are clearly present in other faiths besides Islam.

To reiterate, the Ajmer model is a *universal* model, restricted by neither era nor geography. And renowned mystics like Chisti of Ajmer and Prince Dara Shikoh who changed the course of history are easily found in other parts of the Muslim world. For example, what is now Iraq was home to a female saint, Rabia, born early in the eighth century in Basra. Rabia was the fourth daughter of an impoverished family. According to legend, her father had a dream in which the Prophet of Islam told him that one day Rabia would be loved and revered as a saint. When still quite young, she apparently became separated from her parents and was sold into slavery. Because of her beauty, she was relegated to a brothel and a life of emotional and sexual degradation from an early age but still maintained her love of and faith in God. When Rabia was about fifty, she was able to win her freedom, possibly because some kind patron recognized her spirituality, and devoted her remaining years to seeking and speaking about God and universal love. A mythology grew up around her of a saint who could perform miracles. Her saintliness was reinforced by her rejection of the material world, and when disciples gave her offerings, she would always refuse them. Once when a disciple gave her a bag of gold, she allegedly replied in her simple and rustic manner, "Dear, if you leave that, flies will gather as if a horse just relieved himself, and I might slip in it while dancing."[10]

Rabia's verses of intense love for the divine would be echoed by the mystics who followed her. In "The Sky Gave Me Its Heart," for example, she writes:

Why is it we think of God so much?
Why is there so much talk about love?
My eye kept telling me, "Something is missing from all I see."
    So I went in search of the cure.
The cure for me was His Beauty, the remedy—for me was to love.[11]

Some centuries later, on the island of Java, a boy was born into an aristocratic family of one of Indonesia's last Hindu kingdoms. According to myth, he had established his reputation as a gambler and thief early in life, who spent his money on women of easy virtue. One day he stopped a foreign-looking man—an Arab, so the story goes—and tried to rob him. The man rebuked him, saying that desire and worldly goods are of no value, that we live for a moment and then have nothing. The stranger pointed to a banyan tree that suddenly seemed to turn to gold, its branches dripping with precious stones. At that moment the young man became "aware," a local idiom referring to the realization that the material world is just an illusion, whereupon he asked the stranger to teach him spiritual knowledge. In reply, the stranger asked him whether he had the strength of will and endurance for the task. The young man said he did, and the stranger asked him to wait by the river until his return. He stayed at the spot for many years. Trees grew around him and floods came and went. People stopped to stare, touched him, and went on their way. But the young man appeared to be in a trance. When the stranger finally returned, he declared the pupil a master, named him Kalidjaga, and declared that henceforth he was destined to spread Islam. Indeed, Kalidjaga almost single-handedly brought Islam to Java, now part of the largest Muslim nation in the world.

Unlike Chisti and Rabia, who had grown up in a tradition of Islamic learning and history, Kalidjaga began with a clean slate, and the style and approach to his new faith seemed more in the meditative Indic tradition. Even so, the effect of his teaching and character was as widespread in the Far East as that of Rumi in the Middle East. Even today, Kalidjaga is known as the man who brought Java from *djaman indu*, "Hindu times," to *djaman islam*, "Islamic times." Whatever the historical reality, all three mystics—Rabia in the Middle East, Chisti in South Asia, and Kalidjaga in the Far East—embody the contemplative, pacifist, ascetic, and compassionate form of Islam in popular folklore.

The Ajmer model, with its asceticism and message of universal acceptance, still manages to survive amid the consumerism, turmoil, anger, greed, and ignorance of the modern age. Many in the West are familiar with Rumi's teachings, thanks to the technology of globalization. If the sales of his books and DVDs over the past ten years are any indication, he is the number one poet for Muslims and non-Muslims in the United States, and he counts celebrities such as Madonna, Deborah Winger, and Martin Sheen among his many fans. Rumi's wide appeal stems from his sincere acceptance of all faiths, as reflected in a collection called "Jesus Poems," in which he dedicates one of his most passionate poems to Jesus:

> Where Jesus lives, the great-hearted gather.
> We are a door that's never locked.
> If you are suffering any kind of pain,
> stay near the door. Open it . . .
> Christ is the population of the world,
> and every object as well.[12]

Rumi's love for that quintessential mystic figure, Jesus, and his popularity today confirm the strength of the Ajmer model. At the same time, the struggle between Aurangzeb and his brother Dara, and its outcome—victory for the former and death for the latter—continues to cast its shadow upon our time. For those in India who look for reasons to dislike Muslims, Aurangzeb is an easy target. In the communal riots that occur with frequency in India, the extremist groups contemptuously refer to Muslims as "the children of Aurangzeb." As for Dara, the world will not let him be forgotten either. Dara may have lost the struggle for the throne, but his message still rings true for his admirers.

The Legacy of Aurangzeb

A long drive with Aijaz brought the team to its next stop: Deoband. We stepped out of the van unsure of what to expect. To our surprise, we were greeted by the head cleric himself, Maulana Anzar Shah Kashmiri, and his high command, who whisked us off to one of the main mosques for a speech. The Maulana not only held the grand title of Sheikhul Hadith at Deoband—the highest clerical authority on the traditions and sayings of the Prophet—but was also president of the national All-India Tanzim Ulema Hind based in New Delhi. This meant that he was an authority on the Hadith at Deoband, and also the head of a national organization of religious scholars in India. We were escorted to the large prayer room of the mosque, which was filled with students ranging from young boys to young men similar in appearance to Aijaz.

When Aijaz introduced me, with Hailey and Frankie sitting on the carpets by my side, he spoke with a fiery, affectionate tone about my work and protectively announced my heritage as an "Indian" Muslim who had

At the main mosque in Deoband, young men wash themselves ritually before prayers. The ablution is observed by Muslims before each of the five prayers during the day.

"returned" home from the United States, overlooking the fact I had spent only the first four years of my life in India. Because of the nationalist tensions between India and Pakistan, Aijaz conveniently neglected the middle part of my life in Pakistan. As a sign of prestige, he mentioned the well-known non-Muslim guests at my lecture at the Jamia Millia Islamia, a prominent university in Delhi, which he had attended the previous day perhaps to assess my opinions on Islam in person. Mushirul Hasan, the distinguished vice chancellor of the university, had chaired the lecture. Whatever reservations Aijaz may have had about my work he kept to himself. The Maulana also welcomed us warmly and the introductions set the tone for the rest of the visit.

They listened in silence to my talk in Urdu, sitting with respect on the floor covered with carpets and paying attention to every word. Afterward, during the question-and-answer session, they asked about the United States and Iraq. Hailey and Frankie, unable to understand Urdu, could only make out words such as "Amerika" and "Iraq" and wondered tensely how the students were responding. Within a matter of minutes, it became clear that no words were needed, as Frankie noted:

Mosques are sacred places, and the fact that I, and especially Hailey as a woman, were allowed to enter and participate was an unmistakable gesture of kindness and openness. The people of Deoband were reaching out to us, despite all the boundaries they had erected between them and the non-Islamic world. I was so conscious of the importance of such an occasion that I was almost afraid to move, wanting to make the best possible impression. It was a wonderful experience, but also intimidating, for I was representing not only myself but 300 million Americans and millions more from other parts of the "West." On our way out of the mosque, the boys and young men who had attended our talk came up and spoke to me [,] shaking my hand and patting me on the back, welcoming me to Deoband. There was not a hint of anger anywhere—they, and everyone else we met, seemed genuinely excited to have me, and treated me very respectfully.

We then attended a delicious lunch at the cleric's house. It was here that I observed the strict gender separation characteristic of this form of Islam. I saw hardly any women throughout the day; there were none to greet us, and there were none in our mosque visit. Here at lunch, the separation was very evident. . . . It hadn't quite registered at first, but Hailey was gone. I learned she had gone off to visit with the girls of the house, whom I had not met. I sat eating and chatting with our hosts, along with a little boy who was also there. The men, including the cleric [,] asked where I was from and welcomed me warmly. They also kept having me go back to the table and get more food. "You must try this chicken," they said, "you must try this beef." Like the mosque visit, the lunch at the cleric's home was significant. He had invited Hailey and me into his home to have lunch with his family, probably the strongest gesture of hospitality he could have shown us.

In the meantime, Hailey had been discreetly escorted to the women's section to visit with the sheikh's granddaughters, aged fifteen, thirteen, and seven, who were clothed in typical South Asian dress. Yet when asked about school, their favorite subjects, and their daily life, they said they watched television, Indian mostly, and spent time on the Internet. As to what they wanted to be when they grew up, they responded a journalist, a doctor, and a civil servant of India, respectively. After returning to the

Frankie Martin is surrounded by students of various ages on the steps outside a Deoband mosque. Frankie found that a sometimes frosty atmosphere, wherever he traveled, invariably improved after an exchange of ideas and social interaction.

mixed side for lunch, Hailey was again taken to meet the women of the house, including the girls' mother this time. She later noted, "I thanked her for the hard work she had put in for the elaborate meal and she said it was her honor, warmly giving me a hug. The girls asked for my e-mail address and then inquired, 'When are you coming back to Deoband?' The youngest girl motioned for me to lean down as if to tell me a secret; instead, she gave me a sweet kiss on the cheek and giggled. We then returned to the university to complete our tour. The lunch from that day has become imprinted on my mind and has further confirmed for me that not all Muslims are the same, not even those who live in Deoband itself."

After lunch, we toured the university at Deoband, a well-established institution with a total enrollment of about 3,500 and modern facilities, large dormitories and classrooms, and libraries containing thousands of books. I was surprised by the organization and pervasive sense of discipline—it was not the amateurish madrassah that I had envisioned. The students appeared dedicated to the Quran and Islam, as their founder would have intended. They made no fuss about their beliefs, but every action, look, and word displayed their absorption in their studies. One classroom we passed was filled with several hundred students in white robes and white caps engrossed in reading the Quran. A new addition to the university is its computer department, with about ten computers on dial-up connection and a specialist to teach website design and basic Microsoft applications.

In the English classroom, we had an opportunity to talk to about forty students, all bearded young men. We then distributed our questionnaires and engaged in a discussion about Islam, the United States, and the future of U.S.-Muslim relations with the students and professors. The discussion proved very revealing as to Deobandi views and practices. As Aijaz had made clear earlier, it was the religious duty of Deobandis to take "action designated as Jihad . . . for securing justice for the suppressed, assisting them in their efforts to secure that. . . . Its aim is to resist the oppressors and prevent them from committing atrocities."[13]

Unlike Westerners, Deobandis do not distinguish between the so-called oppressors of the weak who must be opposed because of religious duty and sovereign nations fighting wars for political reasons. However, as our discussion with the class progressed, I could see the students' faces softening. I was confident that my team, the first Americans they had ever met, could help establish rapport and constructive dialogue. We sat debating, exchanging ideas, and interacting with these young men for about thirty minutes. Most of the discussion focused on "Amerika" and its "oppression," but also on the Internet and the use of English throughout the world. Deoband had begun teaching English as a subject three years before our visit, noted the professor, and this was only the third class. The introduction of "secular subjects, like computer studies and English," he continued, "was actually meant for spreading the word of Islam." Thus despite the inclusion of Western technology and subjects, the curriculum holds fast to its original aim to preserve Deobandi traditions. If anything, the intent is to make them stronger throughout the world as well as in India's Muslim community.

Our encounter in the recently opened English class at Deoband established that bridges can be built even in the most unlikely situations, as Hailey recounts:

Computer science classes are taught at the new computer lab at Deoband. Students believe that through technology they can both better understand Islam and spread its message.

We passed by a classroom filled with 500 students in white robes and white caps with their heads down reading the Quran and then entered the English class where we distributed our questionnaires for our study. The students quietly filled them out—without any cries for blood as I had been expecting that morning on the ride in. As we left the class, they asked us for words of wisdom to be written on the board. I wrote something to try to help bring the United States and the Muslim world together in peace: "Learning and education are the most important things for world peace. Let us all continue to work for peace with all. Salaam alay kum." "Salaam alay kum" is the Arabic phrase for "peace be with you," their standard greeting, which unexpectedly gave rise to shouts of delight and friendship. We parted as friends—two Americans, a Muslim professor, and students of the most conservative madrassah in India."

Deoband was established for the express purpose of training religious leaders who would be dedicated to mainstream or orthodox Islam in response to the crisis that befell Muslim society in the nineteenth century.[14] These individuals would become writers, preachers, and teachers who would disseminate their Islamic learning to the community in an effort to preserve Islamic traditions. To gain admission to the school, students were expected to have studied Persian, memorized the Quran, and passed the entrance examination. Only half of the potential candidates examined were actually admitted. Seventy-eight students were admitted in the first year, and thereafter the number increased at the rate of about 200 to 300 a year up to its present level of 3,500.

Initially, the course of study lasted ten years, but this was later reduced to six. At Deoband, students were—and still are—expected to specialize in the three traditional areas of Islamic studies: the Hadith, the Quran, and *fiqh*, or Islamic jurisprudence, logic, and philosophy. There were few other subjects, but today some additions have been introduced, as already mentioned. Teachers have always been extremely dedicated, expecting very little payment in return, many of them influential scholars from different parts of South Asia who gave up attractive jobs with generous patrons in princely Muslim states or even government service. Most of them considered teaching important enough to return to Deoband to teach for small salaries of 10 or 15 rupees a month (currently, Rs60 = U.S.$1).

In time, the name *Deoband* came to symbolize not only the spread of Islamic teaching but also the cultivation of an inner spiritual life. By the end of the nineteenth century, schools modeled on the Deoband madrassahs had spread across the length and breadth of South Asia. When it came to politics, they rejected the idea pursued in the 1940s of partitioning India and creating an independent democratic Muslim homeland, arguing that God has no special country or nation.

With advancing globalization, Muslim culture and religion may again be entering a period of crisis, not unlike that faced by the Muslim community in 1857 under the prospect of a British-ruled India. The Muslims then also had to decide whether to go down the path of integration with the outside world. They chose to maintain their Islamic traditions and identity even at the cost of material and political gain. Deoband today must respond to globalization even if it desires minimum interaction with the outside world and is reacting with the same instincts and attitudes on which it was founded.

We found Deoband unambiguously clear about its self-perception and identity. Its young men—women remain excluded—proudly trace their ideological lineage to Shah Wali Ullah, to the Mughal emperor Aurangzeb (they take special pride in showing visitors his handwritten Quran in a special casement of the library), to Ibn Taymiyya, and straight back to the Prophet of Islam. The Taliban, Osama bin Laden, and members of al-Qaeda also identify with the same spiritual lineage and argue similarly that changes in the world are anathema to Islam, which can only be preserved by retreating to its beginnings, in the Prophet's example and the Quran. Hence on its website Deoband describes itself as "the torchbearer of Islamic renaissance. . . . On the one hand [Deoband] is a central representative of correct faith, Straight Path and true knowledge of Islam while on the other hand it stands out as a 'symbol of guidance' in the face of [a] horrible spate of atheism, polytheism and mental apostasy."[15] The difference between now and earlier times under the British is that the Deobandis completely rejected anything to do with Westernization then, whereas today they have mastered the use of Western technology without compromising their traditional beliefs. Having clear-cut principles and goals as a community, they are able to use technology without losing their sense of identity. They are using the West's own technology to fight against it in a new globalized jihad employing ideology, not the sword. In towns distant from Delhi, however, their daily lives continue to follow the traditional and simple ways based on the study of Islam.

However much the West would like to comfort itself with the notion of a backward Deoband having a poor understanding of global media, the students and faculty know not only how to use modern technology themselves but also how the outside world uses it as a tool of influence. The computer science department that we saw was up to date; its website was professional and extensive, with discussion pages and information on the religion's history, philosophy, and political messages. The website's chief editor, Aijaz, boasted that it was the most widely read Urdu website in

In the library at Deoband, Akbar Ahmed studies with a Quranic scholar who is taught in the traditional manner, seated on the carpet and expected to memorize the Quran by heart.

India. Since the entire institution is run on small donations from average people (which in India would have to be a very large number), the site devotes an entire page to specific directions for depositing funds in a centralized bank. Various publications can also be ordered from the site, including books, magazines, and pictures of the university. These materials are distributed to vast populations throughout the world, spreading Deoband's message in the process. The cleanliness and size of the place, with an entire town of students living and studying there for free, were most impressive. So was the recently constructed mosque, which we were told was the second largest mosque in India and patterned after the Taj Mahal.

After Aijaz had introduced the idea in Deoband, henceforth I would be introduced by Muslims as "Akbar Allahabadi" to indicate that I was a "son of the soil" and born in the historic city of Allahabad on the Ganges River. My hosts would recount my biography with South Asian hyperbole in all its awesome grandeur and—after mentioning my education in the United Kingdom and present activity in the United States—would conclude with an emotional flourish: "And now our Akbar Allahabadi has returned home to us." I was deeply touched but also amused to see that the Pakistan part of my life had been excised. Indian Muslims had once been proud of the idea of Pakistan but in recent decades lost whatever hopes and dreams they originally had about its possibilities. They had also been made to suffer unfairly as "Pakistanis" by the Indian communalists, especially in times of turmoil.

Jawaharlal Nehru, the great international statesman and first prime minister of India, often said that the secret of India's culture lay in its capacity to welcome outsiders. In his definition of Indian civilization, its predominant characteristic was synthesis, not confrontation.[16] He was right.

Nonetheless, with my Pakistani background—and after the particularly warm welcome we received in Pakistan—I alerted my team to be prepared for anything. But I need not have been apprehensive. The Indian charm and hospitality were overwhelming. Indian Muslims, in particular, took great delight in my presence.

To understand how Deoband influences world events, one needs to examine another educational center inspired by Deoband but based in Pakistan. Not far from Peshawar—and on the main highway to Islamabad—stands the Haqqania, one of the most radical, anti-American madrassahs in this turbulent region.[17] Here the lessons of history are relived in battles and skirmishes along the Afghanistan-Pakistan border. From this location students are able to cross the border and provide fighting power to the Taliban whenever they need reinforcements. The Haqqania boasts of having Mullah Umar, the leader of the Taliban, as one of its most prized alumni and is acutely aware of the larger political realities surrounding the events taking place in the region. Haqqania's director, Maulana Sami ul-Haq, tells visitors that whenever the Taliban call for fighters, he just closes down the madrassah and orders his students off to the battlegrounds: "In many ways, then, Akora Khattak [the town where the madrassah stands] represents everything U.S. policymakers most fear and dislike in this region, a bastion of religious, intellectual, and sometimes—in the form of the Taliban—military resistance to Pax Americana and all it represents."[18] Maulana Sami believes that American intervention

in the Islamic world has stimulated Muslim anger and emotion and therefore compelled people to look for answers to their problems within their
own traditions, which has been good for the revival of Islam: "Bush has
[awakened] the entire Islamic world. We are grateful to him."[19] The
Maulana does not conceal that he is angry with Musharraf for his corruption and for "following the wishes" of America.

We saw evidence of the Deoband model's strength throughout our journey. In election after election, Islamic parties are gaining more votes than
ever before, and in countries around the globe—most recently, Palestine,
Egypt, Indonesia, and Malaysia—Islamic parties are gaining popularity
and power. We were able to meet some of the members of these parties.
Abdul Latif Arabiyet, former secretary general of the Islamic Action
Front, which has captured almost 20 percent of the seats in the Jordanian
parliament, sounded like an echo of Aijaz of Deoband. Islam needs to be
revived, Arabiyet argued, especially as it is under attack from the West,
most notably Israel, only a few miles away across the border. Israel and the
United States are attempting to destroy Islam, he said. He described a conspiracy against Islam that aims to keep Muslims fragmented and fighting.
He accused President George W. Bush of launching a "crusade" against
Muslims and referred to the president's use of the word. Islam fell into
stagnation, he remarked, when it was no longer faithful to itself; therefore
Muslims need to return to their central role model, the Prophet of Islam,
and their holy book.

As we had come to expect from other representatives of the Deoband
model, however, Arabiyet was not simply the closed-minded fanatic often
depicted in the media. Rather than reject the state altogether, which
Deoband had done in the past, he approved of Jordan's king, Abdullah,
whose photograph hung in Arabiyet's office in Amman. The king's
dynasty, he conceded, provides both continuity and stability, important
factors in a turbulent region. Although Arabiyet's party admittedly had
links with the Muslim Brotherhood of Egypt, he said he was open to
intellectual influences from outside the Arab world, mentioning his
enthusiasm for Allama Iqbal, the poet-philosopher of South Asia, and for
the Islamic state of Pakistan. His party even boasts the first "Islamist"
female member of parliament in the region, Hayat Mussevi, whom I interviewed shortly after talking to Arabiyet. This shows that the traditionally
orthodox Deoband model is changing its attitude both to participating in

democratic elections and to allowing females to participate in public life. When I sat down to talk to her the same afternoon, she echoed the larger Islamic themes arising in our discussion of Deoband. Even Deoband, once aloof from politics, is expressing a new interest in stepping into India's political arena, and its members have already established links with several religious parties.

Although I could not visit Saudi Arabia and Iran on this trip because of logistics, earlier trips to both countries indicated that Saudi society is dominated by Wahhabi ideology, which is similar to our Deoband model, while the Iranians have adopted a complex mixture of all three models proposed here. The Aligarh model, which dominated Iran under the shah, is now subordinate to the Deobandi. Iranian culture, in contrast to Saudi culture, also boasts a rich mystic and universalist literature that includes works by such renowned literary figures as Rumi, Firdausi, and Hafiz. Saudi Arabia and Iran are important Muslim nations for several reasons: both have oil and holy sites of high prestige, and, in important ways, represent the two major sects of Islam, Sunni and Shia, respectively. Of course, Saudi Arabia is unique for all Muslims because it contains the two holiest places in Islam—Mecca and Medina.

Saudi Arabia and Iran are the heavyweights in the politics of the Middle East and in their bid for regional domination; both countries impose a theological frame on what is essentially a political confrontation and therefore sharpen their claims to represent mainstream and orthodox Islam and denounce the other as a deviant. The Saudis have become the champions of Sunni Islam and its most literal interpretation known throughout the world as Wahhabism. So narrow is the vision of some of its members that they would not even consider Islam's mystics or other sects to be proper Muslims. In opposition to the Saudi position, the Iranians, the preeminent standard-bearers of the Shia sect, announce themselves as the truest of all Muslims within the world of Islam. These conflicting views have taken hold in other countries as well, in some cases with serious effect. In Pakistan, for example, Shia and Sunni slaughter each other in periodic bouts of violence, including in mosques and bazaars.

Saudi Arabia and Iran do have one thing in common, though: in Western minds, both have become symbols of what is wrong with Islam and are thought to be dominated by wild-eyed fanatics with double standards and by an elite that squanders natural resources through corruption and bad planning. Not surprisingly, Western commentators argue these conditions create anarchy, noting that Iranians took American diplomats as hostages and locked them up for months in terrible conditions and that most of the 9/11 hijackers were Saudis. That is why, these commentators conclude, the Islam being taught in these important countries is to blame for Muslim extremism.

In the aftermath of 9/11, there has been a resurgence of a kind of patriotism both in the United States and in the Muslim world. In society after Muslim society that we visited, we talked to many people who represented what I call the Deoband position. They had a clearly defined mission and sense of identity: they are the new protectors of Islam, who have vowed not only to reclaim Islam for our times but also to defend it against all attacks. Their idea of preserving Islam ranges from warding off the "Western cultural invasion" to creating a caliphate or universal Islamic kingdom. At one extreme, some even support using violence in the defense of Islam. In one sense, they could be echoing the words of the Prophet concerning the ummah—or world Muslim community—which he likened to a body: if one part was in pain, the entire body would feel it and therefore be compelled to respond. Events since 9/11 have only strengthened this idea of the ummah under attack and therefore have provided the Deoband model with a common enemy and a valid platform from which to reunite the world ummah. The Deoband model, as we were told throughout the trip, will continue to pray for Bush and his long life because everything he is doing appears to rejuvenate and reunite the Muslim world. The Deoband model, then, is thriving in the age of globalization as a result of the forces of globalization.

Ride the Wave or Drown

Growing up, I attended Forman Christian College in Lahore, one of the premier colleges of Pakistan. Founded by Americans, it was patterned after the universities of Oxford and Cambridge with their tutorials, dormitories, quadrangles, and playing fields. Students dressed in the latest fashions from Europe, played tennis on well-tended grass courts, acted in classic Shakespearean dramas, and debated in English that the Queen would have been proud of. We felt that we could compete with anyone at any level; if we were not better than the West, then we certainly did not feel inferior to

The team at the gates of Aligarh University in India, founded in the nineteenth century and patterned after Cambridge University as a Muslim response to western education. Aligarh has produced generations of political and academic leaders in South Asia.

it. At the same time, we were proud of our Islamic heritage, said our prayers, and kept the fasts. We drew our strength from Aligarh University, founded upon the idea that the only way for Muslims to achieve success was to engage with the British, learn the language, and play within their rules for business and politics. Our history professor was actually an Aligarh alumnus who often talked of Jinnah and his links with Aligarh University in glowing terms. We had a sense of confidence about the future of Pakistan and ourselves. In fact, two students from around my time—Farooq Leghari and Pervez Musharraf—became presidents of Pakistan.

In March 2006, when we took a day of travel to meet with some students and faculty at Aligarh, I half expected the place would be consistent with my vision of it from the time of my youth. Once we arrived, Hadia and Frankie went off on their own to hand out questionnaires and talk to students on campus. When they came back, they were shaken and agitated. While distributing questionnaires outside the engineering college, they had been surrounded by a large crowd of increasingly aggressive students. Frankie, who had stepped in to distance Hadia from the young men, tried to explain the goals of the project, emphasizing that he and Hadia were on an academic trip and were not affiliated with any government:

"Did you vote for Bush?" they yelled, not letting me finish.

"What do you think of Bush?" I asked, attempting to deflect their question back at them.

"No, no," one of the men in front yelled. "Did you vote for Bush?"

I replied that half of the U.S. did not vote for Bush and that America was a democracy. Hadia was behind me talking to some other students. They asked about her, and I told them she was Arab American and a Muslim. They didn't really understand what that meant. These were young students, only about eighteen to twenty, and their English was nowhere near the level of the eloquent graduate students we had been speaking to only ten minutes earlier. Many didn't speak English and simply stared at us. Most wore Western clothes except for one man and possibly a few others in traditional garb. . . . Since they seemed to want to talk about the U.S., I asked them what they thought of America.

"Bush is a terrorist!" one man said. "He kills innocent people and is attacking Islam."

The men were still crowding me, just inches from my face, and the crowd seemed to suddenly increase to about fifty in probably less than a minute. They were not overly hostile but I did not get a good feeling from them. I tried to ask them questions from our questionnaire.

"Who are some of your role models?"

"Bin Laden!" one of the men yelled, in a matter-of-fact tone but also as if to taunt me.

Several others nodded in agreement.

"Does he speak for you?" I asked, raising my voice so the crowd could hear me.

"Yes!" a number of them said. Those that appeared as if they couldn't speak English nodded their head. This part of the conversation they could understand. The crowd was in agreement.

"Why do you say bin Laden?" I asked.

The man in front in the traditional garb said something about him being strong and standing up to the West, and also that the U.S. could not prove that he did all that he is accused of.

"Does anyone have any other role models?"

People shouted out some. One man said President Ahmadinejad of Iran and another Moammar Gaddafi. The man in traditional clothes named a few Indian Muslim leaders whose names I don't remember. When they told me their role model was bin Laden, the man who began talking first had a look as if to say "What do you think of *that*, huh?"

I asked them a question about technology. It was difficult to get questions in because the men were close to my face and kept interrupting me. They did say that they accepted Western technology (they were engineering students) but not the Western culture.

"We reject it!" said the traditionally clothed man.

"It's immoral!" yelled another.

These were young men lacking in etiquette, but they were also pretty immature, as some young men are. Still the intensity of the encounter surprised me. Students at nearly every other university I had been to seemed eager to fill out the questionnaires, but these students really didn't seem to care. It could have been that some didn't speak English; I'm not sure. Finally we gave up and left to rejoin the graduate student conversation.

Just before this incident, we had been sitting and talking to the faculty and students at Aligarh over lunch, which brought me and my team face to face with the deep and seemingly hopeless problems of Muslims in India.[20] Neither my hosts nor I were aware of the aggressive interaction taking place on campus, but I noted the gathering's extreme politeness, to the point of deference. One student said, "The Muslim Indians do not want to live in ghettos, but they are forced to be confined to such ghettos for socioeconomic factors." This was a paradox. Aligarh had been created to lead the Muslims of modern India. It had been so successful in my youth as to become an ideal, but the pessimism of these students was backed by facts and figures. Moreover, they had virtually no representation in the media, which demonized Islam: "We are made to feel guilty every time some Muslim does something wrong."

A related, perhaps greater, paradox was that despite the gulf separating their historical traditions and political positions, both Aligarh and Deoband had mutual sources of inspiration. First was the Prophet of Islam, the leading role model from the past for everyone. While the students at Aligarh dutifully and respectfully mentioned their founder, Sir Sayyed, as a role model, they too felt that leaders of the Islamic community needed to be more aggressive and defiant in order to represent Islam. When we asked them to name their contemporary role models, the list could have been prepared at Deoband: Osama bin Laden, Maulana Maududi, Yasser Arafat, and Mahmoud Ahmadinejad. It was this paradox for which I was unprepared.

Indeed, the lack of leadership in the Muslim world disturbed our hosts at Aligarh. "We live in a stagnant society," one student said. Another added, "We have no role models. There are none for us." There were virtually no Muslim leaders they could point to in India with respect, either. They gave three names of prominent Muslim writers at the national level: M. J. Akbar, Asif Noorani, and Asghar Ali Engineer, and that was it. Muslim leadership, they said with resignation, has no courage or vision. Furthermore, they complained, when color television first came to India two and a half decades ago their religious leaders denounced it as the work of the devil and issued a *fatwa* against anyone watching it. Today, everyone sits all day before their television sets. Muslims are going from one extreme to the other, they sighed.

Although many had read Adam Smith's *The Wealth of Nations* and Thomas Friedman's *The World Is Flat* and were excited by the prospect of success based on merit in a capitalist society, their fascination with globalization was fading. Young Muslims cannot seem to get their foot in the door of globalization because jobs are difficult to find: "People look at our Muslim names on the applications and reject them." In India, where globalization appears to be so popular, too many Muslims take to crime, our hosts continued; their education standards are the lowest in the land, they live in segregated ghettos, and they are lower in caste than the *dalit*, the untouchables.[21] A recent report headed by retired High Court judge Rajinder Sachar indicates that these fears are justified.[22] Muslims are significantly overrepresented in prison, the poverty in their community is alarming, and prospects for the future are bleak. Although Muslims account for about 150 million, or 13 percent of India's population, in 2006 they held only 2 percent of the positions in the prestigious Indian Administrative Service, including district judgeships, and accounted for even less of the student body at the elite Indian institutes of technology. Only 4 percent of Indian Muslims were even attending traditional religious schools such as the madrassahs. According to Abusaleh Shariff, secretary of the panel that issued the report, Muslims have fallen behind even low-caste Hindus. To remedy the situation, the panel recommended free and compulsory education as well as financial support. Such affirmative action has been reserved for low-caste Hindus and others officially considered "backward."

At Aligarh, the admission that the proud Muslims of India had now tumbled beneath even the dalit was a moment of devastating self-reflection, especially since the group reflected the general sentiment of the community. As a South Asian Muslim, I knew the significance of this statement. Here was a community that had prided itself on ruling India for more than half a millennium and giving it some of its greatest dynasties. Only a few decades ago, Aligarh had been on top of the world. Now it was at the bottom of a society obsessed with and defined by caste and hierarchy. Of course, the official position of the Indian government, embedded in the constitution, is that castes have been outlawed in India. The reality there—as in Pakistan—is that individuals are identified not only by their religion but also by their caste, tribe, and sect.

When I pointed out that three presidents of India had been Muslim, which was pretty good for a minority and a tribute to Indian democracy and fair play, our hosts immediately responded that there had never been a Muslim *prime minister* and never would be. In India, political power resides in the office of the prime minister, not the president. The appointment of Muslims to the presidency is only a public relations gimmick for the government and not a real exercise of democracy, they noted. And when I mentioned that even some of the most popular Bombay film stars are Muslim, a professor commented: "While the top musicians, film stars, athletes are Muslim, there is nothing Muslim or Islamic about it. They come from interreligious marriages. They're disconnected from the rest of society." Yes, the Aligarh group argued, certain people would like all Muslims to become like these Bollywood stars. They meant that these Muslim stars no longer behaved, lived, or even worshipped like Muslims. For all practical purposes, these stars had left their faith. Once a Muslim surrenders Islamic tradition and practice, the Muslim community is quick to judge him or her as having crossed the boundaries of the faith and become an outsider. In other words, the Aligarh model, however modern, still sees itself as Islamic.

The group's lack of confidence was matched by its physical appearance. The Western clothes, pants, and collared polyester shirts looked worn and outdated. My mind returned to the people who had been associated with Aligarh a generation ago, who dressed in the smartest fashions from Europe believing they represented a modern Muslim identity, and I began to find the conversation depressing. The bleak present these people faced was bad enough; it was their despair for the future that I found unsettling. Their initiation into the brave new world of modernization appeared to have run aground.

On the journey back to Delhi, the team noted my disappointment at what seemed a dramatic decline in the progressive thinking and self-confidence of Aligarh. Hearing that bin Laden was the role model on the campus created by Sir Sayyed—who admired the English and patterned his college after Cambridge, the quintessential English university—was like witnessing the collapse of the Aligarh model, once a beacon of Muslim modernity and progress, and now reflecting torment, anger, and anguish.

When Aligarh's founder Sir Sayyed faced the onslaught of Western modernity in his time and like many religious Muslims was seriously troubled about serving foreign rulers, he chose a path of adjustment. The same uprisings in 1857 that forced Deoband to go one way had led him to go another. He saw Muslim families ruined and their lands confiscated. He saw his beloved city, Delhi, occupied and large areas destroyed. He saw his favorite buildings demolished. So deep was the trauma that Sir Sayyed contemplated emigrating to the Hijaz in the Arabian Peninsula, far from British influences. Seeing the agony of his community, he decided not to abandon it but to prove that its Muslims were a "useful" people and that Muslims and Christians had a theological bond. He visited England and was so impressed by English culture that he held it up as an ideal for Muslims to emulate. Boldly for that time, Sir Sayyed blamed the British for the uprisings of 1857–58, but his criticism was couched in the language of friendship. He pleaded with the British to take steps to end the sense of isolation and grievance among Muslims. He recommended, for example, that Muslims should be appointed to high office. He pleaded with Muslims not to harbor contempt and hatred for the British and their deeds but to concentrate on what was common between them and what they could learn from these foreign colonizers so that they could survive with dignity. [23]

Recognizing the need for local assistance and for Muslim leaders who would work with them, the British ruling India in the nineteenth century saw immense potential in Aligarh. It was willing to end its opposition to their rule, to end religious fanaticism, and with its aristocratic style, provided a potential nursery for leaders with whom they could do business. Aligarh seemed a perfect antidote to Deoband. The British had not forgotten how the founders of the two institutions behaved during 1857–58: Sir Sayyed of Aligarh risked his life to save the British during the uprisings, whereas Maulana Nanouwoti of Deoband participated in a military jihad against them.

In the opinion of some Muslims, however, Aligarh had compromised Islam. A poem by the satirist Akbar Allahabadi (1846–1921), for example, sarcastically notes that the "stomach" had taken precedence over everything else for the people of Aligarh.[24] Akbar accused Sir Sayyed of selling his religion to the dominant alien power for material gain—much as the familiar "Uncle Tom" of American literature might have done. But this was unfair. Sir Sayyed's lineage (he had deep connections with Muslim aristocracy and Sufism), objectives, and ideas were impeccable from an Islamic point of view. He had spent his life translating philosopher Imam Abu al-Ghazzali and the Quran and writing essays about the problems facing Muslims in India—all still worth reading. His verses in honor of the Prophet's birthday are still evocative.

Despite Sir Sayyed's sincere commitment to the Muslim cause, he could never quite appease the Muslims who accused him of having compromised

Islam. In 1873 Muslims in the Hijaz even issued a fatwa of *kufr*, apostasy, against him, making him a target for assassination. This did not discourage Sir Sayyed. His college at Aligarh continued to thrive. Here, indeed, was a point of intercultural contact between Islam and the West. It would be reflected, for example, in the dedication of E. M. Forster's *A Passage to India* to Ross Masood, the grandson of Sir Sayyed. Whatever its critics may say of Aligarh, it created a space and a philosophy where people and ideas of vastly different backgrounds could—to use Forster's shibboleth—"connect."

Aligarh created a community that not only led the Muslims in India but that could also confidently step into the world within a few decades of the traumatic events of 1857–58. By giving the Muslim community a sense of both confidence and direction, Aligarh demonstrated that Islam was indeed relevant and could contribute to the modern world. In contrast, the mystics and the orthodox of Islam were both finding it difficult to adjust to modern times. By the mid-twentieth century, as the Muslim lands emerged to form independent states, it looked as though the Aligarh model would prevail.

The Muslims who led these movements for national independence seemed firmly planted in the modernist camp—from Kemal Ataturk of Turkey to M. A. Jinnah of Pakistan and Sukarno of Indonesia. Because Ataturk's power rested in the military establishment and Sukarno remained a corrupt demagogue to the end, Jinnah's vision was the closest approximation to Aligarh's ideal of a truly modern Islamic state. Jinnah's Pakistan was to be a land of equality for all and of compassion for the less privileged. He made clear his vision in two seminal speeches to the Constituent Assembly in August 1947, when his country was in the throes of birth: "Now, if we want to make this great State of Pakistan happy and prosperous we should wholly and solely concentrate on the well-being of the people, and especially of the masses and the poor. . . . You are free; you are free to go to your temples, you are free to go to your mosques or to any other place of worship in this State of Pakistan. . . . My guiding principle will be justice and complete impartiality."[25]

Many of the Muslim students at Aligarh supported the Pakistan movement and even migrated to Pakistan. Some became presidents and prime ministers there. The town itself remained in India and suffered an anti-

Pakistani backlash after the separation of 1947. Aligarh's students continue to be hounded by those deep prejudices of the past. As was clear from our visit, hatred and discrimination still make it difficult for the graduates of Aligarh to get jobs. Despite Aligarh's attempts to adapt to modern conditions and its struggle for success, it may well meet with defeat because globalization has not only failed to lift this heavy veil but now poses a dire threat to Muslim culture.

I believe that Hadia and Frankie's unpleasant experience in Aligarh can be explained by the predicament in which Aligarh University and the Aligarh model find themselves because of globalization. Just as in the nineteenth century, Aligarh Muslims of today feel they are losing their language, religion, and identity. How could I have expected its students with their feelings of powerlessness to be sympathetic toward the West any more than Deobandis can when their anger seems focused on the actions of the United States? Few of its Muslims seem to have the patience or tolerance that Sir Sayyed showed in dealing with the West. Instead, they demand a proud, immediate, and visceral answer to what they see as an attack on their core beliefs and traditions. Frankie later told me that he was struck by the eerie similarity between the arguments at Aligarh and Deoband. The only difference was that the students at Aligarh were hostile and those at Deoband were courteous. He felt that Deoband appeared to be more secure about its identity and destiny, whereas Aligarh was on the defensive and desperate, fighting for survival in circumstances that made it difficult to retain its original identity.

In some quarters, however, globalization has induced other mutations and adjustments in the Aligarh model. A Muslim who can speak English, dress in Western suits, and talk the language of high finance and integrated world economic systems can do well. Shaukat Aziz, the prime minister of Pakistan, embodies these adjustments. A smooth-talking, former senior executive of Citibank dressed in smart Western suits, he had been appointed by a military dictator to use his contacts in Washington and New York to integrate Pakistan's economy with the West. "Globalization," he told me during my visit in March 2006, the words flowing with ease, "is like a wave . . . you either ride it or are drowned by it."

Over the decades, the once idealistic and resolute Aligarh model has become a watered-down, insubstantial, and poor imitation of its former self. The leaders of the new Aligarh model are really devotees of Western civilization's consumerism. They are simply "riding the wave." By contrast, Jinnah and other Aligarh leaders of only a generation ago moved forward without compromising their identity or integrity through a conscious revival of Muslim rhetoric and identity. Furthermore, in doing so, they not only created a Muslim homeland in the state of Pakistan but also changed the world.

THREE

Tribes, Women, and Honor in the Age of Globalization

AFTER MY LONG journey across the Atlantic en route to Doha, I boarded the connecting British Airways flight in London along with a planeload of other Western-looking passengers. I traveled in business class, watching the latest American movies on the drop-down screen in front of me, eating snacks, and drinking tea. As the tiny image of our plane on the in-flight screen gradually approached the Arabian Peninsula, the topography below us changed dramatically. The sun was setting, and from my window I could see a vast ochre desert undulating toward the horizon. Our pilot announced that we would be arriving at our destination soon, the last transfer point before Doha.

One after another, the women on my flight suddenly began disappearing into the restrooms of the plane. They filed past in their fashionable European clothes, only to emerge covered from head to toe in black traditional robes, some with black veils over their faces. It was like a costume change in a play in which the actors slipped effortlessly into alternate roles. One minute Western-looking women were chatting confidently with their husbands, and the next they were transformed into reserved, whispering companions, sitting more self-consciously in their seats with a subtle hint of deference.

These women were preparing themselves for the culture in their home countries. Their costume change on the flight epitomizes one of the modern world's great social dilemmas: how to maintain cultural traditions in the face of globalization. In today's world, different societies overlap, are mixed, and juxtaposed—their people forced to walk a tightrope, from which a slight slip could be disastrous. The women on my flight would be at ease in Western clothes sitting in a café in Regent's Park in London but in their home country would acquiesce to the segregation and modesty demanded there. They are caught up in a global charade in which public appearance is locked in with tradition. If these women were to challenge their local customs by revealing another "identity," they would be gossiped about and slandered by their society, which could greatly embarrass their entire family. The best course for them is to observe their society's traditions while assimilating what is convenient from the Western world—carry an expensive Valentino purse with the black robes, say, and employ the Western rhetoric of women's rights while ignoring the poverty and universal human rights violations in their country.

Modern Muslim women like those boarding at London who comfortably synthesize Western and Islamic cultures are following the Aligarh style. On disembarking and submissively walking three paces behind their husbands, they switch to the Deoband model. No subterfuge is involved here, merely cultural values, such as honor. In these changing and difficult times, women are both the embodiment of those values and its primary victims. Furthermore, those values are divorced from the justice and compassion advocated by Islam, and more in line with the vagaries of tribal custom and notions of honor. To understand this phenomenon, one must recognize that it lies outside the realm of theology, and within that of anthropology.

The World Is Not Flat

Thomas Friedman, in his book *The World Is Flat*, gushes with excitement about today's new world.[1] Not unlike "stout Cortez" in Keats's poem ("On First Looking into Chapman's Homer"), who thinks he is the first European to "discover" the Pacific Ocean and stares at it "with a wild surmise," Friedman believes he has "discovered" the new world through the lens of globalization, and it is a "flat," "connected" world. With the increased lowering of trade and political barriers and the exponential technical advances of the digital revolution, large numbers of people are now connected across the planet. Friedman is optimistic about these trends but also implies that if a society balks at them, it will be trampled and soon flattened. Globalization must not be—indeed cannot be—resisted.

From a traditional society's point of view, the world is not flat but uneven, with valleys, ravines, and mountains. Culture, custom, and ideas inherited from the past are highly prized marks of identity and therefore determiners of behavior. They define how people judge one another, and they include notions of honor and dignity. This view is perhaps best exemplified by groups that maintain and perpetuate tradition—such as the tribal peoples of Islam.

In most American minds, the concept of tribal people is limited in scope and has pejorative overtones. Many Americans immediately picture their own native people of a century or so ago, the Native Americans once called "Red Indians" in a derogatory manner and depicted by Hollywood as half-naked, primitive savages. In fact, like many tribal people, they possessed a sophisticated and complex culture directly associated with their natural environment. White European settlers, hungry for land, had little patience with or sympathy for them. The two cultures could not coexist. It was a zero-sum situation. Either the ways of the settlers had to triumph or those of the Native Americans. With the coming of the railways and improved guns in the nineteenth century, their fate was sealed—native custom and culture were all but annihilated.

By contrast, Islamic tribes are not marginal or isolated communities living on the verge of extinction. They are large, powerful, and fully developed societies akin to nations—with a common language, territory, culture, history, and thus a distinct identity. Unlike the modern nation-state, however, a tribe can trace its descent from one common ancestor, whose name the tribe bears. Therefore its members have no doubts as to their loyalties. For example, the Yusufzai, an aristocratic Pukhtun tribe, are descended from a common ancestor, Yusuf. In Pukhto, the language of the Pukhtuns, *zoi* or *zai* means "son of" or "sons of," and thus anyone claiming to be Yusufzai can legitimately trace his ancestry to Yusuf himself.

Muslim tribes have countries, provinces, and districts named after them. Saudi Arabia is named after the tribe of Saud. Since *stan* means "the land of," Afghanistan literally means the land of the Afghan (another name for Pukhtun). Uzbekistan is the land of the Uzbek tribes, and Baluchistan, in Pakistan, is the province of the Baluch tribes. North and South Waziristan Agencies, also in Pakistan, are the districts or agencies of the Wazir tribe, much to the chagrin of the other powerful tribe, the Mahsud, who also live in South Waziristan Agency. The Bugti Agency in Baluchistan is named after the Bugti tribe.

Tribal societies across Africa and Asia, Muslim and non-Muslim alike, now face the juggernaut of globalization. It demands submission to a uniform culture imported from across the seas, whereas tribalism insists on maintaining indigenous customs and culture. Globalization presupposes the dissolution of boundaries; tribalism defines itself on the basis of boundaries. The inherent conflict between these two ways of looking at the world is dramatically illustrated by what is happening in Iraq, Afghanistan, Pakistan, Nigeria, and Somalia, countries that contain large and powerful Muslim tribes. Under the pressure of globalization, those tribes no longer adhere to quite the same nomadic existence of only a few generations ago, when they could cross international borders to remain isolated from mainstream society and thereby safeguard their customs.

At the same time, tribal behavior and the emphasis on self-identity remain strong even in societies considered modern. The tribal cohesion of Muslims in Malaysia and Indonesia, for instance, is heightened when confronted by the large and influential Chinese populations in these Muslim nations. Differences in religion, language, culture, and rites of passage have created bitter tensions between the Muslims and Chinese, which can erupt into violence in both societies. In Malaysia, the ethnic Han Chinese were considered successful capitalists and their wealth envied. In Indonesia, they were considered successful communists and their political influence envied. Thus in both it was a growing resentment among the Muslim majority against the perceived exclusivist success of the non-Muslim minority. Thinking their identity was being threatened by immigrants in their own homeland, Malay and Indonesian Muslims reacted violently, at the cost of thousands of lives.[2] This was a tribal response, quite alien to the Islamic values of justice and compassion.

A Mahsud elder in Waziristan told Evelyn Howell, the British administrator in charge of Waziristan in the mid-1920s, "that a civilization must be judged by the kind of man it produces." It was better, he said, to leave his tribe alone so that they could "be men like our fathers before us—that is men of honor and tradition."[3] The two were discussing the merits of their respective cultures, and the Mahsud criticized British reforms for having "wrought such havoc in British India." Howell, after much reflection, agreed.

Friedman, on the other hand, is more confident about the merits of the world civilization that he represents, yet it may be a salutary lesson for him to recall that only a few decades after Howell's conversation, the British Empire—on which the sun never set—disappeared from Waziristan, leaving behind a few deserted forts and some half-remembered traditions carried on by Pakistani officers.

More recently, Waziristan's refusal to be "flattened" by globalization was tested when the American media reported that Osama bin Laden was hiding here. The media frenzy and speculation brought unwelcome publicity to an area that valued its privacy. In the spring of 2004, American troops launched "Operation Mountain Storm" along the Afghan-Pakistan frontier to look for bin Laden and the remnants of the Taliban. Under direct and immense pressure from the United States, President Pervez Musharraf sent large numbers of Pakistani troops into Waziristan for the first time in the history of the country, thus confirming for anyone with any lingering doubts the domination of the military in Pakistani life.[4] The generals sitting in Rawalpindi, heady with the knowledge that they now possessed the latest American weapons, felt that the subjugation of Waziristan would be an easy task. President Musharraf, appearing on American television, mentioned a "high-value target." Some speculated that bin Laden or his second in command, Ayman al-Zawahiri, would be captured soon. The media were agog with excitement.

Neither the Americans nor city-dwelling Pakistanis like Musharraf and his generals appeared to have done their homework. In their own area, with its high mountains and isolated valleys, the tribes of Waziristan are nearly invincible. Acting upon orders from the United States to find and kill terrorists, Musharraf bombarded Waziristan settlements with American-supplied helicopter gunships. He ended up losing several hundred soldiers, while the tribes complained of the indiscriminate killing of women and children. Musharraf then scaled down the military activity and negotiated with the tribes. When the talks broke down, he sent in the army again, repeating the cycle. Eventually, tribal councils were called and elders consulted. Many lives and much property would have been saved if this had been done in the first place.

Musharraf's Waziristan venture resulted in his ignominious retreat and the establishment of a new variety of Taliban with its own territory and flag, known as the Islamic Emirate of Waziristan.[5] Washington did not know what to make of these developments. Meanwhile, Kabul accused Pakistan of covertly encouraging the Taliban.

Less adroit than Musharraf, the Americans continued sinking deeper into the quicksands of Iraq and Afghanistan, still convinced of the persuasive powers of deadly bombs like "bunker busters" and "daisy cutters" and of the seductive power of the almighty dollar. No community could resist for long, so it was thought. As many close to the Wazir and Mahsud tribes have pointed out, they are "physically the hardest people on earth."[6] In 1920, at the height of British colonization, they decimated an entire British brigade, killing 400 men, including 28 British and 15 Indian officers. In the following years, there would be more British and Indian troops in Waziristan than in the rest of the subcontinent. If there is a lesson to be taken from history then it is that these tribes have always exacted a heavy price from opponents who are ignorant of local conditions. If the invaders are arrogant as well, they are bound to meet disaster.

Musharraf had once told me he admired Napoleon, but obviously the lessons of Napoleon's military failures had escaped him, particularly the dangers of fighting on two fronts. Though fully occupied on the Waziristan front with the hunt for bin Laden, Musharraf sent in his army to pacify the Bugti tribe in Baluchistan. Like the Wazir and the Mahsud tribes among the Pukhtun, the Bugti are renowned among the Baluch for their martial character and tribal sense of honor. Musharraf had landed himself in a dilemma that even the British during colonial times would have taken care to avoid, knowing that it would spell disaster. Instead, Musharraf charged ahead to confront the most fierce tribes in South Asia at the same time and on two different fronts. Musharraf was thus diverting time and energy from pressing issues of national development and integration when the Americans would have preferred him to concentrate on the war on terror.

This was not the first time that Pakistan had attempted a military solution to force its will on Baluchistan and Waziristan. In the 1970s, Prime Minister Zulfiqar Ali Bhutto had sent the army into both areas. The difference between then and now is that Bhutto's motive was an "internal" one—to maneuver his political party into power—whereas Musharraf was acting on behalf of the Americans. Hence developments in the region are now directly linked to wider and more international issues.

Following the Taliban Trail

Shortly after the fall of the Taliban in Kabul as a consequence of the American invasion of Afghanistan in 2001, the tribes of Waziristan became embroiled in a confrontation with Musharraf. In keeping with their tribal code of hospitality, they provided sanctuary to Taliban on the run across the border. In any case, there is always general sympathy for fellow Pukhtuns fighting "foreign" invaders—even if they are elite units of Pakistan's army marching into Waziristan. Tribal resistance to this extent had never been experienced before in the history of Pakistan.

With the escalation of the fighting in Waziristan and Pakistanis pouring in troops under American pressure, the Waziri tribes decided to unite under one platform in order to resist the invading army, which is typical tribal strategy. Furthermore, they allowed religious leaders allied to the Taliban who challenged the authority of their own elders to spearhead the resistance. Both developments would have ramifications for the politics of globalization and its post-9/11 chapter. This is precisely how the Taliban emerged in Afghanistan in the early 1990s, rising from the debris of a long and debilitating Soviet occupation. Local tribal leadership had collapsed, and people welcomed the Taliban to check the resulting anarchy. It was only later that the tribes became disillusioned with this attempt at cohesion. A similar mood to that which had encouraged young Afghans to support the Taliban had now settled in over the young men of Waziristan.

The Taliban on both sides of the border had already made clear their attitude to globalization by banning television and any customs associated with the pop culture of the West. Their identity as Muslims and the ability to uphold their traditions mattered more than joining the world order. When pressed to hand over bin Laden after 9/11, the Taliban couched their response in tribal terms: their code of honor did not permit the surrendering of a guest. This code is poorly understood even by international experts who have dealt with this part of the world extensively. Madeleine Albright, for instance, saw it as "a menu of lame excuses": "They argued that [to turn in bin Laden] would violate cultural etiquette to mistreat the beneficiary of their hospitality and that bin Laden was a hero to Afghans because of his 1980s anti-Soviet role. 'We will be overthrown if we give him to you,' they said. 'Our people will assume we took money from you or the Saudis.'"[7]

While the Taliban's obdurate attitude would cost them dearly and they would be bombed out of Kabul, it elicited sympathy among ordinary people. Pukhtun tribes on the Pakistani side of the border formed their own Taliban organizations, which eventually emerged to dominate Waziristan. Nick Schmidle, a former student of mine who traveled to the Pukhtun areas of Pakistan in February 2006, but not in association with our project, reports the Taliban were widely distributing a DVD showing them hanging five alleged criminals from a water tower: "The five men's bodies go limp, they are lowered, decapitated and then re-strung, upside-down and headless, from the scaffold." These were some of the most "reviled characters" in the area, and "local people, Taliban sympathizers or not, saw it as an act of justice." Similarly, many tribesmen in these areas are still seeking justice from the Pakistani authorities, but with few results. When one tribesman was unable to obtain help for a kidnapped driver, he then turned to the local Talib commander, and "within a few days, he raided a safe house, got the car, and freed the driver. These Talibs are being praised as heroes."[8]

Where the Taliban had failed in fusing Islamic order with tribal custom in Kabul, in Waziristan they succeeded. The precept that Islam must be defended against the West is now colored with tribal notions of revenge: Waziri fighters, according to one man, "are all local people who are seeking revenge for their homes being destroyed and their families being killed." "Every death will be avenged," said another. "This blood is not as cheap as some think it is. One dead creates hundreds of avengers."[9]

Bursting with confidence, their leader, Haji Omar, proclaimed in a face-to-face interview with the BBC from Wana in early 2006: "We will not stop our jihad against the Americans. We are not even willing to discuss anything with the Americans. We just want them out." The Pakistanis received less blame because "we understand that Pakistan attacks us only under American pressure." The location of Haji Omar's interview reveals the extent of Taliban influence in Waziristan: Wana is the headquarters not only of the Pakistan government's political agent (a position I once held) but also of the South Waziristan Scouts, the paramilitary forces that maintain law and order in the area. For the leader of a group declared a terrorist organization by the Pakistani government to be holding press conferences in the agency headquarters is clearly a mark of its power.

As already mentioned, the Taliban emerged in Afghanistan at a time of anarchy in the land. With the end of the Soviet occupation in the late 1980s, tribal warlords had established spheres of influence in an uneasy truce based on brute force. Looting, pillaging, and raping were common. Poppy crops became the number one harvest of the farmers. Tribal relations completely unraveled, however, when a warlord "married" a young boy in Kandahar in a public ceremony, which defied all Islamic and local customs. Religious scholars were incensed and, joined by young, poor, and other supporters, mounted a campaign to cleanse society of its social ills. They called themselves "Taliban" from the word *talib*, meaning student, because many were students of the madrassahs. The Taliban were seen as the good guys, coming to restore order and justice. Their first acts were to ban gambling and alcohol. They also imposed a rigid interpretation of Islamic law, which directly affected women, especially in the cities. Women were not allowed to work in offices, for example, or even appear in public to carry out their daily tasks such as shopping for household goods in the bazaars. Officials were on the lookout for single women, in particular, and punishments for suspected immoral behavior were invariably harsh.

Starting from their base in Kandahar in the early 1990s and supported by Pakistan, the Taliban rapidly moved north to occupy most of Afghanistan. The main opposition they faced came from what was called the Northern Alliance, composed of tribes living in the north such as the Tajiks, backed by Russia and India. After the Taliban were defeated and removed from Kabul, their reputation was attacked: the Western media depicted them as the personification of medieval barbarism. Years later, even with the installment of the American-backed government of Hamid Karzai, Afghan society still adheres to principles from the time of the Taliban and has not entered into a new era of Westernization, as Western commentators had expected. Although women undoubtedly have a much better chance of being educated and even finding jobs, the old customs and traditions are still very much in place.

Simply eradicating a powerful political group in a tribal society does not eradicate centuries of culture and custom. Shortly after taking power, President Karzai appointed Fazul Hadi Shinwari the chief justice of Afghanistan. Shinwari attacked the introduction of television as a harbinger of moral corruption: "As a responsible official I cannot allow cable TV in any part of Afghanistan. People who filed complaints to the Supreme Court said they were airing half-naked singers and obscene scenes from movies."[10] He has denounced the appointment of female ministers to the cabinet, advocated stoning for adultery and the amputation of hands for thieves, and actively opposed the practice of Christianity. Now, however, no one in the Western media appears to be minding the new government's rhetoric or behavior. It is clear that few commentators recognize the differences between tribal custom and Islamic practice in Muslim society, mistakenly clinging to the notion of a monolithic Islamic world.

Tribes and Islam

Although developments in modern Muslim nations may appear to depart from the tradition of tribalism, in fact they simply reaffirm it, as was evident during my stop in Amman, the capital of Jordan, an eminently modern and globally connected nation. A prince of the royal family invited me to look at the grand mosque he was helping to construct in memory of his uncle, the late King Hussein. The mosque's natural colors reflected the same taste and simplicity of the architecture. Despite its new and progressive design, it still carried the traditional towers that date back to the great days of Islam during the Mamluk dynasty half a millennium ago. Their stolid base and thick trunks rose to overlook the city as if they were surveying an empire. Inside the mosque's vast space, the only flash of color was in the calligraphy by the *mihrab*, or the Muslim equivalent of the altar, which proclaimed that God is great and Muhammad was his last messenger. This was to be more than just a mosque. Beneath the hill, an entire office was being constructed for the current king. As the prince explained, the new mosque was in honor of the family, their religion, and heritage in the land—in other words, a symbol of the different strands in Arab society that tie the community together: Islam, tribalism, lineage, and tradition.

Athough the Prophet rejected tribalism—declaring that "there is no Bedouinism in Islam"—Muslim society, with its deep tribal roots, cannot escape the struggle between a universal Islamic vision of the world and a tribal one. Reviving and expanding on the message of the great Biblical prophets, Islam expects society to be based on justice, compassion, and knowledge. But Islam was born in a tribal society with defined codes of honor, hospitality, and revenge. In time, many of these tribal customs came to be associated with Islam itself. Indeed, Westerners often mistake local tribal customs such as honor killings and female circumcision for "Islamic" traditions. On the contrary, Muslim scholars such as Farhat Hashmi have consistently opposed the incorporation of tribal customs into Islamic society. Speaking of Pukhtun tribal custom, for example, she considered it "in some form of opposition to Islam."[11]

In tribal society, an individual's worth derives primarily from one's place on a genealogical chart tracing the descent of everyone in the tribe from a common ancestor. Thus tribes are distinguished on the basis of that ancestor, whose memory is glorified and name often attached to the tribe. The customs and culture of the tribe keep the community tightly knit and distinct. In a conflict between members of one tribe and another, loyalty is expected of and given to the tribe. Members must uphold its honor, which means fighting on its behalf and taking revenge if a member of the tribe is killed or disgraced. Unlike modern culture in the West, in which memory of history rarely dates back longer than a decade or two, tribal culture has a long memory preserved over generations. Tribes in Afghanistan and Pakistan have a well-known saying in this regard: "I took revenge after 100 years, and I took it too soon."

Since women in particular symbolize a tribe's honor, their modesty must be protected at all costs. If a woman is impregnated from outside the tribe illicitly, this is a moral blow both to the tribe's honor and to its carefully constructed genealogical chart. At the same time, marriage outside the group may be encouraged to secure political alliances. Tribes that have been enemies for years can become close allies overnight as a result of a marriage between them.

Tribal custom continues to exert a powerful influence even in states wishing to "modernize." In Jordan, for example, ever since King Abdullah ascended the throne in 1999, he has been attempting to rescind laws permitting "honor killings," which discriminate against women suspected of dishonor. Under Article 340 of Jordan's Penal Code, a husband who kills an adulterous wife will be granted immunity, and any male relative who kills a female relative in observation of honor will receive a reduced penalty. In a case widely reported in the summer of 2006, a sixty-nine-year-old mother, aided by one daughter, axed another daughter to death who had given birth to an illegitimate son.

King Abdullah has tried in vain to tackle this law. Tribal forces remain powerful even in parliament. The king's authority and support, the prince told me, are based in the dominant tribes of Jordan, which constitute 99 percent of the political landscape that matters. As a result, the most frequent crimes against women are those related to honor, and these account for 55 percent of all murders involving women. Although Islamic law has many checks and barriers against precisely this kind of tribal behavior, it is diluted by tribal customs in Jordan.

Throughout Muslim history, tribal chiefs have found it convenient to reinforce their authority by seeking alliances with religious leaders. In turn, religious figures have gained a platform to spread their ideas. One dramatic example from the eighteenth century occurred in the birthplace of Islam itself, the Arabian Peninsula. In Nejd in 1744, an obscure religious preacher named Muhammad Wahhab, who had begun a movement to revive the purity of Islam, met and allied with the local tribal chief, Muhammad Ibn Saud. The man whose mission was to spread the word of God and the man who wished to rule sealed their friendship when Wahhab's daughter became one of Saud's wives. The two men agreed that if the Saud tribe ever ruled the land, it would propagate Wahhab's ideas of Islam. Their compact had enormous repercussions on the world in the twentieth century when oil was discovered in the peninsula. Saud's descendants would capture power and name the entire Arabian Peninsula after their tribe. The Kingdom of Saudi Arabia adopted Wahhabi doctrine and to this day promotes it through madrassahs and Islamic centers.

The Wahhabi concern with maintaining the purity of Islam has parallels elsewhere. During the same period as Wahhab spread his ideas in Arabia, in India, a few decades after the death of the last great Mughal emperor, Aurangzeb, Shah Wali Ullah became alarmed at the rapid collapse of Muslim power, which he felt put Islam too in "danger." He therefore urged that the "pure" form of Islam be preserved. From his work grew the ideas that would flourish in Deoband in the next century. But the difference between the Deoband and Wahhab movements was that the Deobandis never captured political power in India, whereas Wahhab's descendants went on to rule Saudi Arabia and propagate Wahhab's ideas under the ideology of "Wahhabism." Although similar to Deoband, Wahhabism had the power to aggressively exclude any hint of thinking associated with Ajmer or Aligarh. The Taliban in Afghanistan were inspired by both Deoband and Wahhabism, which they saw as two eyes of the same face.

Not coincidentally, bin Laden, a star to both the Wahhabis and the Taliban, patterned himself after Muhammad Wahhab when he sealed a political alliance with Mullah Umar, the head of the Taliban, by arranging a marriage between the families. Wahhab's political alliance led to the emergence of a state that would propagate his message three centuries after his death. Bin Laden's alliance produced benefits in his own lifetime: the Taliban dominated Afghanistan in the 1990s and implemented his vision of Islam.

However divergent Islamic law may be from tribal custom, the tribal Muslim mind can always reconcile the two. During my years in the tribal areas of Pakistan, when I would point out the contradictions between the two in friendly conversations, tribal elders would good-humoredly reply that they were quite aware of their transgressions. Contrary to Islamic tradition, for example, tribal fathers of the bride would claim excessive and often crippling dowries from the father of the groom and then spend it on themselves. For suspected infidelity or sexual misconduct, a woman would be severely punished or even taken to a nearby field and killed by her husband, brothers, or father. The elders of the tribe would invariably approve the criminal act, saying that this was their custom, which their lineage justified.[12] The Pukhtuns trace their ancestry to the thirteenth "lost" tribe of Israel and even to the historic figures of the Abrahamic tradition, including Abraham himself. Thus in their minds, this certifies that they will always be good Muslims, whether they follow the rule of Islamic law strictly or abide by their tribal code.

Even in today's Muslim world, most states retain their strong sense of tribal identity and practices regardless of Western-inspired discussions about democracy and human rights. The problems that the United States and its allies face in Afghanistan and Iraq are the direct result of their failure to recognize or understand the tribal base of these societies. Americans assumed that once free of their rulers, the people would eagerly wish to assimilate into the global system and adopt global values, whereas local people adhered to a very concrete idea of the way things had been done for generations and would continue to be done. The persistence of deeper tribal loyalties and identity that seemed to override notions of the state never failed to surprise Americans, who could not see that tribal notions of loyalty and honor are able to survive in an environment of globalization and compete with ideas derived not only from the West but also from Islamic precepts about justice and compassion. To add to the complexity of Muslim attitudes, a generally unimpressive leadership is failing to provide clear direction—as confirmed by our respondents in questionnaires—and reflects the confusion resulting from the overlapping and parallel religious and tribal identities in Muslim societies.

Women and the Birth of Islam

Muhammad, who belonged to the leading tribe of Mecca, was in the habit of withdrawing to the bare and bleak mountaintop a few miles from the town. On Mount Hira he would meditate about the nature of human beings and the society surrounding him—a pagan society subjected to frequent tribal wars and raids and therefore highly approving of honor and revenge. Being a patriarchal society, it showed little empathy for women, only cruelty and indifference. Female infanticide was a common practice. Islamic literature referred to the age as one of *jihaliya,* or ignorance. A sensitive young man, Muhammad had been deeply troubled by society's behavior. Then in 610 C.E., at the age of forty, he had a vision of the angel Gabriel commanding him "to read." In a state of uncertainty, Muhammad returned from his retreat to the one person he trusted most in the world, his wife Khadija.

Upon hearing what her husband had experienced, Khadija recognized that she was witnessing something extraordinary. She had always been intrigued by his contemplative and gentle nature and impressed by his integrity, so much so that she had taken the initiative and proposed to Muhammad though fifteen years his senior. A bold woman, she had managed successful trading caravans that crisscrossed the tribal lands of what is now the Middle East. She had been a widow for some time and decided to take a chance on a much younger man but also hoped to offer him strength and companionship.

Upon hearing his news, she insisted that she take him to a relative, a Christian priest learned in the biblical tradition. The priest assured husband and wife that what Muhammad had experienced was indeed a revelation in the manner of the biblical prophets. Islam—which means "submission" to God and "peace"—was about to be born. Khadija declared her faith in the religion that was being revealed to her husband, thus becoming the first Muslim in history.

Muhammad became the Prophet—or Messenger—of God. Because the Prophet is the embodiment and ideal of Islam according to the Quran, his wives, notably Khadija and Aisha, and his daughters, especially Fatima, became central to Islamic history and society. They were involved in the development of the religion not merely as wives and daughters but also as warriors, consultants, and scholars; they carried the word of Islam and served as accessible role models for women. Modern women find much legitimate support from the behavior and sayings of the Prophet and the women close to him. For example, when a young man asked the Prophet who is most entitled to his best treatment, the Prophet replied, "Your mother."[13] He repeated this three times, to indicate that only by serving a mother can a good Muslim hope to win the favor of God. The Prophet also reportedly said: "Heaven lies underneath the feet of the mother."[14]

Khadija is significant in Islamic history for another reason. She is the mother of Fatima, who gave birth to two important figures: Hassan and Hussein. Both Hassan and Hussein would be martyred, their deaths reverberating up to modern times. Hussein's death at Karbala in 680—in what is now Iraq—was one of Islam's seminal moments, comparable for some Muslims to the crucifixion of Jesus in Christianity. Hussein and a tiny army were all killed in a battle to challenge the tyranny of the ruling caliph. Fatima's descendants provide Islamic society with a "holy" lineage going back to the Prophet. Both Shia and Sunni Muslims value this lineage, but the former make a point of treating it with special veneration. Indeed, the leading figures in Shia Islam are the descendants of the Prophet.

Aisha, another of the Prophet's wives, was the daughter of his dear and venerable friend Abu Bakr. Aisha was much younger than the Prophet, and he had a protective, loving, and gentle relationship with her. She was able to joke with him and even tease him unlike anyone else. She also transmitted the sayings of the Prophet, called the *Hadith*, to generations of scholars after her. One of the Prophet's sayings quoted by Aisha underlined the compassionate treatment of women: "Believers with the most excellent faith are those with the best manners and those who are kindest to their wives."[15] She was considered a legal authority, and if the "Com-

Shia pilgrims from Iran visit the Sunni Umayyad Mosque in Damascus to pay respect to the shrine honoring Hussein, grandson of the Prophet. Hussein's martyrdom at Karbala in present-day Iraq is a seminal event in Shia culture.

panions," those respected early Muslims who were contemporaries of the Prophet, ever disputed an issue, they often came to her for clarification. She thus became a key inheritor of the Prophet's spiritual and political legacy after his death, even leading a military campaign against Ali, the husband of Fatima.

When the Prophet died, he was succeeded by his friend Abu Bakr, who was elected the first caliph of Islam. Some Shia believe that Ali should have succeeded the Prophet; they do not care for Aisha and even spread rumors about her character. By contrast, the Sunni admire her, and she remains one of their major role models. Early Muslim women were clearly caught in the crossfire of ideal Islamic behavior and traditional tribal attitudes to women. The tension between the Islamic ideal and the tribal reality has remained high ever since and today is particularly dramatic in rural societies.

Honor and Dishonor

On a sweltering day in June 2002 in Muzaffargarh, one of the remotest districts in the Punjab province of Pakistan, three armed men of the Mastoi tribe walked purposefully up to a young man of the Tatla tribe named Shakoor and dragged him into a sugarcane field. Unable to resist the stronger men, Shakoor cried for help as they pulled him into the tall stalks under the blazing sun, just reaching its zenith. Once away from prying eyes, they forced Shakoor to lie face down in the hot soil and took turns sodomizing him.

Mukhtaran Mai, Shakoor's elder sister and a teacher of the Quran to Mastoi children, had heard that he was in danger and in desperation ran about trying to get help from the elders of her tribe. As is often the case in rural Pakistan, the nearest police station was miles away and connected to the district by poor dirt roads.

Members of Mukhtaran's smaller and weaker Tatla clan now began to gather in numbers, as did other men of the Mastoi tribe. The Mastoi accused Shakoor of talking to a woman from their tribe in public and therefore of dishonoring the entire tribe. He was also accused of committing *zina,* adultery, which carries the death penalty in tribal custom. Shakoor continued to struggle against the men late into the evening. When the police finally arrived, they took him, not his assailants, to the local station on charges of improper sexual conduct. Because the Mastoi had influence in the area, the police accepted their version of the story.

Elders from the Tatla clan then proposed a settlement with the Mastoi elders, suggesting that young Shakoor marry the Mastoi girl and, in keeping with tribal tradition, that Mukhtaran marry one of the Mastoi men to prevent more violence. Some members of the Mastoi tribe appeared receptive to the suggestion. Groups of people continued to talk late into the evening, and people soon drifted back to their homes to think the matter over.

Not long afterward, while negotiations were under way in the Mastoi area, Abdul Khaliq, an elder of the Mastoi tribe, armed with a pistol forcibly took Mukhtaran into a nearby home with a dirt floor. Along with two other men, Khaliq raped her while her father and uncle despairingly tried to enter and stop the crime but were held back by other Mastoi tribesmen. After an hour of this ordeal, the men pushed Mukhtaran outside to face the shocked and distraught onlookers. Her traditional shirt had been ripped apart and the loose pants covering her legs had been torn off her now battered and bruised body. In a final sign of humiliation, the men threw her clothes out the front door. Her father attempted to cover her with what he could and hurried her back to their home in the Tatla area.

That Friday, the local imam condemned Mukhtaran's rape in his sermon, then invited a journalist to meet Mukhtaran's father and encouraged her family to file official charges against the rapists. Within days, the story became headline news in Pakistan, soon circulating in different versions. Almost two weeks after it took place, the BBC, on July 3, 2002, covered the story, and a few days later, *Time* magazine picked it up. Pakistan's chief justice called "Mukhtaran's rape the most heinous crime of the twenty-first century." On July 5, President Musharraf announced Mukhtaran would receive a half million rupees (about $8,000) in compensation.

Mukhtaran emerged from the incident as a symbol of the plight of women. She used the money to build two local schools, one for girls and one for boys. Before this, there had been no girls' school in her village, and she had taught herself how to read. Western donors also saw her as a courageous symbol of women's rights and supported her educational program.

Mukhtaran's rapists and those who had conspired with them were sentenced to death by a local antiterrorist court, which specializes in prosecuting cases relating to "terror" or "mass intimidation." It was a new kind of court set up after 9/11 and is widely viewed as an instrument misused by the government. In all, six Mastoi men were sentenced to death. A higher court overturned the judgment, however, and the matter is now caught up in court battles.

Exactly three years after the incident, Mukhtaran was invited to fly to London as a special guest of Amnesty International. When checking in at the airport, she was informed that she was on Pakistan's notorious Exit-Control List, which bars Pakistanis from traveling abroad and is widely seen as a weapon the government uses to intimidate its citizens.

At a press conference on a visit to New Zealand, the matter was brought to the attention of President Musharraf, who now made the first of several public relations blunders: Musharraf stated he was personally responsible for putting a stop to Mukhtaran's trip because the intention of its organizers was to "bad-mouth Pakistan." He went on to attack her hosts as

"Westernized fringe elements," which he considered "as bad as the Islamic extremists." When the *New York Times* and the *Daily Times* of Pakistan strongly condemned the treatment of Mukhtaran in a series of articles, Musharraf backed down with the following message on his personal website: "Mukhtaran Mai is free to go wherever she pleases, meet whoever she wants, and say whatever she pleases." He even awarded Mukhtaran a medal for bravery and courage.

But a few days later, on a visit to the United Nations headquarters in New York, Musharraf appeared to backtrack. In a long interview with the *Washington Post* on September 13, 2005, he dismissed rape cases in Pakistan with shocking callousness, explicitly suggesting that women arranged to be raped: "This has become a money-making concern. A lot of people say if you want to go abroad and get a visa for Canada or citizenship and be a millionaire, get yourself raped." Probably realizing the tastelessness of these remarks when they were condemned as scandalous, Musharraf then denied ever having made them. This induced the *Post* to put the audio interview online, in which Musharraf speaks these very words.[16] As if to further snub Musharraf, the U.S. magazine *Glamour* named Mukhtaran "Woman of the Year." Her memoir, titled *In the Name of Honor: A Memoir*, was published in 2006.[17]

While the Mukhtaran story was making international headlines, another story of rape involving tribes, notions of tribal hospitality and honor, and the clash with modern systems was developing around thirty-two-year-old Shazia Khalid. On the face of it, Shazia seemed not at all like Mukhtaran. She was an educated woman with a medical degree who wished to serve in the more remote parts of Pakistan where doctors are few and far between, particularly female doctors. She had been posted to the headquarters of the Pakistan Petroleum Plant in Sui in Baluchistan, the heartland of the famous Bugti tribe.

In the middle of the night on January 2, 2005, Shazia awakened to a nightmare. A man was attempting to strangle her: "He started pressing on my throat so I couldn't breathe. . . . He tied the telephone cord around my throat. . . . He beat me on the head with the telephone receiver. . . . Then he took my prayer scarf and he blindfolded me with it and he took the telephone cord and he tied my wrists, and he laid me down on the bed. I tried hard to fight, but he raped me." Throughout the night, the man casually watched television between bouts of assaulting her and boasting about his powerful connections in the army. The next morning, Shazia staggered to the nurses' quarters; officials from the Pakistan Petroleum Plant rushed across when they heard about the incident. They warned her not to talk about the matter with anyone for it would not only ruin her reputation but she could be arrested and tried under Pakistan's notorious adultery laws, which are heavily weighted against the female. She was quickly drugged and in a stupor removed to a psychiatric hospital in Karachi.

When Shazia Khalid's story began to filter outside official circles, Musharraf's challenge was to prevent it from connecting up with Mukhtaran's story, which had already become international news. Musharraf's officials put Shazia and her husband under house arrest for two months. A campaign was launched to smear her character, with rumors of her being a loose woman and perhaps even a prostitute. To make matters worse, her husband's father gathered a mob threatening to kill her because she had dishonored the family name. Desperate and dejected, Shazia tried to commit suicide.

Finding Shazia's story beginning to leak to the press, the government encouraged her to leave the country, threatening that she and her husband would disappear and no one would even find their bodies if she spoke up. Shazia and her husband flew to London, unable to bring their son, whom the authorities held back as insurance. She found a one-room flat in a poor neighborhood in London and applied for asylum in Canada, where she has relatives and friends. Canada turned down her request for a visa. Shazia's nightmare has still not ended: "I stay awake at night, thinking, 'Why me?' My career is ruined. My husband's career is ruined. I cannot see my son. . . . If I had died then, it would have been better."

While Shazia remained in a state of limbo, contemplating the ruins of her life, men of honor back in Baluchistan were taking up her cause. Although she herself was not from the province, the elders of the Bugti tribe dominating the Sui region of Baluchistan believed that she had been their special guest and had intended to serve Bugti women. They were therefore obliged to protect her under their idea of honor and hospitality, reminiscent of the chivalrous and gentlemanly behavior in the romantic days of yore depicted in Western literature and history books. The elders of the Bugti tribe pressed for justice in Shazia's case, demanding that the rapist be punished according to tribal law. Because the alleged criminal belonged to the Pakistan army—and was rumored to have connections at the highest levels, as he had boasted to Shazia—important officials helped to stall the case. An important detail in the background to this incident was a long-standing dispute between the Bugti demanding a bigger share of the oil and gas revenues produced from their land and the government of Pakistan.

Thus when the Bugti began agitating for justice, local authorities deliberately misrepresented their demands as an excuse to challenge the government. With negotiations between the local authorities and the Bugti faltering, the head of the tribe, Nawab Akbar Bugti, decided to take matters into his own hands.[18] The nawab demanded that justice be done and that the rapist who had dishonored the tradition of the tribe be punished. The government took strong action to contain the nawab's intervention by "capturing" his house and issuing warrants for his arrest. The nawab then fled to the remote hills to escape arrest.

As Pakistani authorities attacked the Bugti, President Musharraf promised that the tribesmen would "not know what hit them": he planned to unleash on them the latest weapons he had acquired from the United States for the war on terror. In retaliation, the Bugti attacked trains, railway lines, and cantonments. But Musharraf kept his promise. The Bugti did not know what hit them when their nawab was killed along with members of his family and tribe in an army strike in August 2006. American-supplied F-16 fighter planes and helicopter gunships, raining down cluster bombs, phosphorus, and other chemicals, had found the nawab through an intercepted satellite phone call. In the end, the technology of globalization had caught up with the man who, in his behavior, values, and appearance, represented the pride and identity of the tribe more than any one else, the man once called the Tiger of Baluchistan.[19]

In the ensuing protests, riots, and inflammatory speeches, Baluch leaders were quick to connect the use of American weapons with their plight: "All those weapons and aid that the U.S. has given to Pakistan to fight Al Qaeda and the Taliban, the Pakistan army is using against the nationalists in Baluchistan," complained Mengal, a member of the Baluchistan provincial assembly.[20] Further violence was assured as tribesmen prepared to intensify their quest for revenge. The scale of the reaction baffled Pakistan's military rulers.

Musharraf and almost all of the army's generals embrace globalization not only because most of them are from big cities like Karachi and Lahore, but also because it has brought the army significant benefits since 9/11, most notably, new helicopters, tanks, and weaponry. They also appreciate the KFC restaurants, the Internet, and the links with the West that have sprung up in the cities of Pakistan over the past few years. However, these leaders are selective in the aspects of globalization they wish to embrace: they are happy to accept certain economic, military, and cultural gains but equally happy to ignore other more important positive aspects that the West wishes to promote, such as democracy and human rights. To them, globalization presents an opportunity to battle a backward and stagnant form of Islam, represented by the tribesmen, for the future of a prosperous and modern Muslim society.

Musharraf himself would at best have a limited understanding of the tribal populations that he was dealing with in the cases of Mukhtaran and Shazia. As someone who grew up in a big city, he would have expected the aggrieved party to contact the local police and let them deal with the problem. This was, after all, the modern way of doing business in a modern state. Although they are close in terms of distance, the tribes and urban populations in Pakistan are worlds apart in custom, culture, and tradition. In Mukhtaran's case, men of the Mastoi tribe believed that by raping her they were restoring the honor they had lost when her brother spoke to one of their Mastoi women. In Shazia's case, the Bugti tribe took up her cause, equating her honor with their own, since she was in their territory and their guest at the time of the incident.

Unlike tribal relationships, those in the city are based primarily on financial interactions. Neighborhoods are mixed, and there is no way of deciding who should live next door. As people migrate from rural and tribal areas, their original ethnicities begin to blur. Every immigrant to the city quickly learns new ways of dealing with life: how to trade, behave, and interact with a mixture of people. In contrast, tribal life continues along traditionally demarcated lines. Important decisions are still determined by tribal leaders. Commentaries published in Karachi and Lahore may condemn their customs and traditions as a barrier to the march of progress, but the tribesmen would argue that globalization is the menace. With its intrusiveness and unrelenting momentum, it threatens the very core of their traditional identity and way of life. Although tribal codes throughout the Muslim world are changing as they confront the forces of globalization, they still influence behavior. In the case of both Mukhtaran and

Shazia, their fate depended on the interplay of society's different interpretations of honor and justice, particularly in relation to women.

What is noticeably absent from the discussion of these two cases so far is the presence of Islam. In fact, they demonstrate the collapse of the central features of Islam: justice, compassion, respect for knowledge, and the honorable treatment of women. Both women admirably represent the quest for knowledge: Mukhtaran is a teacher, and Shazia holds a medical degree, though this is still unusual for a woman. Nonetheless, tribal custom prevails in both instances, in spite of Islamic teaching. At the same time, the tribal code breaks down somewhat in Mukhtaran's case, because the tribes under discussion live in the Punjab, where tribal customs have become less pronounced and their ideals of honor more compromised with the influx of settled communities, greater interference from the outside world, and the influence of foreign values. In other words, such communities are tribes only in an ethnic sense. Unlike the more isolated and "pure" tribes such as the Bugti in Baluchistan or those in Waziristan, these are more tribal in name than in practice.

When I discussed Mukhtaran's case with Farooq Leghari, a tribal chief living in the area where it took place and a former president of Pakistan, he explained: "What we saw in her case was the equivalent of a lynching mob or a posse from the days of the 'Wild West.' These men had taken the law in their own hands. What we saw in her case was the breakdown of the tribal system, which would never advocate dishonoring women, and the failed justice system of the police." We were talking in Washington, D.C., in the summer of 2006. Aware that the Western media tended to associate precisely such cases with the religion of Islam, he stated emphatically, "The case has nothing to do with Islam."

Musharraf's other dilemma in facing the tribes involved in these two cases stemmed from his economic and political dependence on the United States. Links with globalization gave Musharraf the appearance of a key figure in "modernizing" Pakistan, whose initial sympathy for Mukhtaran and monetary offer would have been met with universal approval abroad. But to the tribesmen, Mukhtaran had lost her honor, and no material compensation from the highest levels of state or words of sympathy from journalists could restore it. In Shazia's case, globalization enabled Musharraf to gain the advantage over the Bugti tribe, which in the post-9/11 environment could easily be depicted as supporters of the ubiquitous al-Qaeda and the Taliban. With the West's limited knowledge of how societies differentiate themselves in the Muslim world, the revolt among the Bugti—and in Waziristan—would have seemed to be yet another expression of Taliban resurgence.

However, it was of vital strategic importance to keep the tribes of Baluchistan friendly and politically calm. With the help of China, Musharraf had developed Gwadar, a small fishing town on the coast of the Arabian Sea, as a port in Baluchistan in order to create a new entry point by land to Afghanistan and Central Asia. Gwadar would also be an improved outlet by sea to the Arab world. Trade and imports from all over the world through Gwadar could potentially transform not only the local economy but also influence the national one. With the Bugti revolt spreading and communications being disrupted in Baluchistan, potential investors were growing skeptical about these possibilities.

At the same time, the United States and its Western allies were finding Musharraf's support more crucial than ever. The war in Iraq and on the eastern borders of Afghanistan was not going well, and the Taliban had reemerged and regrouped on both sides of the Afghan border. Furthermore, tension was building up around Iran's nuclear program, which the United States was determined to squelch. Hence events in Baluchistan, which shares a long border with Iran, were of strategic concern. Indeed, the Bugti have strong tribal connections with other Baluch tribes straddling the Iranian border. If the Baluch revolt spreads, troops moving through Baluchistan, either American or Pakistani, will not have easy access to the border, thus making Musharraf an unwitting ally of the Iranians. The fate of the province, the crisis in the Bugti tribe, Shazia's case, and the war on terror are now intertwined. The outcome of each will thus have an impact on the others and be a harbinger of things to come in the region.

Muslim Tribes in Africa

Islam has a strong presence in Africa, which today is home to one-quarter of the world's Muslims. It is the dominant religion in most of the northern half of the continent. Over the centuries, chiefdoms, tribes, and religion have overlapped, fused, and created a strong local Islamic identity.

The fact that the Prophet himself encouraged early Muslims being persecuted in Mecca to migrate to the Christian kingdom of Abyssinia (present-day Ethiopia) has created goodwill for both the Africans and Christians in Muslim society. As both Islam and Christianity made inroads in Africa, principles of Islamic and Christian theology were grafted onto preexisting tribal social structures, as in the Middle East and South Asia. The synthesis of Islam and tribal culture is particularly evident in Nigeria and Somalia—both important African states located on either side of the continent and both very much in the news in the past few years.

With a population of about 130 million, Nigeria is Africa's giant and the economic powerhouse of West Africa. It has more Muslims than any Arab country. The interplay between our models has also been witnessed in Nigeria, from the Sufis of the Ajmer model who were instrumental in Nigerian trade for hundreds of years, to Aligarh-like Muslims such as President Sani Abacha, a corrupt military dictator who had been trained in the West. Long before the creation of the modern state of Nigeria and even before the colonial period, Sufi networks that spread across most of North Africa encouraged trade and travel, which flourished on the basis of honor and goodwill. In this case, tribal codes of hospitality and honor adapted well to Sufi notions of universal acceptance and trust.

Modern Nigeria did not solve the problems of the people, and its leaders indulged in corruption and mismanagement. In 1999 Abacha's dictatorship fell, opening up the country to other forms of government for the first time since independence from Britain. In the new political environment, the Deoband model appeared as the dominant form of Islam as the Muslims of northern Nigeria immediately voted to institute shariah law, partly in reaction to economic inequality and the disintegration of a society plagued by crime and massive corruption. Nigeria possesses the eighth largest oil reserves in the world, yet Nigerians see little of the resulting wealth: 70 percent of the population lives on less than a dollar a day. Militias in the south frequently kidnap oil company workers and hold them for ransom.

Although all of Nigeria is economically underdeveloped, the northern Muslim areas are suffering disproportionately; unemployment, lack of education, and overall poverty rates are much higher there than in the mainly Christian south, which has been better able to reap the benefits of globalization. The 2006 Human Development Report of the United Nations puts the Edo and Delta states in the south at the top of its list for Nigeria, with a human development index (HDI) score of 0.631. By contrast, the Muslim state of Borno in the north has an HDI of 0.042.[21] If the Edo and Delta states were a separate country, the report notes, they would rank ninetieth in the world, high for a middle-income country. This kind of stark economic disparity within countries that is tearing societies apart is a hallmark of globalization.

The shariah courts have handed down many controversial rulings, a good number of which have had more to do with tribal honor codes and response to globalization than with Islam itself. In 2002 the world's attention focused on the ruling in the case of Amina Lawal, a thirty-one-year-old Muslim woman from the Hausa tribe, who was sentenced to death by stoning for having a child out of wedlock. Although Islamic law requires four credible eyewitnesses to prove adultery, no such witnesses came forward in Amina's case. Nonetheless, she was found guilty of dishonoring her tribe, which prided itself on its traditions, and would have to be punished because tribal custom overrode Islamic law. Meanwhile the father of her child, who was not her husband, managed to escape prosecution altogether. Amina was freed in 2004 in part because of a massive international media campaign waged by American celebrities like Oprah Winfrey.

Christianity, Islam, and animism cross tribal and ethnic boundaries in Nigeria. While different groups have lived together peacefully for centuries, tension between Christians and Muslims has been increasing in recent years, and the clashes have cost lives and destroyed houses of worship. They are rooted as much in tribal rivalries as in religious differences and are stoked by economic inequality and the perception that Islam is under attack from the West, although these factors are rarely discussed in the Western media.

Many cases appearing to be in the realm of religious violence are actually motivated by other factors, often land rights, as in the long-standing conflict between the Fulani—who are related to Amina's Hausa tribe—and the Tarok. The Fulani are a nomadic and predominately Muslim tribe, whereas the Tarok are agrarian farmers and predominately Christian. In September 2001 more than 1,000 people were killed in clashes between Muslim Fulani nomads and Christian ethnic Tarok farmers in the state of Jos, and in May 2004 the Tarok launched a devastating, bloody attack against the Fulani in the same area that left more than 600 people dead and displaced over 60,000.[22] Their dispute is largely over the use of land; the Fulani want to graze their herds on the same land that the Tarok farmers want to cultivate. Indeed, many conflicts in Nigeria and elsewhere in Africa are between indigenous peoples and migrants from other tribes and have little to do with religion.

Attacks from non-Muslim tribes on Muslims in Nigeria, although not primarily motivated by religion, have led to a perception that Islam is under attack inside Nigeria, which, when combined with the perception that the larger world ummah, or community of the faithful, is under global attack from the West, has led to rising levels of anger and disenchantment among Nigeria's Muslims. In February 2006, more than 100 people were killed and 50,000 displaced by rioters protesting the publication in Denmark of cartoons depicting the Prophet Muhammad. This sense of besiegement from the West and anger over domestic injustices has led to a strengthening of the Deoband model in Nigeria.

The model is also spreading in East Africa. Just as the anarchy in Afghanistan gave rise to the Taliban, who promised to carry out Islamic justice and challenge tribal warlords in the region, the chaos of Somalia produced another Islamic group.[23] Shortly after we completed our fieldwork, the "Islamist" takeover of the Somali capital, Mogadishu, began making headlines.

Over the past 100 years there have been major shifts in the kinds of Islam practiced in the country. Sufism first spread as mystics traveled throughout the country seeking a closer, more personal relationship with the divine. Their openness translated well in a society influenced by trade and foreign customs. Sufi Islam in Somalia produced many beloved figures, whose tombs have become pilgrimage centers like Ajmer.

Sufi tradition is still alive in Somalia. When Frankie traveled to Kenya in January 2006 and spoke with Somalis there about our project, he found many of them had an "inclusive spirit and did not see the West as an enemy." However, the conservative Deoband model of Islam appears to be on the rise and the Ajmer model in decline. The latter began to lose popularity in Somalia in the late nineteenth century, with European colonization and the arrival of Christian missionaries. In 1897, so the story goes, a young Muslim cleric named Sayyid Muhammad Abdille Hassan came across a building he did not recognize, a French Roman Catholic mission station. Puzzled by it, he asked a group of boys from the mission what clan they belonged to. "The clan of the Fathers," they answered. Shocked by this rejection of Somali identity, Sayyid Muhammad concluded the

Europeans were trying to destroy Islam in Somalia and forever alter tribal society. He tried desperately to win support for his orthodox form of Islam, preaching in the mosques and streets that Somali society was under attack and urging people to rise up and remove the European "infidels." He also spoke out against the drinking of alcohol introduced by the foreigners. In response to Sayyid Muhammad's anti-European rhetoric, the British dubbed him the "mad mullah."

Despite their inclusive mysticism, many Sufis felt Europeans posed a threat to their society and were uneasy about their presence in Somalia. As Sayyid Muhammad continued traveling and speaking out against the Europeans and the missionaries, he also acquired a reputation as a peace-maker, able to quell interclan strife, and was celebrated for his wonderful gifts as a poet. In mid-1899 he declared a jihad against the Christian col-onizers. He targeted the British and their Ethiopian allies, in particular, Somalia's traditional archrivals. This insurgency lasted until 1920, when the British finally crushed his fighters, and Sayyid Muhammad himself died of disease. After the war, the British, seeking to avoid further trouble, vowed not to interfere in the way Islam was practiced in Somalia. In 1960 sections of Somalia controlled by the British, French, and Italians were united into one makeshift state, and in 1969 revolutionary army leaders, headed by Major General Mohamed Siyad Barre, took control.

Under the façade of Islamic law, Barre's political ideology rested on Marxist philosophy, like that of many Arab leaders of the 1960s and 1970s. Indeed, many young Somalis during this period went to university in Nasser's Egypt. Though leaders of the new Somali government talked of establishing an Islamic state, they really meant an Aligarh version of Islam that separated church and state. Somali nationalists saw Muslim spiritual figures and tribesmen who protested against the government as a threat to their power. Backed initially by the Soviet Union, Barre turned to the United States after the Soviets decided that neighboring Ethiopia was a more attractive ally. The United States proved to be a willing partner throughout the 1980s, although toward the end of Barre's rule, after a series of brutal crackdowns—one of which left 450 Muslims dead who were protesting against him for jailing their spiritual leaders—the United States distanced itself from his regime. Without U.S. backing, Barre was easily ousted in 1991 by "insurgent" forces, and the country soon plunged into a civil war.

In the chaos, tribal warlords moved into the capital and took control of most of the south. Somalia's conservative Muslims thought the ousting of Barre would pave the way for an Islamic state but felt the United States was preventing this from happening and was in fact aiming to establish a military presence in the country. When struck by famine in 1992 and sent food and medicine under the UN's "Operation Restore Hope," Somalia descended further into turmoil: a tribal warlord, who was one of many, blocked food supplies to establish his own supremacy in the jousting for power and became the focal point of opposition against the United States, although anti-American sentiment was widespread. However, the Americans faced the wrath of both the Muslim parties and the warlords, who, according to tribal tradition, rallied to expel the common external enemy from their homeland.

Misreading tribal society and the way politics works in a tribal context, the United States sent in the Marines to help restore order and provide aid, only to be met with hostility. In the infamous "Black Hawk Down" incident of 1993, bodies of American soldiers from a downed helicopter were dragged through the streets. Caught on film and broadcast all over the world, this event caused many Americans to ask why the people of Somalia were bent on humiliating American soldiers in this degrading way when they were only trying to give them humanitarian aid. It created a groundswell of anger in the United States against its perceived weakness in the face of foreign violence and greatly affected its foreign policy thereafter.

By 1995, UN and U.S. troops were gone, and Somalia slipped into a hellish period of anarchy: the warlords and their soldiers did as they pleased, killing, raping, and robbing. Sometimes the warlords cooperated with each other, but they more often fought vicious turf wars in which many innocent civilians were killed or summarily drafted to fight against their will. This was a society plagued by injustice. The guilty went unpunished, and no compassion, thoughtful resolution of issues, or safety was possible. Citizens existed in a state of abject poverty, living in abandoned buildings or shelters cobbled together from whatever they could find—branches, pieces of material, or cardboard. There was little access to clean water. Most international assistance was suspended because of the dangers of operating in the region: aid workers were frequently killed or kidnapped and held for ransom. In addition, piracy flourished off the shores of Somalia after 1991 and since then has become rampant.

The anarchy in Somalia in the 1990s led it to play a central role in the emerging globalized conflict surrounding Islam. When in 1998 bin Laden's al-Qaeda bombed the U.S. embassies in Kenya and Tanzania, the U.S. Justice Department accused him and his group of using Somalia as a base for attacking the embassies and for planning the attack against the Marines in Somalia in 1993. The U.S. government again accused al-Qaeda of using Somalia for the 2002 suicide bombing of an Israeli resort on the coast of Kenya, an accompanying missile attack on an Israeli jet, and a plot to blow up a British Airways jet at Kenyatta National Airport in Nairobi.

Under the Barre regime, Islam melded first with Socialist concepts and then Western ideas in an effort to modernize the country. In doing so, it reflected the Aligarh model, although corrupt and inadequate. Since that time, several attempts to form a national government have failed. In January 2004, warlords and politicians signed an agreement to set up a new parliament, which later elected former insurgent leader Abdullahi Yusuf Ahmed as president. The lack of security, however, prevented the transitional government from installing itself in the capital.

With the complete destruction of society, the collapse of moral values, and the lack of security, the Deoband model emerged as a source of hope for peace and morality, just as it did in the early 1900s under Sayyid Muhammad. Its conservative and "pure" Islam, which seeks to fashion society on the ideal model of the Prophet's community in the seventh century, took form with the help of an organization known as the Union of Islamic Courts (UIC). Just as the tribes of Waziristan united to face Musharraf's government and the United States, the UIC was able to unite Somali tribes traditionally unable to work together since the time of Sayyid Muhammad in his wars against the British and Ethiopians.

The ideals and defined values of the Deoband model seem attractive to the people of Somalia, who are grasping for any semblance of justice and security they can find. Their tribes and Islamic militias believe that the only route to order and normalcy is to maintain territorial independence from the United States and other African nations, notably Ethiopia, and even the United Nations. Many Somalis are probably not expecting a new constitutional government to take shape at this desperate time, nor are they easily able to find the divinity and warmth of God's love.

Instead, they have looked to the UIC for help, a loose network of eleven courts set up in recent years in Mogadishu and funded by businessmen who prefer any semblance of law and order over anarchy. The UIC's stated goal was to restore shariah law and put an end to anarchy and conflict in Somali society. In the first three months of 2006, UIC influence grew as it settled more and more judicial cases by shariah law, often handing down harsh punishments for crimes to control the anarchy. To address educational concerns—the 2004 UN Development Report found that only 16.9 percent of Somali children attended any kind of school—the UIC built many schools over the past few years, a gesture many in Somalia clearly support. Saudi Arabia also donated funds for schools and mosques that promote the Wahhabi version of Islam, which as mentioned earlier is akin to Deoband. The expanding influence of the Islamic courts was met with U.S. resistance, however.

With the growing power and popularity of the UIC, some of Mogadishu's warlords formed the Alliance for the Restoration of Peace and Counter-Terrorism in 2006, which received U.S. backing. The warlords' cynical use of the word "terrorism" in the title of their organization was telling: their aim was to persuade the United States to support them against the Islamic groups, while their publicly stated policy was to root out "al-Qaeda members being sheltered by the Courts." According to a February 2006 report issued by Agence France-Presse, Somali warlords had met U.S. intelligence agents in Jowhar, the seat of the transitional government, just before the alliance became well equipped with rocket-propelled grenades, mortars, and antiaircraft guns, which were used in heavy fighting in the capital in July 2006. It was the second round of fighting that year, following clashes in March that killed more than ninety people, mostly civilians, and emptied neighborhoods around the capital. American assistance to the warlords—some of whom had reportedly fought the United States in 1993—was futile, however, because the UIC defeated them in one clash after another. On July 11, 2006, the Islamic militias defeated the last warlord in Mogadishu.

The UIC, led by Muslim scholar Sheikh Hassan Dahir Aweys, was opposed by the United States, which refused to deal with Aweys because of his alleged al-Qaeda connections. "I am not a terrorist," he told BBC News in June 2006, "but if strictly following my religion and love for Islam makes me a terrorist, then I will accept the designation." By all accounts in the international media, food prices dropped substantially after the Islamic groups took over, the number of robberies and other crimes also decreased, and people were finally "optimistic."[24]

In mid-July 2006 the Islamic courts militia began moving toward the western Somali town of Baidoa, the seat of the weak UN-backed transitional government. Ethiopia, which supported the transitional government, then intervened militarily, sending troops to occupy the town. Seeing the foreign incursion, Sheikh Aweys declared a jihad against Ethiopia, as Sayyid Muhammad had a century earlier.

Somalia is now another focal point of the global conflict involving Islam, with various Muslim countries intervening in Somalia to assist the UIC and repel any possible threat from the West. According to a November 2006 UN report by the Security Council–mandated Somalia Monitoring Group, Eritrea, Djibouti, Iran, Syria, Libya, Egypt, Saudi Arabia, and Lebanon's Hezbollah have provided arms and training to the UIC. Iran reportedly sent three consignments in 2006, including 1,000 machine guns and 45 shoulder-fired, surface-to-air missiles. The UIC apparently sent 700 Somalis to fight alongside Hezbollah in its war against Israel in the summer of 2006. Tactics used by militant Muslims in other parts of the world have also come to Somalia. Abdullahi Yusuf Ahmed, the head of the UN-backed transitional government, was targeted for assassination by suicide bombers in September and December 2006. The December attack marked the first time female suicide bombers were used in Somalia. In late December 2006 Ethiopian and Somali transitional government forces— with U.S. backing—swept through Somalia in an effort to depose the UIC and quickly reached Mogadishu. With their bombers and tanks, the Ethiopians quickly overwhelmed the UIC forces, who fled into rural villages or slipped across the border into Kenya. Just as the Taliban went underground and kept fighting after being deposed by American forces, elements of the UIC have blended into local communities and have threatened to wage a guerilla war against the Somali transitional government, the Ethiopians, and any other foreign power which might intervene in Somali affairs.

U.S. air strikes against the Islamic groups began in January 2007 amid new accusations of UIC links to al-Qaeda, bringing the involvement of the superpower into the open. Soon Oxfam was reporting that large numbers of innocent nomads had been killed, creating panic and uncertainty.[25] With the U.S. air strikes and the U.S. Navy patrolling the East African coastline, the United States, already bogged down in the tribal societies of Iraq and Afghanistan, had now opened up another military front, threatening a repeat of the disastrous "Black Hawk Down" episode of 1993. As of early 2007, the situation in the region remains unresolved and uncertain.

The trends in Somalia confirm those evident in other Muslim societies. American backing of warlords and "seculars" at all costs against Islamic leadership has resulted in widespread discontent and instability. Frankie's research in the field led him to conclude:

> Somalia is a good example of the appeal of the Deoband model. I would guess that if we had been able to distribute our questionnaires in Somalia, many respondents would cite "return to Islam" as a solution to their problems and an exclusion of the West. However, like many other Muslims we met in other parts of the world, Somalis and Kenyans of Somali descent I spoke to in Nairobi said that although they often opposed U.S foreign policy, they wanted to reach out to Christians and Westerners.
>
> Somali Islam, for the time being, generally seems to retain the inclusive spirit of Ajmer. A young ethnic Somali woman I interviewed in Nairobi's Eastleigh neighborhood, who wore the hijab and followed the tenets of Islam strictly, told me her role model was Jesus whom she loved and respected from both the Muslim and Christian traditions, as she had attended a Christian school. She even teased me, asking if I had a girlfriend and jokingly volunteered herself if I didn't, something a woman in Deoband never would have done. But if recent events are any indication, the Deoband model appears to be strengthening in Somalia.

It is easy to see in the context of the Ajmer, Aligarh, and Deoband models why the tribal groups in the Muslim world—from Somalia to Afghanistan—would rely on the Deoband religious leadership model to pull them out of difficult situations. Muslims feel that the mystic Sufism of the Ajmer model or parliamentary democracy of the Aligarh model are almost irrelevant when their religion is under attack, their leaders have failed, their homes are being attacked by American weapons, and they have to escape into the mountains with what remains of their family. A man on the run in these circumstances does not think mystic thoughts of love and compassion or modernist ones about writing a letter of protest to the editor-in-chief of a leading daily paper. He is burning with thoughts of exacting revenge and redeeming honor. It is precisely this sentiment that finds resonance in the Deoband model, and in it the Muslim has a ready-made conceptual frame not only to make sense of the world but also to reclaim it.

Women of the World

While in Damascus, Hailey and Hadia sat down with a group of young Syrian women to discuss how their lives were changing as a result of modern technology, the media, and Syria's evolving culture. In most Muslim countries, men and women still do not mix easily in public, and if they do, women will seldom say what is on their minds. Thus I found it more useful to send the girls out on their own to speak with other young women.

Hadia, because her family is Syrian, had access to the home of two women, twins in their early twenties and the youngest of four girls. Hadia had met them during their summer visits to the United States. Despite the fact that their two older sisters did not wear the hijab, these two sisters decided to do so while in college there. With their friends, they began attending religious circles taught by older female scholars at a mosque. The issues they discussed—such as the soul's immortality and the Day of Judgment—moved the girls to become more committed to Islam and live differently from most of the other girls of their background in Syria. Their older sisters still wore short skirts and tank tops while vacationing in Florida, whereas these two chose more modest clothes, preferably long skirts or pants and loose shirts, despite the summer heat.

When Hailey and Hadia asked the two girls to invite some of their female friends to their home for a group discussion, one young woman among the eight who showed up wore a low-cut black shirt with a three-quarter-length skirt, while another looked like she had just stepped out of a Gap store in her jeans, purple T-shirt, denim jacket, and long earrings. The others wore tight hijabs made of a stretchy cloth covering their hair up to their chins, long skirts, and loose-fitting shirts.

Whatever their style of clothing, all the women said they welcomed the introduction of satellite television, the Internet, and cell phones. One of the twins excitedly said, "I love President Bashar al-Assad. He brought us

Akbar Ahmed with Syrian senator Muhammad Habash addresses an assembly at Friday prayers in the Al-Zahra mosque, Damascus. This unusual picture was taken from a balcony of the women's section.

all of this technology; really he is an innovator." Only within the past few years has the socialist government of Syria allowed Internet usage in homes and schools. About 20,000 Internet connections existed in the country at the time of this gathering. But globalization will not be stopped, even in Syria. Every shack and run-down apartment already seemed to have a satellite dish and every family that can afford it a cell phone. The girls said they watch the BBC, CNN, and Al-Jazeera and also get their news from the Internet.

While they enjoyed access to the latest technology, these girls were all extremely wary of its side effects. One of the twins, Susan, commented: "With all of this new culture coming in, no one is reading anymore. The other day, one of our college friends came up to up me and exclaimed, 'What happened to your sister? I saw her sitting down and reading a book!' People act as if there is something wrong with sitting down and reading, as if it's not a hip thing to do. People are forgetting the true beauty of our own culture."

The young generation, the girls felt, was only reaping the worst of what technology had to offer, rather than the best. They complained that young men are looking at Internet pornography now and sharing dirty pictures on their cell phones. Something new even for my team, one girl showed them how a boy had sent her a picture of a naked woman through a wireless cell phone connection called Bluetooth by passing a photograph from one cell phone to another.

While these girls expressed different religious perspectives, many agreed that technology, though positive in some respects, posed a threat to their religious values and traditional society. It not only helped spread pornography among young men but also induced "slothfulness" and "wasted time." "Can you believe that grown men can spend six consecutive hours playing video games?" one girl asked Hadia in disbelief.

Another girl with long brown hair, wearing jeans and a T-shirt, remarked that the new TV culture has left young teenagers confused about their "moral center": "They can no longer distinguish right from wrong. They wake up watching TV reality shows from the West and fall asleep watching them. The way these people live on these reality TV shows is completely antithetical to Islamic values and morals, but these children don't know any better. For example, they see single guys and girls living together and sleeping with each other as if it's a normal thing."

"The parents have no control over their children any more. It's sad to say, but TV has become the new parent," another girl chimed in. The young women's contemporary role models ranged from religious and political figures to popular talk show hosts like Oprah Winfrey. When we inquired further about Oprah's popularity, the Syrian girls responded that she was a strong and spiritual woman who cared about worthy causes. They expressed appreciation for the shows Oprah hosted on Islam. They said her show moved them, and they admitted watching it often. In fact, nearly all of their contemporary role models came from their exposure to satellite television.

The most frequently mentioned role model was a young charismatic preacher named Amr Khaled. An Egyptian, Khaled gave up a career in accounting to devote his life to speaking and writing about Islam. Interestingly, he was the only role model to receive a majority consensus in the countries we visited in the Arab world. These young women were attracted to him primarily because he presented Islam as a compassionate religion and a spiritual way of life. "His method is light-hearted and easy to listen to," said one. "He doesn't present Islam as a set of dos and don'ts like some of the older scholars. He makes us love Islam."

The most popular political figures mentioned were Bashar al-Assad, the Syrian president, and Hasan Nasrallah, the leader of Hezbollah. Bashar al-Assad, they said, was not only attempting to modernize Syria but also "doesn't bend over backwards to appease the West." As for Nasrallah, the girls admired his eloquent and passionate speeches, which they often watched on al-Manar's satellite channel. They particularly admired Nasrallah's "courage to fight for justice and speak the truth, even if it's against the West." This group of girls clearly reflected Syria's well-known nationalist pride as a country that has opposed the United States for the past few decades. Indeed, all of them expressed anti-Western sentiments to some degree.

However, the girl wearing a shorter black skirt, still below the knees, and a black shirt said that she did not "care for Islam," later adding: "I get in trouble with boys," while her friends shook their heads in subtle disapproval. "What? It's fun to get in trouble!" she responded. She did not accept those interpretations of Islam that were too strict or did not allow room for "fun." Even so, her role models were still the same as those of the other girls: the Prophet, Khadija, and Aisha. The other girls were seriously wondering how far they could bend their Islamic values in the face of so much change, many saying that their parents advised them on Islam, and that the hijab helped them maintain their identity.

Frustrated with the perceived increase in immoral behavior due to the misuse of technology and importation of Western popular culture, the girls are consciously regulating their exposure to technology. Yet their list of diverse and multinational role models reflects the extent to which technology has pervaded even the most controlled Syrian life. They lamented that they may soon be immersed in the sea of globalization and lose the values and traditions that their culture has embraced for thousands of years. Though critical of the influx of Western technology and culture, they also found it hard to resist globalization. Hence they were seeking an alternative, Aligarh-like model that could preserve Islamic values and blend them with the best of Western culture.

We were also able to interview Syria's minister of expatriates, Bouthaina Shaaban, a well-known senior figure in government. An elegantly dressed woman with short hair, she spoke in an expressive and articulate manner, gesticulating profusely and with a charming smile. When questioned about women in Islam, she replied, "I don't feel that Western women are more liberated than Muslim women." To illustrate, she recalled a lecture in the United States during which she stopped midway, covered her hair with a hijab, and then resumed the talk: "I was trying to make the point that the hijab doesn't make a difference. My mind is still the same. Those who speak for Islam should speak in the spirit of the Quran." She, too, revered Khadija and Aisha as her role models.

Women expressed the same sense of Islamic pride during our stay in Islamabad. One evening we attended a large outdoor dinner along with the city's elite as guests of the socially prominent Asad and Nighat Shah. Because of the large gathering, a tent had been set up to take the overflow of guests. After the delicious Pakistani meal, my host asked me to talk about my work and travels and to answer questions.

The women in the audience—almost half of about a hundred guests present—asked about the role of women in Islam, indicating that they were obviously modern and liberated. About half of them wore the hijab, and some were completely covered, only showing their eyes, a dress called the *nikab*. One of the women later complained that she was not recognized. It was difficult to do so because the woman was completely covered. She had studied at the Jesus and Mary Convent in Murree, a town north of Islamabad, which is famous for teaching women to speak English and live in a Western manner comfortably while still retaining their Islamic and Pakistani identity.

Throughout the discussion, I was intrigued and somewhat taken aback by the Deoband trend emerging in the capital of a nation founded by Mohammed Ali Jinnah, the embodiment of the Aligarh model. This was happening under the very nose of President Musharraf, belying his efforts to promote "enlightened moderation." At the same time, the women persisted in asking—or rather lecturing me—about the role of women in Islam and the denial of their rights in society.

When I invited Hadia to offer some comments, she easily won the women over because she was wearing her hijab and identified with them. Upon being asked to give the final word, my daughter Nafees, who had come to Pakistan with Zeenat to be with me, said, "I see Muslim women wearing the hijab in the United States and feel proud that they are ready to identify with their religion. Sometimes this can be difficult for them. Maybe if I had the courage, I would do the same." Several women later told me that Nafees's comment was the best of the evening.

During our discussions throughout the week, we found that one cata-lyst for change is the celebrated female scholar Farhat Hashmi, who while talking about Islam does so in a reasoned, gentle, and logical manner. Amineh Ahmed Hoti, who studied the role of Islam among women (*bib-iane*) in Pakistan, notes that Hashmi's activities are having a significant impact on tribal women, establishing links to the wider Islamic revival movement through branches of the organization she has established known as Al-Huda International Institute of Islamic Education for Women based in Islamabad:

Supported by private funding, Al-Huda centres may be based at homes, schools, or *madrassas* . . . (recently a local *madrassa* in Mardan has been converted into a centre for Al-Huda activities and teaching by a Khan and Bibi, both husband and wife are medical doctors trained in the U.K. and U.S.). When I asked which branch of Islam Al-Huda subscribed to, the answer was always simply: "Islam" and its students said they enrolled in order to learn the meanings of the Quran and Hadith. When I asked one very respected Bibi, a graduate of Al-Huda, whether the Al-Huda women's movement was Wahabi or Deobandi, she answered: "Al-Huda teaches the Quran and Sunnah and they do not follow any particular sect. They call themselves 'Muslim' as was done during the lifetime of the Prophet (peace be upon him)." Dr. Farhat Hashmi, the person running Al-Huda, follows a Hadith of the Prophet (peace be upon him) which says "All my Sahaba are like the stars; follow any of them and you will be rightly guided." She is in fact doing jihad (struggle) against people calling themselves anything but "Muslim."

Al-Huda graduates wear the black abaya (cloak), a garment consid-ered Arab rather than Pukhtun in origin, to mark the completion of the one-year course. More critically, Dr. Hashmi stressed that women could potentially transform society, saying in one dars [lecture] in Urdu: "the example of a woman (aurat)" on her surrounding family and community, "is not like a matchstick but like a flaming petrol pump—as a daughter, sister, wife and mother, her message can spread like fire!"[26]

When Farooq Leghari was president of Pakistan, his wife patronized Farhat Hashmi, adding to her fame. In contrast to the traditional clerics of Pakistan, who usually have long beards and speak in intimidating tones, Farhat appears an attractive alternative for learning Islam. Her popularity in Pakistan is in the same category as that of Amr Khaled in the Arab world. Both represent valid Muslim responses to globalization, and their followers see them as the closest embodiment of the Aligarh model.

While in Kuala Lumpur, Hailey and I heard echoes of these women during a meeting with older professional women, including lawyers, social activists employed mainly by nongovernmental organizations, and government officials. While some wore the hijab and others did not, all were assertively Islamic. When we asked them to name their role models from the past, all placed the Prophet at the top of their list, followed by Khadija, Fatima, and Aisha. Although they participated in public and academic life more than the women we met in Pakistan, they too remained traditional in many ways. Their dress and views about culture, the role of women in society, and issues of modesty were all consistent with Islam. To Hailey, they seemed "more assertive of their Islamic identity and comfortable in their roles in public life. What makes Malaysia so special is that . . . unlike the women in other countries who are struggling to work and to remain traditionally Islamic, [these] women were better able to integrate their faith and professional lives in large numbers with widespread acceptance from the society."

In Turkey, which like Malaysia is a modern Muslim state with a modern economy, women are banned from wearing the hijab in public life. Merve Kavacki was expelled from parliament for refusing to take off her hijab during its sessions and now lives in Washington, D.C. Although women in both countries are vigorously accepting the new challenges associated with professional life in the modern state, Malaysian women feel they can draw strength from their traditional faith more than the Turks do.

Almost all of the women we interviewed in the Muslim world agreed that their personal lives were different from that of their mothers. Complaining about her hour-long commute in the morning and at night and the long day of work at her office, one woman in Jakarta pointed out she has less time for her faith and her family but believed that Islam still provides important guidelines for how women should live their lives.

Women in Malaysia unanimously acknowledged Khadija, Fatima, and Aisha as their role models and mentioned the impact of the three on their lives, which was evident in their balanced lifestyles. One twenty-nine-year-old chose Aisha and Khadija for their "strength, intellect, and bravery." A middle-aged Turkish woman chose Aisha and Khadija because "they were an example by which to learn Islam and practice it in one's daily life and in the best way. They made very important contributions to Islam."

The women we met throughout our journey appeared to be independent, fully aware of the world in which they found themselves, and even assertive. They were a far cry from the miserable and downtrodden stereotypes depicted by the Western media. Both the male and female members of my team confirmed this impression. Jonathan and Frankie even found them "aggressive," as the following comment by Jonathan confirms:

> Some college girls approached me after a session at a university in Kuala Lumpur. . . . I was cornered by a group of young girls who wanted to know all about America, why we came all that way to meet them, and what our research was about. They told me about themselves and wanted to explain Islam to me. They were slightly aggressive and wanted to understand what Americans thought about them and the reasons behind some of our foreign policy decisions. But, they were also very polite and we took pictures at the end. I remember thinking . . . that this was not the picture of Muslim women that we are usually presented with in the West. They were smart, curious, and well spoken. These were not submissive women who are forced to live a life of serving their husbands. They were getting a college education and had a future that would allow them to pursue any dream that they wanted. Malaysia has many elements of the Aligarh model and these women were a terrific picture of modern Muslim women who are very much in touch with their religion, but also living in a globalized world.

Frankie [especially in Jordan] and I both noticed that women in each of the countries that we visited were the most aggressive. After each event or out in public, there were always a group of girls that would approach us to talk about American foreign policy. They were very knowledgeable and always polite. . . . They were the ones most willing to make a point, even if it was a criticism of us or America.

High-profile Muslim women who have held or are holding important public office are also an inspiration to other women. In Qatar, most women named the Emir's wife, Sheika Mozah, as their role model because of her efforts to improve women's education and strengthen family life. With her help, women now number two-thirds of the university students in Qatar and have won the majority of academic prizes. A seventeen-year-old female at Education City in Qatar named Sheikha Mozah her role model because "she's improving things and keeps traditions, even hijab. She makes us proud." A twenty-three-year-old female working with the Qatari Ministry of Foreign Affairs chose her because of her "deep knowledge, promotion of Islam, and love to guide others and benefit society." In spite of strong Wahhabi influences in society, the sheikha is pushing the boundaries of women in public life, appearing on CBS's *60 Minutes* and allowing some photographs to be taken of her. Yet she is still regarded as a model for young women in Islam.

Benazir Bhutto, the first female prime minister of Pakistan and in the Muslim world, provided some interesting insights into her own choices, which reflected how Muslim women saw role models. For her, the women in the Prophet's family were inspirational, especially Khadija and Fatima— she added the title of respect, *bibi*, when she referred to them. She identified with Fatima, in particular, the Prophet's beloved youngest daughter. "She faced many sad days. I too lost my father when I was just twenty-five," she added with a note of wistfulness. But it was not only tragedy that attracted her to those early Muslim women. She mentioned Zainab of the family of Hussein, the grandson of the prophet martyred at Karbala. "She walked to the court of Yazid and looked the usurper in the eye," said Benazir, perhaps hinting at her own ability to look the military dictators of Pakistan in the eye.

Benazir needed to be strong. She reminded me that she was the first female Muslim prime minister in history, that before her appointment women were told their place was either in the secluded home or in the cemetery. In fact, the saying "for a woman, either the *kor* (house) or the *gor* (grave)" is still popular in rural areas in Pakistan. Her other role models

Posing with a Pakistani embassy official, Hailey Woldt and Akbar Ahmed with Benazir Bhutto, the first female prime minister of a Muslim nation, attend the U.S.-Islamic World Forum to promote understanding between the West and Islam. The event was sponsored by the Brookings Institution and the government of Qatar.

were not Muslim. She liked strong, dramatic women who challenged society: Joan of Arc, Elizabeth I of England, and Indira Gandhi of India.

Benazir represents the Aligarh model for women. Having been educated at Radcliffe College and Oxford University, and also at the convent in Murree, she was able to combine Western notions of democracy, women's rights, and minority rights with her own ideals of Islam and national identity. Hence her role models must represent values beyond those of the West, namely the ideals of her society and religion, which are shared by women throughout the Muslim world. Benazir's ultimate role model from the past, the "ideal man," was the Prophet of Islam—she instinctively added "peace be upon him" when mentioning his name. For South Asians like Benazir, the Prophet is *mehboob-i-khuda,* or the "beloved of God," as well as "a mercy unto mankind," the title cited in the Quran. For Muslims, the Prophet evokes strong emotions of affection and reverence.

Several months after returning to the United States, I received the following e-mail from someone I did not know. It was a female student writing from Kurdistan in the western part of Iran. It confirmed everything I had seen on the field trip: the impact of globalization on Muslim society, even in the most remote places, and the desire for change and education, especially among women.

Date: 09/13/2006 03:45PM

Subject: To Dear Professor Akbar ahmad / a Kurdish girl Student of Sociology / Urgent Need Please

Dear my Professor, Professor Akbar Ahmed; Hello

Dear my Professor I hope you are doing well, please accept my warmest greetings; Dear Professor, my name is Negar Ahmadi, a Kurdish M.A student of Sociology at Kurdistan University; Sanandaj City: Iran. I am interrupting you to ask for your kind help, I would be very thankful and indebted to have your kind help for my Thesis and also very interested and need your worthy works; Postmodernism and Islam and Islam, Globalization and Postmodernity;

Dear my Professor this your book is really all my favorite and aspiration to have. It will be very kind of you to get me a copy of your valuable book, used or ragged even. Would you please help me at your convenience, I will never forget your kindness and great assistances. Would you please let me know about your kind help and I will send the address. Thanks again very very much.

Best Blesses

Your Student, Negar

As this chapter has explained, Islam provides an ideal to live up to in society, but tribal customs and traditions challenge, engage, and sometimes overlap with these ideals. Hence there is a constant tension in the Muslim mind between a stylized concept of a perfect society and the realities of sometimes brutal and parochial customs. The question at the heart of the struggle to define Islamic society and of concern to Muslim reformers is how to reconcile the ideal and the actual. This point is overlooked or misunderstood in the midst of the larger clash between Western and Islamic civilizations, which today overshadows everything else.

FOUR

Who Is Defining Islam
after 9/11 and Why?

WITHIN DAYS OF returning from Bali in mid-April 2006, after a long, disorienting flight across the Pacific and the United States to Washington, D.C., I was on the road again. The World Affairs Council of Philadelphia had invited me to a major international conference on Islam and the West—the speakers included a goodly sample of America's high and mighty: Dick Cheney, Henry Kissinger, Bernard Lewis, Joe Biden Jr., and Francis Fukuyama—combined with a celebration of the ninetieth birthday of renowned Princeton history professor Bernard Lewis.[1] Because of the status of the participants, the hotel and the neighborhood in Philadelphia where the conference was being held were sealed off. Men in uniform with guns, dogs, and police cars circled the hotel, creating an atmosphere of high tension not usually associated with scholarly conferences. Equally unusual in view of the theme, few speakers were Muslim (Ayaan Hirsi Ali, who was present, had long declared herself no longer a Muslim).

From Cheney's keynote address and Kissinger's remarks, it seemed clear that their thinking about the Muslim world over the years—and thus that of the U.S. administration—had been greatly influenced by Lewis. When asked to name the single most important step he would take to improve relations with the Muslim world, Kissinger replied, "Well, I would go to Bernard first," then focused on Iran. A nuclear strike from Iran was inevitable, he believed, and the West must try to prevent it from developing nuclear weapons and becoming a global threat. If the use of nuclear weapons against Iran is inevitable, and we "have to do it sometime," he continued, then why not stop Iran now? Because large numbers of people would die and the consequences would last for years, the decision would admittedly have to be approached with caution. However, Kissinger was confident that international powers would quickly move in and ensure a return to normalcy. As is widely acknowledged, Kissinger's views continue to have some influence on the White House.[2]

Speaking after Kissinger, I urged the United States to learn from recent history and not repeat its mistakes, pointing to the anarchy now brewing in Iraq and Afghanistan. The outcome of American intervention in those two countries was far from clear. What, then, could one expect in Iran, which was larger and less impoverished than either Iraq or Afghanistan and whose sphere of influence as the preeminent Shia nation extended far and wide? It was essential to recognize that an attack on Iran would trigger a collective Muslim response: not only would Shia throughout the world respond in passionate anger, regardless of their opinion of Mahmoud Ahmadinejad, but so would many other Muslims. The pro-West Arab regimes would come under such intense pressure as to threaten their existence. Equally troubling, Pakistan's large Shia population—some 30 million—would clamor to deploy its nuclear arsenal in support of a beleaguered and valued Muslim neighbor. The time has come, I emphasized, to remember that the United States stands for and must not forsake the values and practice of human rights, civil liberties, and genuine democracy—concepts badly tarnished by the scandals associated with Abu Ghraib and Guantánamo Bay. If Americans carried on in this way, I cautioned, they would find few friends or allies in the world.

To return to my earlier question about how to improve relations with the Muslim world, I drew on my recent experiences there, noting that the young Americans traveling with me had set an important example of how to build bridges by winning hearts and minds, rather than fomenting opposition. However, such a strategy can only succeed if Americans stop looking at the Muslim world as a monolith and take steps toward bridge building and dialogue. The Muslim world, I pointed out, is angry and foaming with anti-Americanism, holding up Iraq as an example of America's major failure in promoting its own values of human rights and democracy. U.S. policy, in my view, needed to concentrate more seriously on winning hearts and minds and on investing new energy and resources in the Muslim world. It needed to resurrect those ideas that had made the United States a great nation in the first place and once again rediscover them both for itself and for the rest of the world.

Although my words initially produced a chill in the room at the thought that a Muslim of all people was giving such hard advice, the atmosphere began to warm as people responded to what I had to say. Kissinger appeared alert as I spoke and never took his piercing eyes off me. This was an intelligent audience that needed to see the other side of the picture. Gradually, it absorbed my message, many even approvingly.

For me, this one-day conference demonstrated the limitations, dilemmas, and contradictions in trying to define Islam in the United States. One serious limitation, as already mentioned, was that key political players such as Cheney and Kissinger had admitted that for the past thirty years policy toward Islam had been influenced by a single individual, Lewis. Furthermore, policy forums that did focus on the Muslim world made no effort to consider a Muslim perspective or to draw on the important fieldwork of the social sciences to arrive at their assessments. As a result, Americans were not only misreading the Muslim world but were also unable to plan for events that were rapidly unfolding in it. At this conference, too, words such as "dialogue," "understanding," or "compassion" never surfaced. Most disconcerting of all, distinguished as the speakers were, they had failed to open their eyes to the logical conclusions of their arguments—namely, that the United States was driving the world straight toward an apocalypse. The prospect, frightening to anyone interested in peace, created an air of foreboding over the discussions.

Defining Islam, I realized then, had become one of the most important, contentious, and contested arenas of public life. Defined in a certain way, with negative connotations, say, it would assuredly repel the general public and induce a negative response toward the religion. Thus if the word "fascism"—universally reviled because of its association with Hitler and Nazism—were used in the same breath as Islam, ordinary people in the West would be prepared to view Islam as a serious threat to their very way of life and be receptive to the idea of a final battle, however long it took, to eliminate the scourge.

Such terms were indeed coined to describe Muslim terrorists—a recent one being "Islamofascists"—and they infuriated the Muslim community precisely because they tarnished the image of the entire religion. As Muslim leaders pointed out, no one had ever ascribed acts of terrorism committed by Christians and Jews to "Christianofascists" or "Judeofascists." In spite of Muslim protests, the word was widely used, even by President George W. Bush. Defining Islam was no longer a question of grappling with esoteric issues concerning the nature of God and the afterlife but had become disturbingly politicized in a way that cast a shadow over adherents of the religion around the globe. Political careers, intellectual endeavor, and ideological credibility—not only of Muslims—could all be affected by the way people defined Islam. Clearly, it was essential to define and categorize the religion of Muslims accurately. It was equally essential to identify the definers of Islam, none more so than those who were driving the global "war on terror" after 9/11.

The Dark Knights of Globalization

Some Americans have been concerned about the strong connections between the U.S. military establishment, corporations, politicians, and media at the highest levels for their mutual benefit—also known as the military-industrial complex.[3] They fear the United States may be driving the world toward unending warfare for the benefit of the few. After 9/11 they have not quite connected the dots in their arguments or traced them to Islam. I will attempt to do so in this chapter.

Since the end of World War II, this network has worked like a well-oiled machine, its influence and power steadily expanding. In the current war in Iraq, it is not difficult to miss the connections: Dick Cheney was once head of Halliburton Oil, and his wife is a board member of Lockheed Martin, the largest producer of equipment and weapons for the military. Donald Rumsfeld and Paul Wolfowitz, a close and long-standing business partner and a think tank colleague of Cheney, headed the Department of Defense. Halliburton stood to gain directly from the invasion of Iraq, and Lockheed Martin, which cannot survive without defense contracts, produces almost all of the U.S. Army's sophisticated weaponry, including the Star Wars, or missile defense, system being designed to conduct warfare from space. Lockheed Martin reciprocates the contracts for war accessories by donating lavishly to the political campaigns of its favorite politicians, such as Cheney. After the Iraq war, Halliburton stepped in to rebuild Iraq at a high price to U.S. taxpayers under a no-bid contract. Everyone in the network gained. The machine can only function effectively, however, in the presence of a credible enemy. Global war then becomes not only necessary but the very raison d'être or, in this case, the bread and butter of the entire enterprise.

Even during the previous Gulf war during the first Bush administration, the connections between big business and high office led to mutual benefit. At the time, Secretary of Defense Dick Cheney was active in linking big business to high administration officials, as Charley Bartlett, a Washington insider, points out:

> The policy of contracting out military responsibilities was initiated by Dick Cheney when he was Secretary of Defense back in 1990. He awarded a $2 million contract to Halliburton, the company which he was later to head, to examine whether contracting out was a feasible practice. After Halliburton concluded that it was a good idea, Cheney gave the company a contract, without competitive bidding, to take on a number of services previously performed by the military. The public needs to learn a great deal more about Halliburton's performance on contracts awarded since Cheney became Vice President. We need to know further about the work of many of the contractors in Iraq.[4]

For much of the twentieth century, the credible enemy in the eyes of most Americans was the Soviet Union, "the evil empire," to use Ronald Reagan's phrase. The U.S. government, willingly supported by the people, deployed every resource and strategy to prevent the evil empire from invading and enslaving the United States. With the decline and collapse of the Soviet Union in the late 1980s, the gigantic ideological and physical American structures responsible for its demise were thrown off balance. Hence a new global enemy had to be identified.

In the wake of the Soviet collapse, world societies did not convert to liberal democracies with their emphasis on human rights and civil liberties, as some in the West had hoped. Resistance to these Western values was often fierce, not only in Muslim countries, but around the world. Opposition to these values was evident in China, which some in the West accused of suppressing freedom, and in "rogue states" such as Cuba, North Korea, Syria, and Iran. Some of the most violent resistance before 9/11 came from Osama bin Laden, with his attack on the U.S. embassies in Africa in 1998 and on the U.S.S. *Cole* in 2000, while his al-Qaeda group boasted further attacks would take place, even on American soil. Here was a new cause for hostility. "Evil" still lurked in dark corners of the world.

The cold war warriors who had just defeated the Soviet Union argued that this threat was genuine and that the United States needed to maintain the preeminence of its military forces for the sake of both its defense and its global leadership. The strongest calls to do this came from a group of intellectuals dubbed the "neoconservatives," prominent during Reagan's presidency but sidelined under George Bush and Bill Clinton. The "neocons," broadly defined, believe the United States should not be afraid to use its unrivaled power to promote its values around the world. Some openly advocate the cultivation of an American empire. Neocons believe that threats the United States faces can no longer be reliably contained and therefore must be prevented, sometimes through preemptive military action.[5]

To convince Americans of their claims, the neocons established well-funded think tanks providing evidence of the threats—especially from Saddam's Iraq—and promoting their ideology through books, articles, and media appearances. The heavyweights of the current Bush administration—Paul Wolfowitz, Condoleezza Rice, Richard Perle, Donald Rumsfeld, John Bolton, and Dick Cheney—were involved in one way or another with these think tanks. One such institution, the Project for the New American Century (PNAC), founded in 1997 by Cheney, Rumsfeld, and Wolfowitz, argued in a seminal document, "Rebuilding America's Defenses," written in 2000, that the United States needed to "move more aggressively" toward neocon goals, but that the process would be a long one, "absent some catastrophic and catalyzing event" such as "a new Pearl Harbor." These words, the document's critics believe, suggest such a tragedy would almost be welcome because it would give a new momentum to the neocon worldview and its supporting structures. Indeed, September 11, 2001, appears to have been such an event.

To many neocons, including political economist Francis Fukuyama, American liberal democracy is the final stage in human political evolution, its primacy demonstrated by the defeat of the Soviet Union. This, he believed, was the "end of history."[6] Many neocons also believed that every human being has a desire to live in a free society, and that if those living under dictatorships were given the chance to cast off their oppressors and institute a democracy, they would. For many neocons, then, democracy was the "default state" that all societies would eventually embrace. The fall of the Berlin wall and collapse of the Soviet Union were constantly given as an example of this perceived objective reality. This notion of progress as the desired end of advanced societies over time is embedded in Western philosophic thought and can be broadly seen in the works of European thinkers such as Hegel, Darwin, and Marx. It is also reflected in the "civilizing mission" of the British Empire.[7]

Looking at the post–cold war world of the 1990s and seeing "evil" totalitarianism again defeated, Americans congratulated themselves. U.S. forces of freedom and democracy had prevailed, except over the "rogue states," which would eventually be forced to open their societies and join the Western-dominated international system. Western, American-dominated organizations such as the World Trade Organization (WTO), International Monetary Fund (IMF), and World Bank spread out across the world, asking countries to open their markets and encourage free trade, which would also lead to democracy. The force Fukuyama referred to as a movement toward the "end of history" was in fact globalization. Indeed, Fukuyama's thesis would appear in a new guise in Thomas Friedman's *The Lexus and the Olive Tree* and *The World Is Flat*.[8]

In pressing their case for the primacy of democracy and in the runup to the Iraq invasion, the neocons, backed by like-minded political figures, intellectuals, and journalists, developed the idea of equating Islamic extremists with the threat posed by the Nazis in the 1940s. World War II had been morally righteous, they said, and resulted in a total victory over the forces of evil. "The thing that hasn't changed, unfortunately, is that there still is evil in the world," said Wolfowitz, now head of the World Bank. "It is a fascist totalitarianism not fundamentally different from the way it was in the last century—no more God-fearing than [the Nazis and communists] were."[9] The Quran was compared to Hitler's *Mein Kampf* (most notoriously by Bill O'Reilly on his television show). Even mild suggestions of a dialogue with Muslims were dismissed as a means of "appeasing" evil just as Lord Chamberlain, Britain's prime minister, had done with Hitler. Muslim leaders—including Osama bin Laden, Saddam Hussein, and Mahmoud Ahmadinejad—were projected as Hitler reincarnate. The neocons then began blurring the distinction between Muslim extremists and the religion of Islam by introducing terms such as "Islamofascism."

To Bill Kristol, PNAC chairman and a leading articulator of neocon thinking, the fascist Islamic threat emanated from Iran, where it first reared its head in 1979 and has remained a danger ever since. The *Weekly Standard,* at which he served as editor, ran his opinion piece discussing other historical examples of an evil totalitarian ideology that had taken hold in a country seeking to export that ideology: "Communism became really dangerous when it seized control of Russia. National socialism became really dangerous when it seized control of Germany. Islamism became really dangerous when it seized control of Iran—which then became, as it has been for the last 27 years, the Islamic Republic of Iran."[10] In the same article, he suggested that the Bush administration take advantage of the Israeli offensive against Hezbollah in the summer of 2006 to bomb Iran.

The consequences of defeat at the hands of the Islamofascists, the neocons argued, would be catastrophic for the West because they would seek not only to impose shariah law and reinstate the caliphate, but perhaps also to annihilate civilized society in the West. An influential neocon, Richard Perle, coauthored a manual subtitled "How to Win the War on Terror," which he introduced thus: "For us, terrorism remains the great evil of our time, and the war against this evil, our generation's great cause. . . . There is no middle way for Americans: It is victory or holocaust. "[11]

The implication that Islam was akin to Nazism convinced Americans that the post-9/11 experience was like the cold war after World War II. Sacrifices were thus expected from ordinary Americans in order to allow the administration to protect their way of life and freedom. The success of this argument explains the muted response to the cases of torture involving Muslims not long after 9/11 and the introduction of the Patriot Act, which Muslims believed was aimed at them. Faced with a Hitler-like threat, many Americans believed the president should do whatever was necessary to protect citizens. President George W. Bush was a man of action in need of an ideology, while the neocons were thinkers and intellectuals in search of a leader who would translate their ideas into policy. The match between Bush and the neocons was made in heaven.

Despite the neocons' arguments, today's war on terror is vastly different from the cold war but is unfortunately being seen in the same light. In 1947, as in 2001, U.S. policymakers had to deal with new threats facing the United States and chart a new course for U.S. foreign policy. Although U.S. policymakers recognized that communism was going to be the next threat facing America after World War II and had to decide how to confront it, this view was nuanced and the State Department debated how to proceed, noting that communism was simply exploiting preexisting conditions of poverty and despair in Europe. The U.S. government's aim was therefore to "combat not communism, but the economic maladjustment which makes European society vulnerable to exploitation by any and all totalitarian movements."[12] This was part of the justification for the Marshall Plan, but the policy of tackling the root causes of communism did not last long.

In April 1950, Paul Nitze, the director of policy planning for the State Department, presented President Harry Truman with a new document, NSC-68, which was so influential that it would govern U.S. policy and the mind-set of American society until the fall of the Soviet Union four decades later. In this appraisal of the Soviet threat, the previous philosophy of developing countries to stop the spread of communism was no longer on the agenda. Instead, the Soviets were the aggressors, and the document warned of their design to impose an evil ideology on the rest of the world, a mission all the more intimidating because of the strength of their atomic weapons arsenal. The threat now was to America's freedom, the very essence of American livelihood:

> The Soviet Union, unlike previous aspirants to hegemony, is animated by a new fanatic faith, antithetical to our own, and seeks to impose its absolute authority over the rest of the world. . . . With the development of increasingly terrifying weapons of mass destruction, every individual faces the ever-present possibility of annihilation should the conflict enter the phase of total war. . . . The issues that face us are momentous, involving the fulfillment or destruction not only of this Republic but of civilization itself.[13]

Americans would have to mobilize extensively to defeat this "fanatic faith," which represented totalitarianism, slavery, and atheism—quite the opposite of the U.S. values of freedom, liberty, and faith in God.[14]

U.S. policymakers had to make a similar choice after 9/11. Should they do what the State Department suggested in 1947 and attack the root causes of terrorism, pushing hard for Middle East peace and launching a new Marshall Plan for the Muslim world? It could have helped reform the madrassahs, for instance, which were accused of producing fanatic young

Muslims ready to die in a bloody jihad. It could have helped change the curriculum and improve teacher training programs so as to alter the mind-set of future generations. It could have promoted genuine democracy and thereby eased the tensions in Muslim nations where people feel trapped under unelected regimes that are usually corrupt and incompetent.

Instead, the United States chose to return to what was essentially the cold war mind-set of resisting totalitarianism. U.S. policy as laid out in the "Bush Doctrine" emphasizes that the "National Security Strategy of the United States of America" in the war against global terrorism is preoccupied with fighting for democratic values and a basic way of life. Freedom and terror are at war, and there should be unhampered military spending to defeat it.[15] Our enemies, Wolfowitz said, are people who "worship death and not life . . . who worship the devil, I believe, and not God . . . they are an evil that has to be confronted."[16] When President Bush and his administration invited experts on Islam to provide insight into the best strategy for approaching the Muslim world, they relied on figures like Bernard Lewis, whom scholars of Islam consider the quintessential "Orientalist" because like other Orientalists, he tends to apply negative and outdated stereotypes of Muslims and thus misinterprets the Muslim world.[17] Muslims have therefore been suspicious of and vocal about the links between Lewis—and through him the other Orientalists—and U.S. foreign policy.[18]

Bernard Lewis, for example, is credited with the concept of the "clash of civilizations," borrowed by political scientist Samuel Huntington, who penned his internationally famous *The Clash of Civilizations*. One observer writes: "Lewis's basic premise, put forward in a series of articles, talks, and best-selling books, is that the West—what used to be known as Christendom—is now in the last stages of a centuries-old struggle for dominance and prestige with Islamic civilization."[19] Although shaky and easy to challenge, the concept attracted considerable attention. The notion it projected of an ongoing ideological and historical clash between the West and the world of Islam fit perfectly with the administration's mind-set. Despite being ethnocentric and outdated, Lewis's ideas had now become the accepted and indisputable foundation of U.S. foreign policy, identified by the *Wall Street Journal* as the "Lewis Doctrine."[20]

Dick Cheney—the most powerful man in the U.S. administration after the president and the one said to be running its machinery—was so influenced by Lewis that he quoted him on television just before the war in

Iraq.[21] Cheney cited Lewis's insight that Muslims only respond to force and thus need to be approached with firmness. He was saying, in short, that if you show Muslims who is master, they will respect you. In line with this thinking, Cheney justified extreme measures in the execution of the war on terror, including the use of torture. The Lewis-based attitude that guided the planning of the war on terror also influenced the thinking of other officials in Washington and their view of Muslims.

Misguided policies and erroneous concepts in Washington have led to tens of thousands of deaths and injuries in different parts of the Muslim world, which have in turn precipitated more violence and bloodshed, not to mention Muslim anger. Thus, those who advocate violent confrontation with the West have had little difficulty finding recruits. On the American side, the media have kept fresh the images of 9/11 and the "fury" of Muslims. The Muslim rhetoric of retaliation and revenge, couched in the hyperbole of the culture, has served to persuade Americans that their long-cherished security is at risk. The neocons also succeeded in persuading Americans that while they fought for the "civilized world"—as they had done in the two world wars—they may have to fight to win the war on terror on their own: "We are fighting on behalf of the civilized world. We will never cease to hope for the civilized world's support. But if it is lacking, as it may be, then we have to say, like the gallant lonely British soldier in David Low's famous cartoon of 1940: 'Very well, alone.'"[22]

The Afghan invasion in 2001 was at best an uneven war, given the disproportionate military strength of the two sides: one, the mightiest power on earth, and the other a small impoverished Asian nation with a starving population that had been traumatized by decades of resistance to the Soviet Union. Yet the American media, at the time almost an adjunct of the war on terror, with some honorable exceptions such as Seymour Hersh, gave the impression that the Muslim world was a monolith on a crazed jihad against the West. This is just not the case. The Muslim world is divided by nationalism, ethnicity, and ideas about Islam, as in the three models described in this book. Those Americans who wished to justify the brutal nature of the war on terror found enough material to do so in the anger and hyperbolic rhetoric of some Muslims and examples of their violent behavior, such as the beheading of Danny Pearl.

For its part, the administration also created a network of "loyal" Muslims and appointed them to key positions to serve its interests: Zalmay

Khalilzad, who previously consulted for the oil company Unocal, is the present U.S. ambassador to the United Nations and was initially sent to Afghanistan and then Iraq; Hamid Karzai, also formerly with Unocal, is the president of Afghanistan. Furthermore, Shaukat Aziz, formerly with Citibank, was appointed prime minister of Pakistan by Musharraf.

Not long into the war on terror, the famous neocon façade of hubris and intellectual superiority was showing signs of cracks. Fukuyama, one of the most prolific public intellectuals actively involved in the Project for the New American Century since its inception in 1997, saw the unfolding of events after 9/11 and was soon expressing signs of disaffection with the entire neocon idea.[23] After having declared the end of history some years earlier, he now pronounced the demise of the neocons.[24]

But such doubts did not affect the thinking and policies of the administration. In January 2007 Bush announced that he would be sending another 21,500 troops to Iraq to create what was being called a "surge" in military activity. Although about 65 percent of Americans polled confirmed they were opposed to sending more troops, Bush, goaded on by Cheney, was undeterred. Within hours of the announcement, American troops in Iraq assaulted the Iranian diplomatic mission in Irbil, the regional headquarters of the Kurd autonomous region, and captured five diplomats. The Iranians were furious and claimed that diplomatic immunity had been violated, while the U.S. government accused the detained Iranians of being up to "no good" but did not present any evidence of their wrongdoing. Simultaneously, the United States sent aircraft carriers to the Persian Gulf. The tension in the region escalated dramatically. Commentators in the American media wondered in bafflement, considering the dire situation in Iraq, whether a war with Iran was imminent. The neocons beat the war drums once again with gusto.

In retrospect, the fear among American Muslim scholars after 9/11 that the neocons would guide the United States into a "manufactured" confrontation with Syria and Iran seems not unfounded.[25] The neoconservatives' misunderstanding of Islam, and therefore their fatally flawed approach to U.S. relations with the Muslim world, has only led to an American foreign policy blunder and isolated the United States on the world stage. Now an army with the most technologically advanced weapons and communications systems in history faces an impossible military situation in Iraq. That the neocons fail to acknowledge their mistakes appears to confirm a reputation for obduracy and haughtiness. That they show little compassion for the needless death and destruction brought about by their strategies does not go unnoticed. Not surprisingly, critics at home and abroad have come to view them as the dark knights of globalization.

How the Western Media Define Islam

As the foregoing discussion suggests, by 2006 Islam had become a bogeyman for the American people. Whatever their misgivings, Americans failed to challenge the White House's arguments for using torture or domestic spying in the war on terror because they wanted to remain safe from the terrorists. The media had a significant role in convincing them that Cheney's worldview was to be believed. A terrorist alert broadcast round the clock on television, colored "red" for a high threat or "yellow" for a moderate threat, kept everyone's nerves on edge. Interestingly, it was never "green."

Reports of foiled terror plots and attempts at infiltration into the West by Muslims bent on mischief were fed to the media and kept people nervous, wondering when and where the next terrorist attack would take place. Although not to be ignored, these threats were made out to be more intimidating than the reality warranted. Details were vague and facts difficult to establish because the administration did not wish to divulge them. Some critics of the war on terror thus began to question their authenticity. Craig Murray, for one, a former British ambassador to Uzbekistan and an outspoken critic of Tony Blair and his blind support of Bush's policies, was skeptical about the alleged plot of twenty-four British Pakistanis to blow up ten planes over the Atlantic in August 2006. In several media interviews, he pointed out that many of the accused did not possess passports, airline tickets, or any training for such high-precision activity. Pakistani intelligence officials confirmed the accused were "amateurs" who could not have been a credible threat. Despite these facts, those who cast Muslims in the guise of a credible threat treated the story as another unrelenting attempt by Muslims to cause damage to the West.

According to widespread reports, the media also received support from the administration to promote the neocon ideology aggressively through television channels such as Fox News, with its exciting news presentations and controversial right-wing contributors, and a host of radio and newspaper outlets. The media chose to sensationalize news related to terrorists, yet many Americans took what they saw and heard as fact. Commentators on Fox frequently began selling the threat from the Muslim world as an imminent danger that could abruptly end "Western civilization as we know it." Fox also produced a glitzy and popular television series, *24*, which sensationalized terrorists of all nationalities and races. Early episodes showed U.S. authorities fighting Muslim terrorists depicted as average immigrants living in the house next door, thus implying that the threat may be present everywhere at all times. In 2005 an episode had Muslims gaining control of a nuclear plant in the United States and causing it to melt down. One of the leaders of the plot killed his wife and shot his son because he feared they would prevent him from carrying it out—all this after he kidnapped the defense secretary and tried to behead him live on the Internet. Muslims were outraged and several advocacy groups protested.

But the point had been made, and it reinforced the negative perception of Muslims as minatory and violent. The threat became so inflated in the media and the element of fear so high that the public tacitly agreed that there should be no limitations to government actions in order to prevent another attack, allowing the policy of zero tolerance to be implemented whether it pertained to listening in on phone conversations without warrants, the controversial U.S. Patriot Act, or torturing terrorist suspects. Another neocon, journalist Charles Krauthammer, suggested that the United States should also adopt policies of torture if they would help extract information from "Islamist" prisoners.[26]

The mainstream media thus portrayed the threat of "Islamism" along Lewis's lines—as a widespread ideology in the Muslim world intent on re-creating an Islamic caliphate to engulf the world. Neocon columnist and historian Daniel Pipes has long warned of the dangers posed by "Islamists," stressing that since 9/11 they could be anywhere: "Individual Islamists may appear law-abiding and reasonable, but they are part of a totalitarian movement, and as such, all must be considered potential killers."[27] Pipes launched a program called Campus-Watch to monitor teachers who may be spreading anti-American sentiments or Islamic principles. "What we need to do," Pipes said, "is snarl, not be nice. What we need to do is inspire fear, not affection. You can't inspire fear and love at the same time, so one has to choose."[28] Remarks like these drew praise from Krauthammer, who called Pipes a "prophet" for understanding that "militant Islam is the problem, and moderate Islam is the solution."[29] With the connotation of evil now surrounding it, "Islamism" appeared to be the very antithesis of what the United States stood for. The confrontation between the two assumed the nature of a cosmic struggle between liberty, justice, democracy, and freedom, on one hand, and extremism, terrorism, and violence, on the other. The argument implicitly equated the entire Muslim world with these negative concepts and constructed a monolithic and frightening picture of Islam in the minds of Americans, who before may not have had any opinion on Islamic history and culture at all. Americans, unaware of how this "construct" had arisen, began to associate the word "Islam" with terrorism and the enemy. These sentiments made the idea of dialogue and diplomacy irrelevant. As Pipes put it, the "season for understanding is over."[30]

With the idea of a permanent threat both outside and inside the United States convincingly conveyed to the American public, those behind it now had an identifiable enemy with which to justify an open-ended global war. Muslims, whether they followed the Ajmer, Deoband, or Aligarh model, were all perceived as potential suspects predisposed to violence. Yet this enemy had been identified as "Islam" in a scandalously loose and essentially inaccurate manner, in tandem with the myth of Islam as an inherently violent doctrine dating back to Medieval Europe. Passages of the Quran are taken out of context to support this argument, and the true nature of Islam is ignored. No mention is ever made that Muslims each and every day refer to God as "Merciful" and "Beneficent," that the Quran states "There is no compulsion in religion" (Surah 2, Verse 256), or that the Prophet's most significant title—given by the Quran itself—is a "Mercy unto mankind." War is to be waged only in defense of one's family and community, and never in aggression. The principles of war codified by Abu Bakr, the first caliph of Islam, forbade the killing of holy men of all faiths, women, and children and the destruction of trees, crops, or any other vegetation.

On the heels of U.S. policy equating Islam with terror and evil, the media have become so heavily indoctrinated that a large section of the American public now believes Islam is an evil and inherently flawed religion that condones violence. Few have stopped to consider that a countless number of people have been killed in "terrorist" attacks by non-Muslims, such as Christians and Jews: for examples of the former one only has to look at the murderous attacks of the Irish Republican Army in the United Kingdom, and for the latter the massacre in the Hebron mosque in 1994 when Baruch Goldstein killed 29 Muslims and wounded 150 while they were praying. Even members of traditionally "pacifist" religions such as Buddhists and Hindus have bombed and killed innocent people. The Hindu Tamil Tigers, for instance, have killed thousands of people in Sri Lanka, including prime ministers and presidents. Seldom have the acts of these people, though contrary to the central tenets of compassion and wisdom of their religions, been equated with their respective religions.

A question asked frequently and often with some exasperation since 9/11 is "Who speaks for Islam?" Outside the inflammatory statements of media commentators, interest in the nature of Islam has now reached unprecedented levels, but unfortunately too few appear to have studied Islam adequately, and too few Muslims themselves have been asked to join the discussions, thus compounding the confusion surrounding the subject. I cannot imagine Judaism being discussed by a panel consisting entirely of Christians and Muslims or Christianity discussed by a panel composed only of Jews and Hindus. But this is precisely how Islam is being discussed, much to its detriment and the frustration of Muslims.

Meanwhile, Muslim scholars have remained largely invisible, reduced to watching their subject, faith, and tradition being mangled and distorted by a range of opinion over which they have no control. Many have reacted to attacks on Islam by writing for Muslim outlets and pleading the case of Islam as a religion of peace. They have sounded defensive, powerless, and helpless, unable to speak for themselves directly in U.S. forums, sometimes because they were denied entry. Two such individuals refused visas are Arab scholar Tariq Ramadan from Switzerland, a descendant of Hassan Al-Banna, and Yusuf Islam from the United Kingdom, known as the pop singer Cat Stevens before he converted. Western commentators find Ramadan and Islam enigmatic and controversial although they were both frequently cited as role models in our questionnaires. These commentators see Ramadan as Deoband in Aligarh clothes and Islam as Ajmer in Deoband clothes.[31]

Americans therefore do not see or hear Muslims as normal, average, everyday citizens talking about a variety of issues that affect the nation. Muslims are defined and discussed almost entirely by non-Muslims. A distorted understanding and perception is therefore guaranteed. In the end therefore Americans have an incomplete understanding of Muslims. Considering how involved Americans are with the Muslim world and need to be making decisions, often of a life-and-death nature, this lack of understanding can be catastrophic.

The result was that the majority of commentators—judging from their remarks on television and their book titles—viewed the post-9/11 world simplistically through the lens of security, terrorism, and the war on terror. Most were explicitly hostile to Muslims in a general and even irrational way. Others just pretended Muslims did not exist. There was not, for example, a single Muslim among the eight authors of *The Muslim World after 9/11,* a major Rand study that ran to 525 pages.[32] Worse: not a single anthropologist who could have told us about Muslim culture, traditions, sects, and values was listed among the authors.

In pursuit of sensationalism, the media ignored authentic Western scholars—not necessarily Muslim ones—who had labored for decades on their subject. Established academics such as Clifford Geertz, Lawrence Rosen, John Esposito, John Voll, and Tamara Sonn were seldom called upon to deconstruct what was happening around the subject to which they had dedicated their lives. Instead, the media demanded the services of those who understood Islam in terms of security threats, terrorist attacks, and violent extremists. It had little time for or patience with objective discussions about history, society, tribe, and sect. Commentators therefore lectured on "Islam and terrorism" without explaining "Islam 101."

The negative depiction of Islam in the Western media did not go unnoticed in the Muslim world. Throughout our journey Muslims consistently expressed their concerns to our team over Western misperceptions and misunderstandings of Islam. Our questionnaires showed a clear majority cited "Western misconceptions of Islam" as the number one threat facing the Muslim world. Presidents, princes, sheikhs, and students, all were concerned and even alarmed at the gap between what they knew of Islam and how they imagined the West saw it. The closing of this gap, Muslims felt, would be the great challenge in the future.

Many Muslims have been angered by figures with no academic or community background whom they often see as speaking for Islam in the Western media. Ayaan Hirsi Ali in Europe, Irshad Manji in Canada, and Asra Nomani in the United States emerged overnight to challenge traditional Muslim leadership, values, and ideas. Each has written a widely publicized book, and each has talked of "reforming Islam," which even the most respected Muslim religious scholar—*alim*—from an established religious school would hesitate to do.[33] To ordinary Muslims, these women appear deliberately provocative, challenging some of the core cultural values of Islam in both their writing and behavior. Conservative Muslims consider all three notorious: Ali for working on the script of a film featuring a woman with verses from the Quran painted on her naked body; Manji for declaring her lesbianism; and Nomani for bearing an illegitimate son, and for campaigning to lead prayers at her local mosque, a position traditionally reserved for a male cleric. So irrational is the anger among some Muslims against these particular women that when I appeared with them on different programs, I faced severe criticism. By talking to them, I was admonished, I was giving them legitimacy.

My impression after meeting all three is that of intelligent women who desperately want to contribute to the discussion about Islam, hoping that the sympathetic ear being extended to them in the media will help them "reform" Islam. In an hour-long, one-to-one television discussion on C-SPAN with Asra Nomani in 2005, I raised the problems of reform in Islam, which she had been advocating. I explained that reformation would entail complicated theological and legal issues. The theology of Islam is so firmly rooted in one book, the Quran, and one man, the Prophet, that mainstream Muslims are unlikely to ever support attempts to tamper with either. What required attention, I suggested, were the long overdue rights for women, improved educational standards, and the introduction of democracy. I was able to persuade Asra that a better word to use than "reformation" would be a renaissance within Islam. I could not see Asra— or either of the other two—as a Martin Luther of Islam. If change is to come—as it must—it needs to be from *within* an Islamic framework and introduced by Muslims who have credibility within their own society. In the opinion of most Muslims, the behavior of these women is contrary to Islamic values, goes against their traditional culture, and therefore indicates they are not "true" Muslims, but outsiders.

Needless to say, the media, always on the lookout for some controversial issues surrounding Islam, patronized these women enthusiastically. In Philadelphia, at the World Affairs Council Conference mentioned earlier, I heard Ayaan Hirsi Ali described as a "hero" who was "brave to stand up against the tyranny of Islam." The career of "the Honorable" Ayaan, as she was addressed, illustrates the ongoing relationship between the West and Islam. At the age of fourteen, Ali arrived in Holland from Somalia as a refugee, later gained notoriety when she attacked aspects of Islamic culture, particularly what she perceived as the mistreatment of women. She shot to international fame when she wrote the script for a short television documentary on violence against Muslim women titled *Submission* and directed by Theo Van Gogh, a descendant of the famous Dutch painter. Theo was murdered in Amsterdam in 2004 by a Muslim with a Moroccan background who left a note pinned to the body of his victim promising that Ali would be next. Subsequently she required full-time bodyguards and to Muslims became a symbol of Islamophobia in Europe.

A certain segment of European society strongly defended Ali's right to express her opinions. Others were more critical, seeing her attempts as self-publicity and cheap shots at a depressed community. On the whole, Muslims were agitated and angry, even more so when Ali publicly stated that the cartoons of the Prophet, which Muslims felt had insulted him, should be republished. It now appeared that she was simply baiting the entire community, which did not care that Ayaan had already renounced Islam. It seemed she was either being deliberately provocative or being used to humiliate Islam.

In May 2006, a major international story broke reporting that the Dutch government had threatened to revoke Ali's citizenship because she had lied in her official documents when she sought political asylum in 1992. Perhaps anticipating the move, Ali had already made arrangements to leave the country. She had been offered a lucrative position at one of Washington's well-known right-wing think tanks, the American Enterprise Institute. Her ignominious exit from Holland and warm welcome in Washington confirmed Muslim suspicions that a Muslim was being used to humiliate Islam.

By contrast, many Americans see Ayaan as a heroine in the mold of Rosa Parks or Coretta Scott King—as a brave and courageous woman standing up to the forces of tyranny in her own society. They can relate to her and seem unaware that she used her knowledge of Islam to play on Americans' worst fears and prejudices toward Islam. While she projected herself as a reformer of Islam, she had in fact overstepped all sorts of cultural and religious boundaries for Muslims, to the point where she no longer represented any aspect of their community. If anything, Muslims such as Ayaan are thought to have betrayed the community, crossing the line at a time of crisis. Though few Americans would recognize Ayaan's deliberate use of Islam for her own gain, her American hosts may well have darker political reasons to welcome her than simple hospitality. Her presence could be used to show the alleged backward and intolerant nature of Islam and hence the need to continue fighting it. Why else would commentators in the West promote such figures aggressively when most mainstream Muslims have strong reservations about them—indeed, no one considered them role models in any of the interviews that we conducted. One such commentator, Andrew Bostom, has argued that Ayaan is an "intellectually honest reformer of Islam," while attacking me for still writing about the Prophet with "respect and affection."[34] Bostom used the same argument in an exchange with Judea Pearl, who was promoting Jewish-Muslim dialogue with me. People like Bostom are suggesting, I suspect, that only those Muslims who reject Islamic tradition altogether, as Ayaan has, are acceptable as the "correct" Muslim. Here is an experiment in the reformation of Islam being attempted from outside Islam.

The unfavorable and marginal portrayal of Islam only further widens the chasm between the West and mainstream Muslims. If the West were sincere about understanding Islam, Muslims believe, it would consult the serious or established scholars. Instead, Islam is being viewed as a religion of violence and extremism and a credible global enemy for the West, which has transformed the religion of peace-loving Rumi, Rabia, and Chisti, the saint of Ajmer, into a religion of terror.

How Muslims Are Defining Islam

Our team's questionnaires and interviews captured the frustrations, thoughts, and candid hopes of a range of Muslims—people on the street and in their homes and in community gatherings—voices that are not often heard today (see appendix). Respondents were able to define themselves and their ideals without being directly asked to state them, a useful approach since many Muslims are reluctant to speak openly about such matters because of the repressive atmosphere in some countries. Authorities might misunderstand even harmless questions about Islam and issues of modernization as implied criticism of the regime. To circumvent this restriction and avoid putting respondents in an awkward position, we asked them about role models and contemporary icons. Their replies revealed a common disappointment in the lack of globally recognized Muslim leaders who represented the scholarship, justice, or compassion that Muslims wished to see in their society. But the idea of a heroic Islamic past was also widely shared. The Prophet of Islam was the most inspiring figure for Muslims everywhere, followed closely by his companions and family, who represent ideal Muslim society. Finally, our own three models—Ajmer, Deoband, and Aligarh—are visible everywhere in the Muslim world and appear to be undergoing various interesting mutations as they adapt to a post-9/11 world.

American Muslims who are able to express themselves freely are in a unique position between Western and Muslim civilizations and feel they are the leaders of the future on behalf of the ummah. But faced with the stereotype of Islam's supposed violent nature, even those living in the United States have sometimes been unable to convey the true nature of their faith to non-Muslims and have often ended up by reinforcing the negative image. This is what happened at the annual Islamic Society of North America (ISNA) conference in Dallas in July 2006, where the remarks of a Muslim community leader, the head of the society representing the Muslims of the entire continent, cast a shadow on the legitimate Islamic concept of jihad before an audience that included non-Muslims. As I was expected to give a keynote address immediately afterward, I could see from the stage the look of horror and discomfort on the faces of my American guests—which included Hailey and her family, who live in Dallas—sitting in the front row.

What the Muslims in the audience saw and heard was a well-known and respected leader of the community with the requisite generous beard and passionate look in his eyes inviting them to join him in jihad—they knew he meant of the spiritual kind—and asking them to show their commitment by loudly repeating *Allah hu Akbar*, meaning "God is great." His South Asian accent would have sounded familiar and comforting to the majority of the audience as there were more elderly immigrants in it than young American-born Muslims. But what the Americans saw was a bearded man with a sallow complexion and a wild look in his eyes shrieking a call for jihad into the microphone in a foreign accent and rousing the audience into a frenzy by making them yell the name Allah repeatedly. Surrounded by hundreds of Muslims wearing traditional Islamic clothes and shouting words like "jihad" and "Allah" without any explanation, the Americans felt intimidated. For all they knew, the stereotypes now so familiar to them could be confirmed momentarily by someone pulling out a grenade, shrieking "Death to the infidels," and blowing them all up in order to proceed on his way to heaven to claim the seventy-two virgins highlighted in media accounts. I knew that to Americans, the word "jihad" meant military aggression by Muslims and would be instantly misunderstood. I changed my opening remarks to explain that what the man had meant by jihad was not a military action but a spiritual dialogue and the intellectual and democratic empowerment of the Muslim community within the United States.

The hard work and commitment of Muslim leaders like ISNA's Mohammed ElSanousi, who was present and later said he was uncomfortable with the use of the word "jihad" in that context, was thus almost derailed by the easily misunderstood remarks. If Islam is not defined in a culturally sensitive manner for non-Muslims, the vacuum of information surrounding the religion grows only larger and allows the misconceptions of others to fill it and distort the true definition of the religion. But such sensitivity is slowly emerging in the community with changes such as the recent election of Ingrid Matteson, a female white convert to Islam and a prominent professor at Hartford Seminary, as ISNA president.

Some Muslims are defining themselves proudly as American Muslims and not as Arab, Pakistani, or Black Muslims. A new identity is thus being forged. The Hasan family is an example. Malik Hasan, born in New Delhi, India, before its independence in 1947, migrated to the United States in the late 1970s, establishing a highly successful neurology practice in rural Colorado. His devotion to his patients eventually led him to open a health maintenance organization (HMO), designed to challenge the restrictive practices of other HMOs. Through his persistence, the HMO grew into a Fortune 100 company, one of the few to be headed by an American Muslim. The Computerworld Program of the Smithsonian Institution and *Forbes* Magazine also presented him with awards for his technology prowess.

His wife, Seeme Hasan, a graduate of Pakistan's Kinnaird College, in Lahore, became a tireless activist in their hometown of Pueblo, Colorado: participating in and raising funds for various civic activities, including the local symphony and ballet; organizing eyesight testing for low-income children; and even protesting zoning changes and liquor licensing in residential neighborhoods. She has been recognized for her work with young Latino children, specifically for integrating these children into arts programs that were previously offered only to white youth. The same organization named its annual primary award the Seeme Hasan PEACE Award after her. On appointing her to the Colorado Council on the Arts, the state's governor, Democrat Roy Romer, recognized her devotion to the performing arts and education, constituting more than 10,000 hours of volunteer service. Seeme's personal passion has been overseeing the Hasan Family Foundation, which has contributed more than $5 million to various causes in the United States. The foundation's main purpose has been to promote understanding between Muslims and Americans, a goal laid out even before 9/11. Seeme is particularly focused on presenting the culture of South Asia in a positive manner to the American community, which has led her to start her own record label, called iSufiRock, which publishes South Asian, Muslim, and Sufi-styled rock music.[35]

She has also been named "Woman of the Year" by the cultural organization Safeer-e-Pakistan and TV Pakistan. After 9/11, she threw herself into creating better understanding between Muslims and Americans and specifically lobbied the White House and Congress to end the post-9/11 registration program and stop its frequent incarceration from being applied indiscriminately to Muslims, especially Pakistanis living in the United States. These political efforts led Seeme to found Muslims for America and Muslims for Bush.[36] Together, Seeme and Malik have promoted health care, art, culture, and education. They have contributed over $2 million to the Colorado State University–Pueblo, where the Hasan School of Business and Hasan Amphitheater are located.

Continuing the tradition, their children are involved in medicine, media, law, and art. Their son, Muhammad Ali, is a filmmaker, who often uses his films to enlighten the life stories of American Muslims. He also writes frequently and appears on television to discuss foreign policy issues related to Islam. Their daughters Aliya and Asma are a doctor and lawyer, respectively. Asma is also the author of two books on Islam in America. Both daughters speak frequently and are also interviewed about Islam and being American Muslims. Asma describes herself as a "Muslim feminist cowgirl" in her book, *Why I Am a Muslim: An American Odyssey.*[37] When Asma lectured in my class at American University, the students enjoyed her talk and the casual approach to her own celebrity. She discussed her appearance on Bill Maher's *Politically Incorrect* while talking about traditional Muslim marriage. The Hasan family represents what is possible in being both American and Muslim.

American Muslims can clearly be an asset for the United States. As one Washington, D.C., student pointed out in a questionnaire, "Muslims in the West [can] provide the bridge between the two sides. But, Western states need to realize that how they treat Muslims at home will affect their reputation in the Muslim World. I also think that young Western Muslims should reach out to their peers in the Muslim world, through the Internet, for example, and share with them their experiences in the West and what they've learned about freedom and civil liberties." The real hope for the future of the U.S. Muslims lies with the younger generation, which feels strong ties to the United States and has grown up synthesizing and negotiating between the different cultures of their parents and their new homeland.

Although they live in a Western democracy, Muslim immigrants and their children in the United States still strongly adhere to their religious identity. Their historic role models resemble those for the rest of the Muslim world. As revealed in further questionnaires administered in and around Washington, D.C., the most inspiring figure from the past for American Muslims is the Prophet of Islam, followed closely by Abu Bakr, Ali, and Khadija. The selection of Umar and Saladin, considered victorious generals for Islam, shows the desire to look to models that are needed today. Other role models include Muhammad Ali and Malcolm X, who Muslims see as having stood up for Islam under difficult circumstances and emerged with their reputations enhanced. Still other interesting figures mentioned by U.S. Muslims are Jesus, Rumi, Jinnah, Hamza Yusuf (the American scholar who converted to Islam), Amr Khaled (a popular preacher in the Middle East), Mughal emperor Aurangzeb, and Ayatollah Khomeini (who led the Islamic revolution in Iran). The last two figures are connected with the Deoband model. A small percentage of American Muslims name bin Laden, a surprising and daring choice considering the political climate in the United States.

Because Muslims have been living far longer in Europe than in the United States, the discussion about defining Islam will benefit by crossing the Atlantic. Among Europe's Muslim leaders, Mustafa Ceric, the Grand Mufti of Bosnia, admires as role models the great Muslim scholars of the past—Ghazzali, Ibn Rushd, and Ibn Taymiyya—as he explained to me in Doha in 2006 where we were attending the Brookings conference on U.S. relations with the Muslim world. The fair-skinned Ceric, wearing a long Muslim-style coat and red fez, spoke with the logic and style of a European intellectual: "I am most angry with Ghazzali," Ceric said several times, aware that he was being provocative considering the high esteem that Muslims have for Ghazzali. He loved Ghazzali more than any other intellectual but felt that after Ghazzali's dramatic soul-searching toward the end of his life, he took the ummah down the wrong path by denouncing the philosophy that set the precedent blamed for stifling Muslim intellectual thought. "When I meet Ghazzali in the hereafter," said Ceric with a wry smile, "I will ask him what he thought he was doing."

Of the Muslim intellectuals that Ceric admires, it is Ibn Taymiyya who has triumphed. His philosophy of orthodox Islam permeates the madrassahs. His more literal reading of the Quran and charter for Muslim action—in contrast to Ghazzali's flirtation with Sufism—appeal to the temper of Muslims today. He is an iconic figure among religious groups in Saudi Arabia and Pakistan. "It is a time," Ceric added with a hint of regret, "of Muslim activism, not intellectualism," noting that today's Muslims live in a time of great "cultural insecurity" and "low self-esteem." As a result, they are constantly looking at the past for inspiration: "Our history is the history of yesterday and we have left the future to the West." A series of disasters has not helped matters. As Ceric pointed out, 70 percent of the refugees in the world are Muslim; the tsunami that hit Asia and the subsequent earthquake took mostly Muslim lives; most of the current wars are being fought in Muslim lands; the problems of the Palestinians, Kashmiris, and Chechens have still not been solved. He told me that thousands of Muslims had been killed in his homeland, in the Balkans. Each such crisis generates countless numbers of displaced people and the list of discontented Muslim refugees grows.

Yet when I pressed him for solutions, he appeared unusually upbeat considering the gloomy analysis he had just presented. "We need to understand the West better," he argued. "We need to balance the trends in Muslim societies between the secularist model of Ataturk and the completely Islamic models of Qutb and Maududi" (between the Aligarh and Deoband models, in terms of our discussion). The answer, for him, was not Muslim integration into the West, but cooperation between different peoples.

Though unimpressed with contemporary Muslim intellectual leadership, Ceric had faith in the future, drawing on the optimism implicit in the Quran. When I pushed him to explain the dearth of Muslim intellectuals like Ghazzali or Ibn Rushd despite vast Muslim resources, a point easily made sitting in a luxury hotel in Doha, and challenged him to give me one name, he was at a loss for a moment, then said, with a twinkle in his eye, "But we have produced Akbar Ahmed." This was a convenient escape from the discussion but, for me, coming from one of Islam's leading intellectuals, not unpleasant to hear.

Lacking such leadership, many Muslims throughout the world do not know what to make of globalization's winds of change and are reacting to them in anger.[38] After September 2001, most people in the West associated young Muslim terrorists with Arabs because nineteen of the hijackers were Arabs from Arab countries. It was assumed that Muslims living in the West had been fully integrated into society and were not a potential threat to the security of Western nations. It came as a shock, then, to learn that many of the Muslims involved in the aborted attempt to blow up airliners over the Atlantic in the summer of 2006 were British citizens of Pakistani origin.

I was not entirely surprised because I had been seeing—and writing about—the dramatic changes taking place over a generation both in the United Kingdom's Pakistani community and in British society. I first came to the United Kingdom in the 1960s as an undergraduate, returned in the 1970s to complete a Ph.D., and returned once more in the late 1980s to join Cambridge University as a fellow, where I remained until my appointment as Pakistan's high commissioner to the United Kingdom from 1999 to 2000. By the turn of the century, Pakistanis constituted the largest ethnic group among British Muslims, many of them living in isolated communities in northern towns. Unlike the previous generation, these Muslims were born in the United Kingdom and had little intention of returning home. Deprived of real political and economic power and often the target of racism and discrimination, they resented the negative depiction of their religion and culture in the media, which intensified during the controversy surrounding Salman Rushdie's novel *The Satanic Verses* as Muslims were portrayed as little more than an angry community of book-burners. They saw this media attention as a Western-inspired, postmodernist blitzkrieg against their cherished traditions and values.[39]

At Cambridge in the 1990s, I witnessed these trends developing in the United Kingdom's Muslim society with unease: in one case, bearded young radical males, influenced by Iranian politics, captured a local mosque and denied access to the elders who once ran it; in another case they threatened to disrupt and beat any Muslim joining a Pakistan Society event because it wished to sponsor a folk dance from rural Punjab and they saw dancing as un-Islamic.[40] As the tensions in Muslim society heightened, and while their complex causes remained unresolved, I feared even more tragic, possibly violent encounters in the future unless Muslim and British leaders stepped forward to address the growing Muslim problem with wisdom and compassion.

Along with many others, I wrote commentary on what was happening, joined interfaith initiatives, and was a member of the Runnymede Commission to study the problems of the Muslims of the United Kingdom and suggest recommendations.[41] In addition, I made frequent media appearances challenging some of the trends in Muslim society.[42] It was in this context—the need to explain Islamic issues both to Muslims and non-Muslims—that I launched the Jinnah Quartet, a project to revive the Aligarh model, discussed later in the chapter.

The 1990s marked the coming of age of a new Muslim generation that was essentially marginalized and even alienated from mainstream society, not only in the United Kingdom but also in the rest of Europe. Although Muslims had migrated to the region as a result of different historical experiences—South Asians predominantly to the United Kingdom, North Africans to France and Spain, and Turks to Germany—the principles underlying the new mood among these Muslims are the same. In the context of our three models, one can see the Ajmer model growing faint, the Aligarh model becoming increasingly weakened and marginalized, and the Deoband model gaining followers and becoming assertive. It is the Deoband model that captures Western headlines and convinces people of the irrelevance of the other two.

Several international and national developments contributed to the new Muslim mood of anger and defiance. The successful Afghan war against the Soviet Union, the fervor of Khomeini's Islamic revolution in Iran, his fatwa against Salman Rushdie, and the increased racism against Muslim immigrants persuaded Muslims to stop taking gross injustice against Muslims passively, as their émigré parents had been doing.[43] Their patience finally snapped with the raping and killing of Muslims in Kashmir, Chechnya, and the Balkans—most graphically symbolized by the slaughter in Srebrenica, captured on television, where thousands of Muslims were murdered while in UN custody. Outraged, the Muslim community saw the need to become active and vigilant in international affairs. Many felt that however integrated and Westernized they might try to be, their "Muslimness" would still keep them from being accepted as part of Western society. Unfortunately, Muslims were not reacting with wisdom, knowledge, or calm rationality. This lack of a coherent and universal Muslim response meant that others could easily define Islam. The bombings in London in 2005 and the plot to blow up civilian planes in 2006 are a product of this cultural environment.

Yet a nonradical element emerged from this environment as well that defined Islam as peaceful and accepting. The different choices made by two young students of Pakistani background at the London School of Economics in the early 1990s illustrate the point. They were contemporaries although they never met, and both dedicated their lives to what they saw as Islamic causes. One, Omar Sheikh, decided to fight for the rights of Kashmiris, was eventually captured by Indian authorities, made a name for himself as a London-educated student prepared (paradoxically) to commit acts of terror, and then gained notoriety as the main figure in the brutal slaying of Daniel Pearl in Karachi in 2002. The other student, Amineh Ahmed, my daughter, looked to more traditional Islamic methods of building bridges through the pursuit of knowledge and friendship. After graduating, Amineh went on to do her Ph.D. in anthropology at Cambridge University and worked toward interfaith dialogue and understanding aided by her supportive husband Arsallah Khan Hoti. She returned to Pakistan for fieldwork and brought her experiences with the community back to the United Kingdom, where she focused in particular on young Muslims. In 2006 she was appointed director of the first Jewish-Muslim Center at Cambridge, which was inaugurated by Sir Jonathan Sacks, chief rabbi of the United Kingdom, on February 1, 2007.

Amineh Ahmed and Omar Sheikh reacted differently to the challenges of living as Muslims in the age of globalization. The task for Europe is to determine whether it wishes to nurture a future generation of Omar Sheikhs or Amineh Ahmeds and develop an appropriate strategy for dealing with the Muslim community.

It will not be easy. Even modern Muslim nations like Turkey with an image of themselves as more European than Asian have problems in finding a balance between Islam and modernity. Cited by the West as the ideal secular and progressive model for other Muslim nations, Turkey is precariously situated between East and West. Under the tradition of its founder, Ataturk, it has strived to remain staunchly secular, firmly looking to the West for political, military, and economic support, while consciously distancing itself from its Islamic history and identity for most of the past century. Despite purporting to be a democracy, Turkey has actively suppressed outward signs of religion—especially Islam and the orthodox Deoband model—by, for instance, banning the hijab for women and beards for men. The state clings to the idea of itself as rigidly secular.

Yet the Islamic faith has remained strong in Turkey, and it is moving in interesting directions. The most recent elections were dominated by the AK Party, a modern political party with a strong Islamic identity. Since its rise, girls frequently appear in public wearing the hijab, although it is still banned in official settings, a rule that our team found still being enforced strictly. My assistant Hadia was almost not allowed to enter certain universities because of her headscarf. At the same time, the resurgent trend toward Islam is disconcerting for some brought up in the secular ethos of the last century. Gunsel Renda, a prominent public figure and art historian, was dismissive of the new Islamic expressions. An unabashed supporter of Ataturk, she called the hijab trend "ridiculous," "terrible," and "confused" and blamed the Arabs bitterly, especially the Saudis, for having introduced this new and, to her, strange form of Islam, perhaps through the media or various spiritual settings.

While the hijab creates some tension as a symbol of a backward past and more orthodox form of Islam, another emerging movement is developing wide appeal: namely, Sufism, or what I am calling the Ajmer model. With its capacity to absorb every spiritual position and yet maintain its own internal balance and integrity, Sufism has even incorporated Ataturk himself, the man who outlawed Islamic expression. When I attended the traditional Sufi dance in Istanbul organized by the Contemporary Lovers of Mevlana Society formed in 1989, it was a sold-out event. The visitors were gentle-looking people from all over the world, including the United States. The society's official pamphlet celebrated "the exalted Mohammad, the exalted Ali, the exalted Mevlana [Rumi], and the hero and head teacher

Mustafa Kemal Ataturk." By grouping the greatest Islamic names with the greatest critic of Islam, Ataturk, the Sufis showed that they could reverse the tide of secularism through their characteristic philosophy of universal acceptance. In less than a century after Ataturk's death, the religion was back with a new vitality.

Sufism is even appearing in the modern galleries where Turkey's most fashionable artists display their work. The Miracname series—named after the Prophet's celebrated night journey in the Quran—is a stunningly beautiful collection by Erol Akyavas depicting time, the universe, and the stars and planets as symbols of that miraculous journey and is on display at the New Gallery in Istanbul. According to the gallery's Turkish director, Sufism is now a popular form of expression but lies outside the realm of traditional Islam advocated by orthodox clerics. In its peaceful way, Sufism is carrying the argument forward for acceptance and tolerance. Another collection of paintings combined homosexual themes with Sufi calligraphy, but the gallery director and I agreed that such themes would be found controversial by many Muslims, even Ajmer followers.

Trying to make sense of these trends in Turkey, we spent an evening talking to one of the country's leading intellectuals, Mim Kemal Öke. I had met him in the 1980s when as a young man he was rediscovering his Islamic identity in a difficult environment almost hostile to religious identity. We had become friends, and he had translated my books into Turkish. This time, I found him oddly at peace with his society yet somewhat withdrawn from it.

The current clash in the Muslim world, he explained, is between two forms of Islam. One emphasizes violence and literalism, as personified by bin Laden, the other love and justice. In his view, the latter, Sufism, is "true Islam." In a community lacking in both love and justice, men like bin Laden are able to manipulate Muslim emotions more easily, especially when Sufism's characteristic self-reflection, contemplation, and withdrawal give it a low profile in Islam's internal debate. The most assertive argument usually wins the attention of the people. The Sufi does not believe in active engagement with worldly affairs but prefers to sit in quiet stillness contemplating the divine and feeling compassion for humanity with no personal desire for power.

Though veiled in the language and spirit of Sufistic love and compassion, the recent reemergence of Islam in Turkey cannot be seen in isolation from its political and cultural context. Alongside a desire to reconnect with the past, we found a strong desire to assert Turkish identity and guard against the perceived evils of globalization, as reflected in fierce anti-American sentiments. To our surprise, Turkey expressed the most anti-American sentiments on our journey.[44] That Turkey has been consistently refused European Union membership no doubt adds to this wave of Turkish nationalism. Our meetings with both the secular and more Islamic political parties confirmed our impression of a reemerging Islam. While looking to the West for certain technological and societal advancements, the Turks are able to identify their own traditional, widely respected Sufi Islam with pride. This quiet revolution—it is not noisy, or violent, or even immediately apparent—remains undetected by the West, though it marks a return to Islam and a strong assertion of identity, largely in protest against the uncomfortable currents of globalization, even if veiled in Sufistic love and compassion.

Our questionnaires concerning role models again reflected interesting trends. Since one of the most celebrated of all Sufi figures, Rumi, is buried in Konya, Turkey, we were not surprised at his popularity. Among contemporary role models, Sufi writer and activist M. Fethullah Gülen was overwhelmingly named the most popular. One nineteen-year-old student in a girl's dormitory felt Rumi and Gülen "remind us of the Islam we have forgotten."

Gülen has a large following in the United States, where he lives, as I discovered when invited to give the keynote address at a conference in his honor at the University of Oklahoma in November 2006. Visiting beforehand with Muhammed Cetin, an important figure in what is called the Gülen movement in the United States, I asked him for his favorite Gülen quotation. A devoted Muslim in Western dress and clean shaven, Cetin recited without pausing: "Be so tolerant that your bosom becomes wide as the ocean and is inspired with faith and love of human beings. Let there be no troubled souls to whom you do not offer a hand and about whom you remain unconcerned."[45] Gülen's message was to act Islam, not just to speak it, and the way to do this is through the discovery of love: "A soul without love cannot be elevated to the horizon of human perfection. . . . Those who are deprived of love, entangled in the nets of selfishness, are unable to love anybody else and die unaware of the love deeply implanted in the very being of existence."[46]

Gülen, said Muhammed Cetin, had become a *hafiz,* or someone who memorizes the entire Quran, at the age of four, and by nine had become a Sufi master through the inspiration of the great Sufi master himself, Maulana Rumi. A few years later his teachers said they had no more to teach him and asked him to go out to the world and preach. More than a thousand schools and colleges were directly inspired by Gülen's teaching, said Cetin, which emphasized nonviolence as much as love and an aversion to partisan politics. In Istanbul, at the height of his fame, his audiences would number up to 40,000 people, many of them students.

In 1999, Cetin added, the Turkish government charged Gülen with terrorism and treason, even though he had been lecturing against terrorism and anarchy for a quarter of a century. Furthermore, on September 12, 2001, he strongly condemned the terrorists who had struck the United States. Fortunately, good sense prevailed, and the case against Gülen was dismissed, but he left Turkey and took up residence in the United States. The environment in Turkey was inimical to overt Islamic teaching and symbols. In the past few years, said Cetin, more than 44,000 girls wearing the hijab had been expelled from Turkey's colleges and universities.

Upon meeting Gülen, Barbara Boyd, director of Interfaith Religious Studies at Oklahoma University, felt "he was like Jesus." When I asked why she compared a Muslim to Jesus, she said, "He radiated love." These were significant words not only because they were coming from a Christian but also because Oklahoma City is part of the Bible Belt in the United States. In her generosity of spirit, Boyd was reflecting the essence of Christianity. Gülen further won her over by saying she should lead the change of heart between Muslims and non-Muslims. I could not imagine a similar request coming from many in the Deoband or even Aligarh model.

I was trying to understand Gülen through Cetin yet failing to grasp the essence of his character until I asked Cetin how Gülen responded to the Prophet. Gülen, he said, would cry with love whenever the name of the Prophet was mentioned and stand up to show respect. That deep love of Muslims for the Prophet, I later explained in my address in Oklahoma, is why some become extremely angry when they think he is insulted. I asked Vahap Uysal, a Turkish professor on campus sitting in the audience, to explain what the Prophet meant to him. As he stood up, Uysai's eyes filled with tears, and trembling with emotion, he began weeping uncontrollably. His tears said it all, he whispered, and sat down. Barbara Boyd said she saw many wet eyes in the audience. Even journalists in the Bible Belt recognized from this public display of emotion that Muslims felt deeply about the Prophet. The local newspaper reported:

> By the time the microphone found its way back across the room and into the man's hand, he could barely control his wavering and sobbing voice. "I can't say anything but tears," the man said. Ahmed said this love for Muhammad pervades the Muslim world in a way comparable to Christians' love for Jesus. "This love could easily be turned to violence," Ahmed said . . . . Christianity and Islam are two ocean liners on a collision course in the middle of the ocean. He said efforts like Gülen's movement will "change the direction of an ocean liner in the Atlantic."[47]

Findings in the Field

Many of the people we talked to in the Arab world, especially in Qatar, named Yousef al-Qaradawi as a contemporary role model. Al-Qaradawi became notorious in the West after 9/11 when commentators scouring books by Muslim scholars came across one titled *The Lawful and the Prohibited in Islam*, in which al-Qaradawi argues that suicide among Muslims is justified when the ummah is under attack, as in the case of the Palestinians.[48] He also addresses everyday behavior ranging from hygiene and sexuality to prayers, and today he discusses similar topics on a television program. Though entertaining and helpful for his audience, his discussions also call upon Muslims for social action.

For purposes of comparison, we also grouped the responses to our questionnaires about role models in the Muslim world by region. Thus we learned that Ali, the fourth caliph, is far more popular in South Asia than in the Arab states, which is primarily due to the fact that South Asia has a large Shia community. Second, after the Prophet and three of the caliphs, Mohammed Ali Jinnah, the founder of the Islamic Republic of Pakistan, is considered a historical role model in Pakistan. Third, as in most other countries, the Prophet and Umar are the most popular historical role models in India. Other popular historical figures overall are Hassan Al-Banna, Muhammad Ibn Abdul Wahhab, and Ibn Taymiyya, who represent the Deoband intellectual Islamic tradition and are exclusivist in their

Jinnah's mausoleum in Karachi, Pakistan, a major tourist attraction, pays homage to the founder of the largest Muslim nation in the world, established in 1947. Jinnah's early death created the conditions for military rule, and his vision of a modern Muslim polity still remains an unfulfilled challenge.

approach. Banna founded the Muslim Brotherhood in Egypt, and Wahhab founded the Wahhabi movement in Saudi Arabia, while Taymiyya, who lived centuries earlier, inspired both. Other role models in South Asia included Mohammad Iqbal, the Islamic poet-philosopher of Pakistan, and Sir Sayyed Ahmad Khan. All three models—Ajmer, Deoband, and Aligarh—were prominent in South Asia.

In Malaysia and Indonesia, the Prophet and the first four caliphs were again the most popular role models. In addition, there was a strong inclination toward intellectual figures in Islamic history, from Ibn Khaldun, Ibn Sina, and Al-Khawarizmi to Imam Ghazzali and Imam Al-Shafi'i. Not surprisingly we discovered a strong intellectual tradition in Malaysia because Malaysians relied more on text and literature as primary sources than those in any other country.

In Egypt, data from an earlier trip gathered with the assistance of Krystle Kaul, another of my American University students, confirmed what we had found on our longer journey in the Muslim world. Some respondents named bin Laden and Arafat as contemporary role models. Although people may not support bin Laden's views on Islam, they feel "he is putting up a force against influence that may corrupt Islam." It was not surprising to see Gamal Abdel Nasser on the list in Egypt. Nasser's charisma mesmerized the Arab world in the 1950s and 1960s, and his memory still fills some with nostalgia. Another name evoking national pride was um-Khatoum, the celebrated female singer. The Prophet of Islam remained the most inspiring role model from the past. Among women, the hijab was more popular than ever before and visible everywhere.

A common theme running through both questionnaires and interviews was that Muslims are misrepresented in the media, some even calling it a "conspiracy." Out of hundreds of images, they complained, the ones the Western media would choose to run on a continuous loop were those of angry bearded men or scenes of violence. Moreover, many people in the West fully accepted these misrepresentations as reality.

The media now have a strong presence throughout the Muslim world. In every city, I saw satellite dishes perched on many poor homes—a potentially dangerous situation for the war of ideas. What people choose to watch colors their worldviews and their actions in the Muslim world just as it does in the United States. Thus the media exert considerable influence over what actually happens overseas and the direction of international affairs. Along with global technology and transportation, the media have also strengthened the ties between Muslims, in part by broadcasting the pains experienced by the ummah—television shows women and children dying and enables members of the Muslim "family" to share their stories. What used to be isolated incidents and problems have become more numerous, with more serious ramifications. Furthermore, in an impulsive, sensationalist culture goaded on by globalization, there is less responsible deliberation about what should and should not be shown on television.

From Qatar to Indonesia, the overwhelming majority of Muslims have access to satellite TV and the Internet, and many told us that their primary source of news is the BBC and CNN television, as well as the Internet. In other words, Muslims all over the world are able to see themselves being described as "terrorists" and "extremists." To add to their frustration, few statistics are reported on Iraqi or Afghan civilian deaths, which suggests a lack of sympathy for Muslim suffering. Instead of being as unbiased as possible, Western media reports are considered gratuitously Islamophobic and insensitive. As a result, even the vast majority of so-called moderate Muslims, who are not terrorists and not interested in prolonging the war on terror, have come to distrust and be annoyed with the United States.

A young, female Jordanian University student angrily mentioned that a television series on the cultures of the world by Oprah Winfrey showed the best of each culture except for the Middle East, where Arab culture was portrayed through an interview with a victim of domestic violence. To add to the problem is the lack of Muslim voices in the Western media speaking for their communities. Muslims are left to admire the likes of Saddam or Ahmadinejad, or anyone who can give vent to some of their frustrations. If anything, news channels are inadvertently exacerbating the problems between the two civilizations rather than bringing understanding and truth.

The Muslim media have not helped matters either.[49] Al-Jazeera, the Muslim "answer" to Fox and CNN and widely viewed in the Arab world, presents images of Muslim deaths and carnage—as in Lebanon in the summer of 2006—that are not often shown in the West. Another Arabic news channel, Al-Arabiya, has been launched with the patronage of the king of Saudi Arabia, a friend of the West. Al-Arabiya and Al-Jazeera broadcast dramatically different views of the same reality. *The Economist* noted in 2005, "Watching their contrasting takes on November's offensive by American marines in Fallujah, for example, one might have thought they were covering different events: while Al-Jazeera focused on civilian deaths and heroic resistance, Al-Arabiya pictured the storming of a terrorist haven."[50]

Although the media have been giving Muslim leaders more opportunity to explain Islam to Americans since 9/11, this has been a "hit-or-miss" strategy. Some appear on television and, in cliché-ridden language, state that Islam is a religion of peace but fail to explain what is actually happening in the Muslim world. Some fail even to understand the cultural context in the West and hence merely add to the frustration and humiliation of Muslim communities.

At the same time, the media are reaching out to young Muslims in the Aligarh model living in the West or middle-class elites in their own countries who admire the "progressive" Westernized leaders of a newly emerging Islamic pop culture. These men and even some women use technology to communicate and advertise a modern, "trendy" version of Islam. Some examples of these icons are Sami Yusuf, an Iranian-born British singer; Farhat Hashmi, a popular Pakistani female preacher (see chapter 3); Ahmad Dhani, an Indonesian pop star; and those mentioned earlier— Yusuf Islam, Hamza Yusuf, and Amr Khaled. While they are known and admired throughout the world, thanks to globalization, these pop culture figures are at the height of popularity in their own regions where Islamic identity is on the rise. There was a sense among our respondents that the image of Islam and Muslims is being defined by current political events rather than theology and that Deoband, while it meets the Muslim need for religious identification, seems too restrictive for young Muslims trying to integrate into the global society.

Ahmad Dhani deserves special mention because his album has sold more than two million copies in his region, and his song "Laskar Cinta" (Warriors of Love) has topped music charts throughout the Far East, yet he is little known in the West. His music uses the sayings of the Prophet and verses from the Quran to develop themes of love, acceptance, and mutual respect. The music videos of Sami Yusuf, another popular performer, play in cafés in the Middle East, and he gave a live performance at the conference we attended in Doha. His music is a mix of electronic sound and catchy beats with lyrics revering the Prophet and Islam. His videos show him walking around as a businessman, soccer player, or family man in a Westernized or Western country.

Amr Khaled, on the other hand, needs no introduction in the West as he has been given wide coverage in the mainstream media.[51] His popularity in the Arab world is unrivaled. Selected by about half of our respondents in each Arab country, Amr Khaled appears to be popular because he presents Islam in a manner perceived to be accurate, sincere, moderate, and relevant to contemporary issues for the youth. He is also able to instill pride and happiness in people for being Muslim and has helped strengthen faith in Islam at a time when it is thought to be under assault by Westernization, secularism, and nationalism. Furthermore, he has helped restore Islam's dignity in the Muslim ummah.

Contemporary icons such as Amr Khaled reflect a subtle but significant shift within the Aligarh model. These new-age "feel-good" role models help Muslim youth live in a Westernized, global society and yet remain "Islamic." They encourage young professional Muslims to succeed, enjoy leisure activities such as going to the beach, and improve their communities. They represent the "pill form" of Islam designed specifically for the comfortable middle and upper classes, which have time to watch television and the resources to improve their daily lives. One young Western-dressed female at Georgetown University in Qatar felt that these figures "do not present Islam as a religion of rules, but as the best way of life. They provide me with the real combination of body and soul. Above all, [it is] the spirituality they have." Another fan received a letter from Amr Khaled signed "your elder brother" and gushed, "He is so tender and most adorable!"

Such visions of Islam coincide with the characteristics of young and newly affluent middle-class Muslims, whose cultural influences derive from globalization as represented by the Internet and mass media. In our questionnaires, many of these Muslims complained it was difficult to connect with religious clerics and other traditional religious leaders, all of whom seemed out of touch with present reality. In contrast to the intimidating and aloof style of the clerics in robes and beards, these young Muslims have a relaxed manner as they stride onto public stages or into homes via television wearing Western clothes and talking about mundane "issues" in modern life.

This version of Islam may be harmless enough and even beneficial for the community, but it fails to address the central concerns of millions of Muslims facing political tyranny, poverty, and injustice. When taping a fifty-episode series titled "Life Makers" suggesting ways to improve the Arab world, Khaled mentioned good works—"teach illiterate Arabs to read . . . fix potholes in the streets . . . buy new prayer mats for the local mosque . . . and to walk the length of a marathon before the next broadcast." However, these suggestions hardly comport with the realities faced by many in the Muslim world struggling to alleviate their living conditions, improve education, locate work, and simply find peace. In particular those of the Deoband model would find suggestions of walking the marathon little more than a ruse to introduce Western culture into Muslim society and a diversion from its more pressing problems.

Even so, the Deoband model is learning to adapt tradition to the age of globalization. Another pattern evident throughout our journey was that

Muslims would cite role models who represent the politically pragmatic approach within the Deoband model. These included leaders who acknowledged the legitimacy of the modern nation-state system and wished to participate in it to safeguard and promote Islam. Hassan Al-Banna and Syed Qutb from the Middle East and Abu A'la al-Maududi from South Asia were examples of such figures and were identified in nearly all of the countries.

Among Muslim leaders, including heads of state and political figures, the most popular role models were those perceived as having "stood up to the West" or to Israel. Some people in this category are Mahmoud Ahmadinejad, Mahathir bin Mohamad, Yasser Arafat, Hasan Nasrallah, and Ayatollah Khomeini. These leaders are widely recognized because of the coverage they have received in the Muslim media as heroes, although the international media depicts them as "extremist" and even "terrorist" leaders.

To our surprise, however, many Syrians looked up to President Bashar al-Assad, just as many in Pakistan named their own dictator, Musharraf, as a role model. These two choices epitomize the paradox of the post-9/11 world. Syrians felt a sense of pride because Bashar has repeatedly defied Israel and the United States, yet his regime is one of the most repressive in the region. Moreover, it is minority-ruled and socialist, or secular. When the UN Security Council called for an investigation into Syria's involvement in the assassination of Lebanon's Rafik Hariri, for example, the Syrian government resisted. And when the United States and Security Council accused Syria of aiding the insurgency in Iraq and being a sponsor of terrorism, Bashar was again defiant despite having no Arab allies rushing to his support and facing the threat of UN sanctions. The Syrian people perceived this as an act of honor and pride. This sentiment was also evident in banners our team saw hanging in the main Hamadiya marketplace in Damascus in Arabic and English, one of which read:

> From Syria the country of peace and loving to the aggressive Israel and its allied America. . . . We are in Syria the country of self-esteem and home-bred, we refuse your democracy after what we had seen in what happened in Iraq and Palestine and how your democracy build on people's bodies which you bombed on civilians innocents, and when the matter reached the Council of Security in the United

Nations and how you used the rejection right (the vito) to save Israel for only a suspicious matter, and how America pushed the council to issue a decision against Syria followed by new decision even Syria executed the first one, but the Syrian people not afraid what ever the difficulties could be, and they are resistant by leadership, dearest President Bashar al-Assad.

When one young girl in Damascus said, "I love our President, I really do," we felt we were seeing the same heroic ideal based in notions of honor under attack gaining a foothold throughout the Muslim world and being abetted by U.S. attitudes.

Another name that cropped up as a role model during our travels—alas, with some frequency—was that of Saddam Hussein. Because I had been writing about Saddam as the model of tyranny, this came as a shock to me. Muslims had apparently already forgotten the diabolical excesses of Saddam's Soviet-style dictatorship, often targeted at the good and decent citizens who resisted his regime. Only the current desperation of Iraqis combined with an urge to express anger against the United States could possibly explain why anyone would be looking at Saddam with nostalgia. Perhaps the sight of Saddam on trial and of a former Muslim head of state being humiliated by a government propped up by the Americans generated some sympathy for him. Despite his alleged atrocities, many felt he deserved some degree of respect and justice as a former head of state and as an elderly man. The notion of justice is central to Islam, but it is applied with the practice of compassion.

The television in the courtroom was becoming a double-edged sword for Americans. Saddam's own arguments in court, defending his actions and criticizing those of President Bush, were also being heard and making an impact. The fact that three of Saddam's defense lawyers were assassinated also raised questions about whether Saddam had any hope of getting a free and fair trial, and thus about the very ideals the United States wished to promote in Iraq. Although Saddam's death sentence did not surprise anyone given the long list of his crimes, the credibility of the court trying Saddam came into doubt.

Images of his hanging, which occurred during the last hours of 2006 and were captured by an eyewitness on a cell phone, only confirmed suspicions concerning Saddam's trial. The video showed him being cruelly taunted while the jailers put a noose around his neck and then danced around his dead body. The pictures were broadcast on television and the Internet across the world almost immediately, feeding into the anger already felt by mainstream Muslims—especially Sunni—who believed that Saddam's execution was deliberately staged by the Iraqi government and encouraged by the Americans to humiliate them. Many Sunni saw the treatment of Saddam as nothing more than a continuation of the pattern of sectarian revenge and retaliation. The irony was not lost on commentators who were quick to point out that Saddam, a villain and a tyrant in life, was dignified and even sympathetic in death. The improbable had happened. The bungling manner of his trial and execution had softened the image of one of the most notorious despots of the twentieth century. Even President Hosni Mubarak of Egypt, most loyal of American allies, publicly declared Saddam a "martyr."

As mentioned earlier, another common complaint of our respondents was the dearth of leadership in the Muslim world, the roots of which are discussed in chapter 5. For them, Aligarh figures are thought to be lacking in a sense of social justice and action for the masses, while the Deoband leaders tend to be close-minded and parochial. Sufism, despite its many advantages, is unfortunately drowned out by the voices of intolerance and ignorance and seen as irrelevant to the problems of our world. What most Muslims want are human rights, justice, and civil liberties in an Islamic context; yet the foresight, vision, and integrity entailed in securing those rights have been in poor supply recently.

Muslim establishment figures, in particular, seem unable to provide meaningful direction to the ummah or to apply the principles of *ijtihad* that allow Muslims to adapt to changing times while still maintaining the integrity of their faith. There is little innovative and inspiring leadership to deal with the challenges of globalization and to help ordinary people meet those challenges. One professor at Aga Khan University in Karachi told us that the gap in intellectual leadership is widely felt in Pakistan: "People are looking at radical leadership because people think they are the ones who are going to bring change. Take the MMA [Muttahhida Majlis-e-Amal], the alliance of religious parties. It's not a popular party or a grassroots party, but they are gaining power here." The MMA in Pakistan promises change and an answer to ummah problems through a return to the Prophet's traditions. Here, as throughout the Muslim world, the political pendulum is swinging toward the Deoband model.

Muslims in beleaguered circumstances in all societies have rallied to those leaders that best embody present sentiments and promise a just and hopeful future. Leaders that strongly identify with Islam and advocate reading the texts to apply key notions of Islam to their present situations belong to the Deoband model. At the same time, they are also actively and controversially redefining the notion of jihad. Today, many Muslims will argue passionately—as did Aijaz of Deoband—that civilians, including women and children, are acceptable targets in a war imposed on Muslims. Some groups are using this ijtihad license to redefine some of Islam's central features relating to injustice and anger but lack the wisdom and restraint required to apply the concept in its true definition.

Of the groups identified with an aggressive Islam that stands up for ordinary Muslims, the best known—certainly the most notorious in the West—are al-Qaeda (the base), Hezbollah (the party of God), and Hamas (HAMAS, the acronym for the Islamic Resistance Movement). Although these organizations are fused as one in the minds of Western commentators, who see them simply as "terrorist organizations bent on abduction and murder," they are in fact different responses to different situations. Al-Qaeda, for example, has even publicly criticized Hamas for wishing to join a legitimate government or talk of a peace process.

Al-Qaeda grew out of the Soviet occupation of Afghanistan and was founded by bin Laden in 1988. With help from the United States, bin Laden and his followers fought to free the country of Soviet influence. They cast themselves as the David against the Soviet Goliath in the cause of Islam and believed they were directly responsible for defeating the Soviets, who had suffered heavy losses, and forcing them to leave Afghanistan. Heady with confidence, they found in the United States a new giant to challenge.

Hezbollah and its active militant wing emerged in the late 1960s, energized by the overthrow of the shah of Iran and Ayatollah Khomeini's revolution. Its roots are in the Shia population of South Lebanon, motivated by the Israeli invasion in 1982 to develop an explicit agenda for expelling the Israeli army. It gained international notoriety in 1983 with the bombing of the U.S. Marines' barracks in Beirut, which killed 300 soldiers.

It has enjoyed the patronage of Syria. Hasan Nasrallah, the leader of Hezbollah, appeared as a role model in some of our questionnaires. Judging from Muslim newspaper accounts after the Israeli invasion of Lebanon in 2006, I suspect Nasrallah would capture an even greater percentage of any future role model votes, especially in the Arab world.

Unlike al-Qaeda, which is a purely militant organization, Hezbollah also organizes philanthropic and commercial ventures in the community, including hospitals, schools, orphanages, and even a television station. In the absence of an effective Lebanese administration, which is deeply divided by ethnic, regional, and religious loyalties, Hezbollah often provides the only services available to the Lebanese people, regardless of their religion. Most important, the Shia population sees Hezbollah as embodying an organization heroically championing their cause in difficult and changing times. When Beirut appeared to abandon Hezbollah in favor of a Western-dominated peace initiative, which included the expulsion of the Syrians, people once again had high expectations for the peace process, later dashed by Israel's bombardment and invasion of Lebanon in 2006. Hezbollah took the lead in defending the Shia population during the fighting and helping them to rebuild their shattered lives afterward, thus reaffirming the organization's importance as the most innovative, caring, and efficient organization in Lebanon.

Traditionally, the distinction between Sunni and Shia has mattered to Muslims, but because both Hamas, a Sunni group, and Hezbollah share a common enemy, Israel, they have developed considerable sympathy for each other. Hamas was established in 1987 by Sheikh Ahmed Yassin, head of the Muslim Brotherhood in Gaza and assassinated by the Israelis in 2004. Hamas won credibility among the Palestinians because of its emphasis on social and political initiatives in addition to its more militant activity. In January 2006 Hamas won 74 of the 132 seats in the legislative council, thus becoming the majority party and filling the gap left by the Palestine Liberation Organization, which had failed to deliver on its political promises, continued in its corrupt and incompetent ways, and was unable to resolve Palestine's problems. Because they consider Hamas a terrorist group, Israel, the United States, and most Western nations refused to accept the clear results of a democratic election. Many Muslims began to question the credibility of America's commitment to genuine democracy in the Muslim world. Commentators in the region asked whether the results of democratic elections would only be accepted if the successful candidates were those approved by the West.

Hamas has had an acrimonious relationship with Israel from the start, abetted perhaps by its very name, which in Hebrew means "injustice" or "violence." Israelis point to Hamas bombings, killings, and kidnappings as confirmation of the anti-Semitic sentiments openly expressed in the organization's literature. It not only quotes *The Protocols of the Elders of Zion* in its founding charter of 1988 but also threatens to "obliterate" Israel, warning that "after Palestine, the Zionists aspire to expand from the Nile to the Euphrates" (article 32 of the charter). When Israel launched a military invasion of Gaza in the summer of 2006 and kidnapped dozens of senior parliamentarians from the Hamas Party, any hope of dialogue came to a standstill.

However dark and unsavory some Hamas and Hezbollah characters may seem in the international media, Muslims in search of ummah defenders find the organizations heroic in comparison with the supine "legitimate" Muslim leaders. The Sunni girls we talked to in Syria in March 2006 said that Hasan Nasrallah spoke for all Arabs. One twenty-year-old Jordanian female identified Khalid Mishal, a former Hamas leader who is now in exile, as her role model because "he is intelligent and open-minded and modern in his role of thought and action." She considered the late Ahmed Yassin, the spiritual leader of Hamas, "a historic figure, although he existed not too long ago. He walked the path of reform, in spite of difficulties, and kept Islam as his true resource." A young Sunni female in Syria placed Hasan Nasrallah at the top of her list because "he's very open-minded and an authority in his own right." Another Muslim girl added: "He does and should represent Islam."

Interestingly, Muslims are not the only ones in the Arab world who look up to these figures. A young Christian Jordanian female told us that Nasrallah is her role model because of his "justice, courage and [protection of] the rights of individuals." The members of Hezbollah and Hamas are thus developing a legitimate and powerful voice in the Arab world as adept politicians, not just as renegade "Islamic jihadists." In the summer of 2006, Hezbollah's reputation gained added strength in the Muslim world because of its "just and valiant" fight against a once-invincible Israel.

By contrast, Israel's actions drew widespread criticism, despite genuine concerns for its safety—indeed its future, considering how many people in the Middle East were openly talking about "exterminating" it. The kidnapping of its soldiers had triggered the crisis, but its "summer adventure" had resulted in many civilian deaths and had merely served to elevate Hezbollah's Nasrallah and Iran's Ahmadinejad to superstar status in the Muslim world. Because the United States had so publicly and unequivocally supported Israel, it too shared the blame.

Thus the definition of "terrorist" in the war on terror seems to depend on what side one supports. It is all a matter of perspective. The point is effectively made by St. Augustine, one of the great theologians, noting the confrontation between Alexander the Great and a captured pirate: "For when that king had asked the man what he meant by keeping hostile possession of the sea, he answered with bold pride, 'What thou meanest by seizing the whole earth; but because I do it with a petty ship, I am called a robber, whilst thou who dost it with a great fleet art styled emperor.'"[52]

How Muslim Leaders Are Defining Islam

After clearing intensive security checks, we sat waiting in President Pervez Musharraf's official drawing room in Rawalpindi, an army base about an hour from Islamabad, for our interview with him in March 2006. I noticed the only two portraits hanging in the room were of Jinnah and Iqbal and wondered whether my team appreciated the irony of a military dictator drawing inspiration from their democratic legacy. My two American students busied themselves with their notebooks and pens in anticipation. Only the week before, they had seen President Musharraf on CNN teaching President Bush how to play cricket on the presidential lawn in Islamabad.

President Musharraf, in gray suit and silk tie, strode in with his army staff in uniform trailing behind him. We sat down together on two plush couches, and he cordially said, "Please, have some tea, Akbar *sahib*." I began the interview by asking him about his own role models. He said that he admired the Prophet of Islam first, then Jinnah, and Napoleon, in that order. It was not difficult to see why he chose the third. Napoleon, patterning himself on Caesar, wanted to be more than a military commander come to save a desperate political situation. His grand mission was to institute widespread social reforms. Musharraf may feel he has the same destiny as head of one of the most important Muslim nations on the world stage (and the only one that is nuclear). Musharraf is neither an Islamic scholar nor does he have the popular mandate through the democratic process to speak on behalf of his overwhelmingly Muslim population. But as commander-in-chief of the army, he has the military power to back his claim to the presidency and political mission.

Responding to my question about Islam's approach to Western modernity, Musharraf made three basic points. First, he affirmed his Muslim identity: "I may not be a very orthodox Muslim, but I am a Muslim. And I believe Islam is compatible with modernity."

Second, Muslims do not have to become *Westernized* in order to become *modernized.* That is to say, they do not have to behave like those in the West—have Western values, dress like people in the West, or become secular like those in the West: "We have our own culture; we have our own history. We are proud of that. We must be modern; we must have modernity, which means civic government, a good system of administration, justice, good education, democracy. All these features are characteristic of modernization, and that we can have as Muslims." Reiterating that "Islam is not incompatible with modernity," President Musharraf explained how this related to his own role, even in the war on terror: "I have put my neck on the line. I am a victim of assassination attempts, but I believe in what I am doing because I am doing it for Pakistan. It is also beneficial to America and the West, because it helps them if I can control terrorism." But, he emphasized, the interests of Pakistan were still uppermost in his mind.

Third, Pakistan can play a pivotal role in the Islamic renaissance. "We are the leaders of the Muslim world," President Musharraf said. "We are the only nuclear power. We have a population of 160 million. Our geopolitical situation makes us absolutely vital to understanding the Muslim world. And we have a history of leading the Muslim world in terms of [new] ideas. So Pakistan cannot be ignored."

On this trip I also discovered that Pakistan had moved markedly toward public expression of its Islamic identity, even among those who, like Musharraf, would normally speak of a liberal and secular Islam. Musharraf told me an interesting story to illustrate his Islamic fervor. On a visit to Mecca, he was given the rare privilege of climbing to the top of the Kaaba, the central structure in the courtyard of the Grand Mosque and the holiest of holies for Muslims. Once there, Musharraf looked down at the circling mass of pilgrims and cried, "Allah hu Akbar"—"God is the greatest."

Akbar Ahmed interviews President Pervez Musharraf of Pakistan in Rawalpindi. Shunned by the West when he took power in 1999, Musharraf became a key ally in the war on terror after September 11.

The crowds responded by shouting, "Allah hu Akbar." He had made the pilgrimage six times and told me this, he emphasized, to establish his Islamic credentials. Although critics might call him a sequacious "Busharraf"—a clone of President Bush—Musharraf argued that being modern does not mean giving up your religious values and cultural norms; indeed, his Islamic roots remained strong and had not become as Westernized and secular as some were claiming. Temperamentally, ideologically, and culturally, Musharraf appeared to be grappling with the Aligarh model and quite consciously reaching out to the issuant Deoband model.

Regarding the negative perception of madrassahs in the West, Musharraf noted that educational reforms are under way: "We are introducing subjects other than religion, so we are studying religion and subjects like geography, history and other religions, not just Islam. Even computer training—in madrassahs!" When I asked why he chooses not to close the madrassahs, as many Westerners demand, he replied, "In the West, they think the madrassahs mean a terrorist camp. But all madrassahs are not violent or extremist. Some are, but not all. I have one million students in madrassahs. Now if you close all of them, you'll have one million kids out there in the street. So what I am doing is—by persuasion, by discussion, bringing them into the mainstream—helping them to raise their standards and become absorbed into the mainstream."

Musharraf appears genuinely committed to ideas of change and to grappling with Pakistan's problems, rather than just trying to please the West. "Look," he pointed out, "I have a lot of critics in Pakistan who say I'm pro-Western, but I'm simply trying to bring my nation more in line with the vision of Pakistan's founder Mr. Mohammed Ali Jinnah, who believed in a modern, democratic society based on human rights and women's rights. The Americans are my friends for a short time. They are helping me and I am helping them, but beyond that we have no other arrangement."

Achieving a compromise between the Deoband and Aligarh models while not appearing to "sell out" to the West, as Musharraf conceives it, seems an onerous if not impossible task. Yet in his balancing act since 9/11, he has managed some success. Many of our Muslim respondents within and even outside of Pakistan referred to him as a role model or good leader in the Muslim world. They admire him for his negotiating skills under pressure, especially with the then U.S. secretary of state Colin Powell, who rang Musharraf immediately after 9/11 on the eve of the American invasion of Afghanistan, offering him a stark choice: you are either with us or against us. Richard Armitage, Powell's deputy, had already made it clear to Musharraf's head of intelligence that if Islamabad did not support the war on terror the United States would bomb Pakistan back to the "Stone Age," according to Musharraf's memoirs.[53]

Musharraf was caught on the horns of a painful dilemma. Pakistan had been supporting the Taliban and helped it grow as a movement. Pakistan's foreign policy required the "strategic depth" that Afghanistan could give it in case of a war with India. To abandon the Taliban now would require a U-turn, which the nation—and more important, the army itself—might not take to kindly. But Musharraf's instincts for self-preservation at that moment perhaps saved Pakistan from a direct confrontation with the United States, which after 9/11 was like a raging bull ready to charge at any object that stood in its way. Musharraf handled the situation calmly, using his position to emerge as a key ally in the war on terror. Thus even those outside the borders of his country cited him as a role model.

Nevertheless, he is still extremely unpopular with the more Deoband-oriented Muslims, who frequently speak out against him and have twice attempted to assassinate him. During our visit to Islamabad, anti-Musharraf rhetoric spewed openly from the main mosque, a mere two miles from the presidential palace. Demonstrations against him were also frequent and since then have continued and increased in number. In his view, such activities are fomented by strict Deobandis, traditionally the most widespread interpreters of Islam in Pakistan, and who only emphasize empty rituals. "So far, the fanatics are interpreting Islam," he said, and their strict interpretations create points of contention that lead to violence within Pakistan. The recent riots between Shia and Sunni in the Northern Areas, he noted, began because one group objected to the other's style of praying with their arms across their chests. "That's the kind of Islam we have to avoid," Musharraf told me. "The defenses of Islam are progress and compassion. In order for that to happen, the scholars of Islam have to be engaged so that the people in the streets begin to appreciate what Islam really is." He understood the necessity of reinterpreting Islam from within the tradition. Although he did not state it outright, he was obviously grappling with the use of ijtihad.[54]

In fact, the precepts of many textbooks used by the madrassahs are far from the spirit of compassion and tolerance preached by Islam's philosophers and thinkers. Recent reports by Freedom House, an independent monitoring group in the United States, indicate that textbooks used in Saudi Arabia and distributed throughout the Muslim world from the first grade on and distributed abroad to madrassahs in Pakistan and elsewhere contain statements such as "the apes are Jews; while the swine are the Christians, the infidels of the communion of Jesus."[55] Students are also encouraged to demonize other Muslims, including the Shia and Sufi mystics, who are called "polytheists" to be condemned as wayward and misguided Muslims. The hatred contained in the teachings of some Saudi-funded madrassahs translates easily into a call for religious intolerance and even violence against those seen as deviant Muslims.

The often exclusivist Saudi version of Islam is being met with a negative response among Muslims outside the Arab world, creating a new "anti-Arabism" phenomenon in concert with anti-Americanism and anti-Semitism. Non-Arab Muslims—of whatever class, gender, or age—resent what they see as Arab arrogance in wishing to impose their own version of Islam on others and in assuming that they possess all the answers. The wide respect for Arabs because the language of the Quran is Arabic and the Prophet was an Arab has been dampened by a general cynicism and even anger. After my talk at the university in Jakarta, Tarmizi Taher, former minister of religious affairs for Indonesia and the picture of urbanity, launched into a tirade against "Arab Islam" that bore no relationship to anything I had said. "The Prophet may have been Arab," he fumed, "but there were often villainous Arabs at the time like Lahab and Jahal. We reject the Islam of Saddam Hussein." In his cantankerous outburst, he was echoing what one minister in Lahore told us over lunch: "Pakistanis are better Muslims than the Arabs in every single way—no, better human beings in every single way." Educated Indian Muslims too looked at the Middle East and saw "the defeated and demoralised Arab."[56]

At the same time, we found that "Arab Islam" was not without its supporters. In Pakistan, many people admire King Faisal of Saudi Arabia because of his open identification and sympathy with the Islamic ummah. Although the hijab is foreign to Pakistan's cultural tradition, the rise in Islamic identity is persuading more girls to turn toward the Saudis and their customs, because they are considered the "true leaders" of the Muslim world. This, in turn, invites greater emphasis on Saudi Wahhabism. With its strict and literalist interpretation of the Quran, Wahhabism preaches that every Muslim can worship God directly and does not need intermediaries such as priests or holy figures to do so; it imposes harsh restrictions on women and in some locales is even critical of the excessive reverence Muslims show for the Prophet himself. It was this environment that nurtured bin Laden.

Bin Laden's adult life gives him credibility with many Muslims. The son of a Saudi millionaire, he was a member of the idle rich until he attended college in Jeddah. There, he made the acquaintance of Muhammad Qutb, the brother of the late Syed Qutb, who had written *Signposts on the Road*, the standard text that some radical extremists later used to promote their interpretation of Islam. Soon bin Laden was a character looking for a role on the global stage. Recognizing that the battle for Afghan freedom of the 1980s marked an important global crisis for Muslims, he packed his bags for the hills of Afghanistan. Bin Laden's years in Afghanistan—with a sojourn in Sudan—gave him both an insight into tribal politics and a platform from which to wage his battle against the United States. With a shrewd understanding of how tribal society functions—he himself was a descendant of a Yemeni family from a tribal society and since childhood was familiar with Saudi tribal politics—he cemented his political friendship with Mullah Umar, the reclusive leader of the emerging Taliban in Kandahar, through a marriage alliance. Thus he had a direct entrée into Afghan tribal politics and a claim to Afghan loyalty. Even after he was bombed out of Tora Bora, he found support among the tribes along the Pakistan-Afghanistan border. He may have been an "Arab" outsider to the Afghans, but through marriage he had become part of their tribal network.

Bin Laden is at the focal point of several currents in globalization. The Western media have made him one of the most easily recognizable men on the planet, adding to his status with the Muslims. His tape recordings, globally transmitted on international television, have shown the power of technology and the effect it can have on the world community. More important, bin Laden's leadership demonstrates a notable change in the rules of the game once controlled by the leaders of nation-states. Furthermore, the fact that the U.S. superpower, with all its technology and resources, had been unable to capture "the number one terrorist in the world" in the several years after 9/11 turned bin Laden into a living legend.

But bin Laden has many vocal critics in the Muslim world too. In large part because of him, many say, the West is loath to accept Muslims. These Muslims we found, especially in the Arab world, pointedly distance themselves from him in public. As one nineteen-year-old Jordanian at the shariah university put it, "Islam is the religion of tolerance and not all Muslims are like Osama bin Laden or other extremists. We have concepts in our religion and strong ties to our Prophet who personified true Islam. Muslims need to prove themselves in this world and should be governed by the religion of justice and equality."

In the view of others, bin Laden is unafraid to express the sentiments of the "true" or "ordinary" Muslims, which many rulers are too tactful or timid to state. One should hasten to add, however, that many Muslims who sympathize with bin Laden in a broad and general sense would by no means support his more murderous or violent activity. In a recent Gallup poll, 70 percent of Muslims interviewed were angry with Americans, but only 7 percent felt that the attacks of 9/11 were justified. At the same time, bin Laden's main criticisms of the West have wide appeal to Muslims around the world.[57] He has opposed the presence of American troops on the same holy soil as Mecca and Medina, has consistently supported the Palestinian cause, and criticized the devastation wrought by the Americans in Afghanistan and Iraq. He also accuses the Americans of destroying "nature with your industrial waste and gases more than any other nation in history. Despite this, you refuse to sign the Kyoto Agreement so that you can secure the profit of your greedy companies and industries." Addressing the political situation in Muslim nations, he warns the United States "to end your support of the corrupt leaders in our countries. Do not interfere in our politics and method of education. Leave us alone, or else expect us in New York and Washington."[58]

Bin Laden repeatedly invokes the loss of Muslim "honor," which resonates with Muslims everywhere. Not surprisingly, Aijaz from Deoband called him "Sheikh" Osama, and even some of the students of Aligarh University referred to him with the same fervor and respect. Many people we met cited his complete dedication to the Muslim ummah because he gave up his luxurious lifestyle to fight for Islam in the barren hills of Afghanistan and donated his personal fortune to the cause. Throughout our travels, we saw evidence of his charismatic popularity, which has been reported elsewhere as well. Bin Laden is now considered a global if mythical champion of downtrodden Muslims everywhere. Randolph Persaud, an American University professor from Guyana, told me that 45 percent of that country's population is East Indian (South Asian)—about 10 percent are Muslim—and faces racial tension. After a number of assassinations targeting mainly South Asians, Persaud said he saw some people in Guyana hanging a portrait of bin Laden festooned with garlands in their homes. Thus bin Laden has become a talismanic figure even in the most remote parts of the world and even among non-Muslims. At a 2004 soccer game between Mexico and the United States, for example, 60,000 Mexicans broke into chants of "Osama!" to the outrage of many Americans.

One must be wary of generalizations, however. As I have repeated earlier, our three models are neither static nor watertight. A leading Malayasian figure provides an example to illustrate the range and complexity of our models, in this case, a Deobandi one.

Anwar Ibrahim, deputy prime minister of Malaysia from 1993 to 1998, was widely expected to succeed Mahathir Mohamad as prime minister. But their relationship soured, and Anwar was sentenced to fifteen years in prison on trumped-up charges. Simultaneously, a smear campaign was launched to ruin his reputation with charges ranging from political corruption to homosexuality. He was released after six years, during which he was subjected to solitary confinement and beaten repeatedly. Since he has emerged from jail, Anwar has become a popular speaker on the international academic circuit, from Oxford to Washington, D.C., where he is currently a visiting professor at Georgetown University.

Anwar Ibrahim and Mahathir Mohamad had followed the post-independence generation of Malaysian leaders into power by challenging what had gone before. They attempted to shift both the substance and form of politics by bringing to it a more sharply focused Islamic identity. It would make them well-loved leaders not only in their own country but also in the wider Muslim world. Mahathir Mohamad's name, we saw in our questionnaires, came up as a role model again and again outside his native land.

I had heard much about Anwar Ibrahim and was curious to meet him because he represented the classic Deoband model with an interesting sociological twist.[59] He was the modern face of tradition itself. I was not disappointed. In person Anwar is warm, alert, and well-read and exudes an easy Malaysian charm. He smiles easily and is fluent in English. When he first met me over dinner in Washington, he said he had spent his time in solitary confinement reading my books on the Pukhtun tribes along the Afghanistan-Pakistan border, mentioning *Pukhtun Economy and Society,* in particular.[60] His remarks made me thoughtful. I was impressed that this Muslim leader chose an obscure book on anthropology to read during such a trying period, and with obvious appreciation, and moved to hear that it was one of my own.

Anwar may at first appear to fit our understanding of the Aligarh model, but his words and his ideas suggest another interpretation.[61] He is a powerful and clear-headed thinker for traditional Islam. Indeed, he is one of its leading exponents, who has not only spoken about its ideas but also attempted to implement them when he was in charge of the Ministry of Finance and Education in Malaysia. Anwar was able to show in a practical way how a traditional Muslim society might not only adjust to modernity with success—in its hotels, infrastructure, tourist industry, technology, and so on—but also resist the tidal wave of globalization and Westernization. Because he was considered one of the architects of what in the last decades of the twentieth century was called the Asian renaissance, he gained credibility not just as a thinker of Islam, but also as a practical leader able to balance the past with the present.[62] He came to personify the successful modern Deoband model in power.

Anwar's success and somewhat flamboyant style exposed him to attacks from both sides—Muslim traditionalists, especially those of the Deoband model, found him a bit too accommodating to the West for their comfort, while Western critics saw him as too Islamic in his position. (One of the hosts at a leading think tank in Washington leaned across to me to remark, after he heard Anwar extol the virtues of democracy and civil liberty within an Islamic framework, "It's a pity he did not advocate these virtues when he was in power and in a position to do so and has only now discovered them in Washington.")

During Anwar's visit to my home shortly before his return to Kuala Lumpur in November 2006, our conversation turned to contemporary role models. His choices both surprised and pleased me. He said Jinnah, and then added, the Quaid-i-Azam, giving Jinnah the title that his admirers use. Anwar added that his grandfather had a colored photograph of Jinnah in his living room in his village in Penang in the 1950s. Interestingly, Anwar has been a champion of both Iqbal and Jinnah and often cites them in his public lectures as role models. Iqbal's ideas, as already pointed out, turn up in all three models, while Jinnah's reflect the Aligarh model.

As his thinking matures, Anwar is obviously moving toward a broader and more inclusive interpretation of Islam. As a non-Arab, he is quick to point out that Muslims, especially those in the Arab world, need to appreciate non-Arab leaders such as Jinnah and thereby take advantage of the full breadth of Muslim culture. When I asked him to name the greatest ever role model in history, he said, without hesitation, the Prophet of Islam: "Not only was the holy Prophet a great spiritual master but he embodied compassion and love of knowledge."

What I found impressive about Anwar was his personal journey. He had been a highly successful public figure who had faced a traumatic and humiliating downfall, but then was able to transcend memories of his entire past and attain an inner calm, reflected in his bearing, thinking, and responses. Now at peace with himself, Anwar, I felt, was on the threshold of discovering the Ajmer model.

Mystic figures are more difficult to locate than the visible and vocal Muslims who adhere to the Deoband and Aligarh models. A question some have raised is whether Sufis—who represent the Ajmer model—exist in our time outside Turkey and its cultural influences. The answer is they do, and I was privileged to meet one in Amman. Sheikh Nuh Keller is an unlikely Sufi master with an American background—he left the United States three decades ago and while traveling in Cairo discovered Islam—but his following is strong within the Arab world.[63] His conversation with me was largely about the *ruh*, the soul, which has a beginning but no end. To him, the Prophet of Islam is the ultimate standard of human behavior, which raises the position of Muslims above that of others and makes Islam a superior religion. The best way to persuade people to follow the standard is not through press releases but by example. The sheikh was dismissive of the traditional religious clerics of the Deoband model, whom he called Salafi. He described them as "hairy mullahs," in reference to the more extravagant expressions of facial hair preferred by some religious clerics; he himself had a well-trimmed beard. Sheikh Keller was clearly troubled by what he viewed as their close-minded and bad-tempered tendencies: "Something is the matter with them. They emphasize the body and rhetoric of faith but miss out on the ruh." It is a "Salafi burnout."

Sheikh Keller's role model was Imam Ghazzali. God's light, or *nur*, shone on Ghazzali, and he could "gaze above the horizon and see Allah and worship him." The imam, he recalled, abandoned a successful academic career for a decade in order to give deep thought to spiritual questions, and on his return began to write books that changed the course of Islamic thought. Ghazzali, the sheikh said, is still relevant and teaching Muslims a great deal.

Although Sheikh Keller uses a computer and receives many inquiries about Islam through the Internet, he criticizes technology because it creates confusion in the mind and "hardens the heart." It is abstract bifurcation. All Americans know is "how." As for "what," they "haven't a clue." These days, people everywhere are not studying liberal arts subjects or gaining any knowledge of world civilizations. That is why they can fly planes into buildings without any feelings, he argued. There is a thirst for spiritual awareness in humanity, and most people do not even realize it.

In the same breath, he excoriated American culture. Half a million people have died in Iraq, but to Americans this is just another statistic on the television screen. Children grow up playing video games and then assume everything is a game, and thus fail to develop human feelings. Despite the terrible toll of alcohol and drugs, people seem unable to give up their dependencies or to find answers to questions of life. He believes that a secular society cannot say no to such indulgence: "The substanceless will by its very nature break. Humans need a sustainable way of life. Secularism does not give anything." America is dominated by a government and industry closely allied in interest: the sheikh called this the "essence of fascism. My culture wishes to sell wars." The downside of globalization, he noted, is, precisely, materialism: "What is globalization for? It is for selling things to people. Your big cigar doesn't look so good when you are trying to survive. With what you eat, what you wear, or you buy, you realize there is very little that can make you happy. The same is true with the spiritual ambience of the heart. Less is more." The sheikh was not particularly concerned about the attacks on Islam, however. Allah has promised us protection, he said. After all, the Mongol onslaught was far worse in the thirteenth century. That, he reminded me, ended with the Mongols converting to Islam.

The sheikh was a modest man and deeply spiritual in his responses to my questions. Initially reserved—something I found very American or European, as opposed to the way native Muslims received me—he eventually began to warm to me. When I asked if we could film our interview for a television series, he said he never gave media interviews but agreed to waive his policy in my case because he thought it might be of benefit if his message was conveyed to others. After the interview he became animated with good will and wished to personally show me the new Zawiya, a place of *dhikr*, or recitation of the names of God, for him and his students. It was a simple and even classic Sufi structure that allowed his followers to gather and sing the praises of Allah and his Prophet. When he saw me to the door, I left with the impression of an extremely perceptive man who had attained a high level of spiritual awareness through the Sufi path. Here, then, was an embodiment of the Ajmer model, whose mystics must fight the same battle that Dara failed to win.

The next logical question to ask is how a Muslim leader in the Aligarh model might be faring in the post-9/11 world. In the case of M. Syafi'i Anwar, executive director of the International Center for Islam and Pluralism in Jakarta, he finds himself waging a losing battle to promote dialogue and understanding in an increasingly hostile environment.[64] Americans, he complained to our team, just did not understand how important the moderate Muslim position was in his country. He had no support from the West. "Every Muslim is a potential terrorist," he said with exasperation, "because no one seems to care about us." By not supporting people like

The team, including Jonathan Hayden, Akbar Ahmed, and Amineh Ahmed, interviews M. Syafi'i Anwar of the International Center for Islam and Pluralism at a hotel in Jakarta, Indonesia. He expressed his unhappiness with the lack of support given to him in his efforts to promote interfaith activity and pluralism in society. The hotel had been bombed earlier as a sign of protest against the West.

him, he added, the Americans do not realize they are actually helping the radicals. These radicals are now imitating what Anwar called "Arab Islam." Even names such as Hamas, Ikhwan, and Hizbut Tahrir from the Arab world were being adopted and used by groups in Indonesia, local versions of the Deoband model.

According to Anwar, Muslims are unable to respond to the world critically and therefore lash out aggressively and irrationally. His was a more reasoned and thoughtful—yet Islamic—response, he believed. Although Anwar had once been on several committees looking after mosques, religious scholars were now attacking him for promoting liberalism and barring him from even visiting a mosque. The *ulema* (religious community) had issued fatwas against pluralism and interfaith dialogue, stating "Pluralism is against Islam," and thus as head of the center representing pluralism, he had become a major target for terrorists.

Anwar made it clear that he was not a blind follower of the West, however. He saw globalization as Americanization and expressed distaste for

Western television and especially the pornography available. He felt this promiscuity fed into the strong sense of anti-Americanism in his society. Despite all of his talk of liberalism, he shook with anger at the thought of some televised material that offended his Muslim sensibilities. Muslims, he noted, believe the West has constructed a "conspiracy theory" against them that equates Islam with terrorism and violence. Frustrated by such gross misrepresentations, even more reasonable Muslims are pushed toward extremist rhetoric. Anger against the West escalates into the emotion that drives those who volunteer for suicide. For the first time, he pointed out, Bali and Jakarta (indeed, the very hotel we were meeting in) were beginning to see their own suicide bombers.

These remarks are supported by the findings of a recent study of radical religious attitudes and behavior in Indonesia.[65] This investigation was based on interviews with men and women in agricultural and urban environments conducted face-to-face and on a national level. The conclusion was inescapable. Almost 50 percent of the respondents desired shariah law and supported actions such as the Bali bombing as true jihad, which would strengthen Islam. These same voices were opposed to having a woman become the president of the nation and insisted that thieves be punished by having their hands amputated, adulterers be stoned to death, men be allowed to practice polygamy, and daughters inherit half the amount claimed by sons.

Anwar spoke ominously of the "creeping shariatization" around him, warning that Indonesia's more secular legal system and traditionally more accepting and tolerant plural society are slowly being infiltrated by Deoband thinking. This was, after all, the same island as that of Kalidjaga, the mystic saint. He felt overcome by despair, anger, and even hopelessness at this prospect, reduced to an articulate, albeit edentulous, leader of the Aligarh model. Both the Ajmer and Aligarh model are clearly under attack in Indonesia and in danger of retreating.

Unfortunately, Anwar is not the only example of a lonely and embattled Aligarh model. His counterpart in Kuala Lumpur, Ismail Noor, head of the Altruistic Leadership Center, complained about the very same situation and personal predicament. Both men are of middle age, distinguished looking in Western suits and bespectacled and are articulate, intelligent, nationalistic, and devoted Muslims. While believing in Islam, both also believed in ijtihad, or change in Islamic tradition. Both talked of the highest levels ever of anti-Americanism as a result of the events of the past few years. Both believed that Western media, hostile to Islam, create support for the radicals. Both named the Prophet of Islam as their ultimate role model, followed by Umar. Both pointed to the dangers of fanaticism in their societies, seeing "no compassion in this vision of Islam, which is angry, desperate, and violent."

Muslim leaders at every level of society are aware of the scale of the crisis. Abdurrahman Wahid, Indonesia's first elected president, issued a call in the summer of 2006 for "a spiritual regeneration within Islam itself." Alarmed at the influence of the "extremists," he believed "the most effective way to overcome Islamic extremism is to explain what Islam really is." These leaders were also bitter about what they saw as the West's indifference to their plight. Sadly, the West failed to grasp the strategic importance of people like them and therefore showed no interest in assisting them. What these Muslim leaders themselves failed to appreciate was that Western politicians, policymakers, and commentators, for their own ideological and strategic reasons, made clear throughout this book, were shining the spotlight on the Deoband model as if it were the only representation of Islam. Amineh Hoti, who has been actively involved in promoting dialogue and understanding between Islam and the West, believes that although the trend appears to be away from the "moderates," the tendency to focus on the "extremists" does not help the cause of understanding:

> The dwindling moderates and growing extremists are a dangerous and challenging development that lies not only on the Muslim side. Ordinary people in the West I have spoken with hold many negative and often false perceptions of Islam, Muslims, and Muslim women. Being Arab, for example, is immediately associated with being Muslim and Muslim with being Arab. Yet the present bishop of Jerusalem in a fascinating talk at Cambridge pointed out that he was an Arab Palestinian Israeli Christian and that Jesus himself was not a blond blued-eyed Hollywood-looking figure but that he originated from the Middle East.
>
> Similarly, Dr. Anwar in Indonesia pointed out that Indonesian Muslims are a diverse community. Indeed, I would agree with him: Islam is inclusive and accepting of others, and it shares many common

beliefs with Christians, Jews, and other monotheistic faiths; Islam gave human rights to men and women as early as the seventh century; all life is sacred in Islam and suicide or murder is haram (absolutely forbidden); Muslims have many colors, faces, and behaviors; women are given many benefits, sometimes more than men.[66]

Our findings in the field, however, confirm that although figures in the Deoband model attract considerable sympathy, their significance may well be magnified because of current events and the exaggerated importance these leaders are given in the Western media. Jonathan Hayden, who arranged my interviews with both Noor and Anwar, believes this to be the case:

> When we were meeting with Dr. Anwar in the hotel in Jakarta, his nervousness was palpable. He is basically risking his life fighting for a moderate, modern Islam. Fatwas calling for the head of people like him had been issued. During the entire meeting, in the cocktail room of our hotel lobby, he was looking over his shoulder, sweating and talking in hushed tones. The hotel had been bombed in 2003 by terrorists and while security was tight, there was a tension in the air. He was being persecuted for arguing for pluralism, one of the most important features of modern democracy. Indonesia is the largest Muslim country in the world and was described to us many times during our visit as a "sleeping giant." With the United States putting so much money into "planting democracy," it is frustrating for me to see people like Dr. Anwar struggle to promote the basic tenets of democracy in such an important and often overlooked country. He, like the other Muslims in Indonesia arguing for equal rights, pluralism, and liberalism, is a friend to the U.S., arguably doing as much to fight terrorism as the soldiers on the ground in Iraq, and he is being left alone in the trenches to face the threats of conservative clerics.

Indonesia is indeed a sleeping Islamic giant—with a population of about 250 million—and what happens there will affect the entire region. Therefore, the struggles of Noor and Anwar do matter. While they are battling for the Aligarh model of resolve and substance in their society, too many people are seeing compromises and distortions in their version of

Islam. Muslims will always resist the imposition of an ideological frame colored by Western ideas such as "secularism," which many people see the West as promoting. Having been surprised at my own warm reception in the Muslim world, I realized why Muslims had responded to me so positively, but so defensively to these two genuinely sympathetic figures. While acknowledging a crisis in Islam, I have never suggested using new or Western-inspired phrases such as "reformation of Islam" or "progressive Islam" to address the underlying issues. I believe that it is important for a culture to work within its own beliefs and traditions as much as possible. Because these two individuals are assumed to be attacking the foundations of Islam itself in their efforts to revitalize it, they have been condemned, despite their credentials as good Muslims. There is a lesson here for both Muslims and non-Muslims wanting positive change and true dialogue in society.

My Battle to Define Islam

My commitment to the Aligarh model was first inspired by Jinnah himself and later strengthened during my years in what was then called the Civil Service of Pakistan (CSP), the elite cadre of the Central Superior Services of Pakistan. In word and deed, Jinnah embodied a true democratic order, respect for the law, the rights of others, and protection for the weak and oppressed.[67] He believed in hard work and merit and condemned nepotism and corruption. I saw in his vision an ideal Muslim society with the central features of Islam—justice, compassion, and knowledge. The ordinary people who lived in the villages and tribal areas in Pakistan inspired me with their faith, integrity, and hospitality. I knew that by providing them with responsible governmental power, swift justice, and accessibility to officials, I could help them in the spirit Jinnah would have wished.

The CSP, hailed as the "steel frame" by the founding fathers of Pakistan, descended directly from the Indian Civil Service, which was established by Imperial Britain and designed especially for India. Its admirers looked up to it in awe, and books were written comparing it to the "Guardians" of Plato and the "heaven-born" of the upper-caste Brahmins.[68] Chosen through competitive examinations and drawn mainly from Oxford and Cambridge Universities, its officers ensured stability in changing times and neutrality in local politics. A centralized and powerful civil service recruited on the basis of open examinations, whose primary duty was to ensure law and order, was a great boon in societies dominated by ideas of tribal and religious loyalties. The story of the district officer continues to fascinate writers.[69] To its critics, however, the Indian Civil Service was not really Indian, rarely civil, and hardly a service.

Despite its social prestige and status, the CSP was a field-based system. With his first posting as assistant commissioner, usually at the age of about twenty-five, a young man would be placed in charge of a subdivision containing anywhere between several hundred thousand and several million people. He could implement development schemes and create new schools, but his main duty was to maintain law and order and act as the chief revenue officer for the government. At a young age, unless his direct superior was visiting, he was lord and master of all he surveyed. Tribal people, invariably more perceptive than those in the more settled areas, called the head of the administration "bacha" (the political agent in South Waziristan Agency was generally called the "Waziristan Bacha").[70]

An early lesson I learned was that the dictum about absolute power corrupting and power corrupting absolutely applied to the ruling elite of Pakistan. When I became a young district officer in the 1960s, I carried the ideal of Jinnah's vision in my mind, hoping to make a difference in the lives of the people in my charge. But I was also aware that Jinnah's vision of Pakistan was slowly being corrupted and that the Aligarh model itself was in danger of becoming distorted. A succession of regimes recognized that the CSP structure was a stumbling block to securing the unlimited powers they desired because it represented a defined concept of law and order and finally dismantled it. There was no great hue and cry in the public because over the years the CSP had begun to acquire a reputation for arrogance and even corruption. What replaced it, however, was not an improvement. Today, in the vacuum caused by its demise, tribal, sectarian, ethnic, and ideological passions compete in society and easily translate into violence. Clearly, the substitution of a military administration for a civil one has failed in Pakistan. This is a lesson that needs to be remembered by anyone designing the future of Muslim societies, whether in Pakistan or indeed in Iraq or Afghanistan.

I faced my first major moral crisis only a few months after being posted to the Okara subdivision, in the district of Sahiwal, south of Lahore. A colleague who was trained with me at the academy was posted to the same district, and our superior, the deputy commissioner, one of the most powerful CSP officers in the land, arranged for a welcome dinner at his home. The elite of the district were there—members of parliament, heads of departments, police officers, and the rich and influential. The men were segregated from the women and were drinking. My colleague and I, the most junior guests in the gathering, sat as unobtrusively as possible in a corner when the deputy commissioner, looking slightly inebriated, approached us and asked why we were not drinking. He gave us a lecture on the merits of drinking, which he said was imperative for good field officers and asked a waiter to bring drinks for us and left. As neither my friend nor I had touched a drink before, we were determined not to compromise our principles. I had learned from my father to say no politely in such situations but also not to condemn others who may behave differently.

The deputy commissioner returned a few minutes later with some senior officers and they began to put pressure on us to drink. They were cordial but intimidating. Some of them were swaying with the effect of their drinks. My friend abruptly put his glass to his mouth and drank. The attention now turned to me. Others joined in to persuade me to imbibe. I continued to refuse and prepared myself for an ignominious transfer out of the subdivision the next morning and a shaky start to my career as a district officer. At this point, someone announced dinner, and people began to file into the dining room. As the host, the deputy commissioner hung back at the end of the line. My colleague and I followed suit, conscious of the hierarchy. When he was out of the hearing range of the last guest, the deputy commissioner spoke to me, and I saw that he was cold sober: "I was testing you. Well done, Akbar. I am proud of you. You'll have my full support in your charge," he said. He directed a withering look that spoke volumes at my colleague and drew himself up as we entered the dining room.

Just twenty-five years old, I was already seeing the bewildering clash of the different models in Muslim society between which I had to navigate in order to maintain my own moral bearings. At that dinner, those of the Ajmer model would have maintained their own Islamic integrity by not drinking but adopted a live-and-let-live policy toward the others who clearly saw themselves as "modern" Muslims of the distorted Aligarh model. Those who believed in the Deoband model would not have been invited to a gathering of this kind—recall it was the 1960s, when the Aligarh model dominated Pakistan, and Deoband was marginalized—and in any case would have condemned the gathering as a violation of Islamic principles.

The golden days of the CSP and the Aligarh model are a thing of history. But even I, living in the midst of Muslim society, could not foresee the pace and nature of change beginning to take place. Starting from the late 1980s, from my vantage point as the Iqbal Fellow at Cambridge University, I should have seen the larger effects that globalization was having on the Muslim world and the threats it posed to my society. I knew that the Aligarh model was at risk, but I had no conception of the scale of the change that was in motion. I decided then to join the fray and to support the promotion of the Aligarh model in any way I could. I decided to launch an ambitious program to revive the Aligarh model by making films and writing books about Jinnah, its triumphant and ideal embodiment. I called the four-part project the "Jinnah Quartet." I completed it eventually, although it took me almost a decade. In the process, I was almost destroyed—physically, emotionally, and financially. Most dispiriting for me was the disappointment with the behavior, which included the violation of written commitments and contracts, of those who in their Western education, appearance, and spoken words appeared to reflect the Aligarh model and I assumed would understand the scope and depth of what I was trying to do.[71]

The project was clearly seen as an attempt to revive the flagging spirit of Jinnah and the honor of the Aligarh model. While filming in Pakistan, I was warned not to show Jinnah as a "liberal" or even to hint that he had a daughter because she had committed the sin, in the eyes of the more orthodox, of marrying a non-Muslim. It was demanded that I remove Christopher Lee from the role of Jinnah because he had played Dracula in the past and Shashi Kapoor from the film altogether because he was a Hindu and an Indian. When I refused, I aroused the fury of far more people than I could ever have imagined. I had expected opposition but not a steady smear campaign in the press, demonstrations, court cases, and even death threats. Newspaper reports hysterically announced that they had uncovered a "Jewish conspiracy" and a "Hindu conspiracy" against Islam in the making of the film. On my return to Cambridge, I felt strangely disjointed and unsure of what had happened and how to make sense of it. But I was aware that I had clearly encountered deep currents in society.

While I received immense support from those who believed I was struggling to revive the memory of Jinnah, I was also seen as the symbol of that revival. Umar Bakri, who became internationally known after 9/11 for claiming he was bin Laden's chief spokesman in Europe, attacked me as an "Uncle Tom," accusing me of being too fascinated by Western civilization and too keen to have a dialogue with Jews and Christians.[72] At about the same time, he launched a vitriolic attack on Jinnah in his magazine *Khilafah,* accusing him of exactly the same sins in the December 1996 issue. The title of the special feature summed up its tone: "Mohammed Ali Jinnah Exposed! Jinnah Defies Allah." Bakri's attacks echoed those of Jinnah's religious critics who called him the Kafir-i-Azam, or the Great Kafir (*kafir* means "unbeliever"). I dismissed Bakri, assuming that he was representing what many Muslims saw as the "lunatic fringe" in Islam. This was a failure on my part to read the deep and fundamental shifts taking place in my own society.

I could understand the malice of those who did not wish to see me succeed because of the well-known jealousy in Muslim society, but I could not explain the genuine hostility or even ambivalence of so many other people until my present travels in the Muslim world. What I had actually been witnessing was a dramatic decline of the Aligarh model. I had grown up hearing my parents and their friends talk of Jinnah as though he were a Moses, someone they would follow into the sea if he so commanded them. After all, he had almost single-handedly created a nation for them. I could not imagine any Pakistani not being in thrall to the man who gave them their freedom and their own state. So when I heard young Pakistani students from an elite Westernized school in Karachi, the first school I ever attended, extolling the virtues of bin Laden during our 2006 trip, I finally came face-to-face with the reality of the dramatic collapse of Jinnah's modernist vision of Pakistan.

The Aligarh model embodied by Jinnah meant tackling issues that demanded social reforms involving the economy and politics, Muslim representation in parliament, and the struggle to preserve the safety and security of Muslims in real-life situations. This struggle requires hard sacrifice and critical thinking in our personal lives. We cannot be diverted by anger, greed, laziness, or ignorance in the pursuit of this greater goal. In the Islam being interpreted by Amr Khaled and Shaukat Aziz—the nearest thing possible to a contemporary Aligarh model—I saw these important issues being sidelined to make way for more emphasis on personal gain. I feel that this interpretation does not spiritually challenge anyone, but rather provides a false sense of security and temporary sense of well-being.

Since the completion of the Jinnah Quartet in 1997–98, the world has become even more polarized and violent, and globalization has accelerated. On the 2006 trip, it became clear that the hostility to my Jinnah project was anchored in societal changes. The progressive and active Aligarh model had become enfeebled and in danger of being overtaken by the Deoband model, which never had much sympathy for Jinnah. I felt like a warrior in the midst of the fray who knew the odds were against him but never quite realized that his side had already lost the war.

FIVE

The Clash of Civilizations?

"THE MUSLIM SITUATION is so desperate. I would gladly give my life for their cause." These were the chilling words of my dinner companion on a balmy spring evening in Amman. A seasoned diplomat in smart attire, complete with pink silk tie and handkerchief, this former Iraqi ambassador, now head of a major Arab think tank, spoke in measured and quiet tones shaped by years of service, making his message all the more forlorn: "I have nothing to live for. I have lost my culture, my homeland, my honor. I have lost my religion."

We were at the Tannoureen, an elegant upscale restaurant famous for its Lebanese food, at a dinner hosted by Pakistan's ambassador to Jordan, Arif Kamal. The guests were the elite of the city, Westernized and living comfortable lives, able to travel abroad at will and dine at the finest restaurants. They were examples of the successful Aligarh model in Amman.

Kamal, an old friend, had arranged the dinner following my talk at the Royal Institute for Interfaith Studies, the brainchild of Prince Hassan, uncle of the present king and one of the leading thinkers of the Arab world. It was a well-attended event, chaired by former ambassador Hasan Abu Nimah, the institute's director, and had drawn scholars, journalists, ambassadors, and senators living in Jordan. Although the atmosphere was cordial, I had faced some hostile questions about the United States and Israel of the kind I would have expected from less polite audiences. A young man in a dark suit and glasses pointedly asked why I appeared to sympathize so much with the death of one Jewish boy—referring to Danny Pearl—and ignored the deaths of hundreds of thousands of young Muslims. Nonetheless, the dinner afterward seemed a pleasant enough evening of diplomats expressing well-rehearsed and inoffensive platitudes—until the former Iraqi ambassador released his despair.

Only a few days earlier, on February 22, 2006, explosions had destroyed one of the oldest mosques in Iraq, the Golden Mosque of Samarra. It contained tombs from the ninth century of two of the holiest imams in Shia Islam, one being Imam Hassan Al-Askari, the father of the Hidden Imam. As every Shia knows, the coming of the Hidden Imam will herald the end of the world. According to Shia theology, he will fight side by side with Jesus Christ to defeat the Muslim version of the anti-Christ. The destruction of the mosque triggered a bloodbath between Sunni and Shia in Iraq and attacks of vengeance on each other's mosques.

The Iraqi ambassador did not blame the Muslims for what had happened, however. Like President Mahmoud Ahmadinejad of Iran, he accused the Americans and Israelis of planting the bombs in the mosque. "No Muslim," he said indignantly, "Shia or Sunni, would ever think of destroying such a sacred mosque that had withstood some of the world's bloodiest conquerors—even the Mongols." The ambassador's quiet remarks, almost as if directed at himself, now took an ominous turn: incidents such as the one at Samarra, he said, were a prelude to the eventual destruction of the Noble Sanctuary in Jerusalem itself, planned in detail by the Americans and Israelis. Muslims were already at the "boiling point," and the destruction of what Muslims call the Noble Sanctuary with its internationally recognized mosque with its golden dome, their third holiest site after Mecca and Medina, would be a point of no return that would, he was certain, trigger violence on an unprecedented scale. This was not the first time I had heard this notion, recounted only a few days earlier in Damascus by the Syrian minister of expatriates. Overcome by a sense that the world had spun out of control, the Iraqi ambassador had apparently been moved to talk of suicide to a stranger. This was not an al-Qaeda terrorist, a young fanatic, or economically deprived individual—some of the stereotypes of the Muslim suicide bomber. Here was an intelligent human being of the diplomatic world engulfed by despair and anger.

The conversation at this point was interrupted by the former foreign minister of Jordan, who had declared himself a Christian, launching into a tirade against the controversial Danish cartoons of the Prophet of Islam. "How dare the West insult the Prophet?" he said. "He is my biggest hero." The West, he fulminated, knows nothing of true Christianity, a gentle and accepting faith that would never condone such brutal disrespect toward other faiths.

The idea of a Christian extolling the virtues of the Prophet of Islam may seem unlikely to a Westerner. Yet in the cultural context of the Middle East, the Prophet is not just a religious figure, but a historical one considered responsible for bringing peace to the Arabs. Arab Christians lived in the Middle East long before the coming of Islam and in their cultural milieu have learned to see religious figures of the Muslim tradition with reverence and sensitivity.

When the conversation turned to further humiliations, notably Abu Ghraib, my companions drew a direct link between American policies and Muslim anger and despair in this part of the world. America's actions led directly to more violence and talk of revenge among Muslims, which could spiral into more "terror plots" formed and foiled, more distraught families on both sides of the ocean, and more Muslim and American recruits for the war on terror. Even the most optimistic observers would hasten to ask, "Are we finally in the grip of a clash of civilizations?"

It was difficult not to believe that political scientist Samuel Huntington may have been right: perhaps a "clash of civilizations" was under way between the West and Islam, from which there was no escape.[1] The wounds being inflicted were deep, and it would take sustained work and prolonged compassion to bring the different sides together again. In Iraq and Afghanistan, it seemed that the two civilizations were trapped in a quicksand of blood and terror. With each new horror story, people's most dreadful nightmares had turned into reality. When I heard about the Israeli assault on Lebanon in July 2006, I remembered all too vividly the conversation that night in Amman. How would the Iraqi ambassador be coping with the news, I wondered. It was not hard to imagine his deep resentment and anger at the United States, which claimed to fight for justice and peace, yet consistently vetoed a cease-fire at the United Nations to stop the destruction of Lebanon.

Americanization

This turmoil can only be understood in the context of globalization and Americanization, which are synonymous, according to commentators such as Thomas Friedman.[2] While globalization seeks to spread such cherished American ideals as democracy and human rights, it also corrodes values that many people admire about American society, such as individualism. Unrestrained, the American emphasis on individualism can override duty and responsibility toward the family and community, traditional values that Muslims hold in high esteem. Indeed, the overarching message of globalization and the American spirit, also of sociologist Max Weber's Protestant work ethic, is independence in all its forms, rapid results, and material self-indulgence—all of which can have deleterious effects on the individual and society as a whole.

The term "globalization," though relatively new, encompasses phenomena that have been infiltrating the American psyche and culture for years, particularly the effects of advanced technology with its overnight success stories. Although Americans have always highly valued hard work, today many also seek the "fast track" to success. Emphasis on developing the right experience or skills, which takes time and dedication, has been supplanted by a desire for the "right image." Qualifications are based on "manufactured" talent, rather than on the more solid traits acquired through experience and education. Politicians of both parties are carefully groomed by public relations firms and political advisers, their speeches based on a "sound-bite" formula that is a far cry from the eloquent substance of words by a Lincoln, Jefferson, Franklin, or Washington. Republicans and Democrats alike acknowledge the "genius" of Karl Rove, for example, crediting him with the "creation" and two-time electoral victory of President George W. Bush.

Leading the way in endorsing the value of image is the entertainment world, with its celebrity culture. The success of pop icons such as Britney Spears or Paris Hilton is due to physical appearance, popularity, and public relations; they are products of the two-dimensional world of the television screen more than the real world. Yet many Americans fail to make that distinction and even draw role models from the flat-screened version.[3] When I am invited to speak before distinguished audiences and given accommodation in some of the best hotels in the United States, I find chocolates and flowers in my room, along with cards containing pearls of wisdom, not from the Bible or Shakespeare, but from Donald Trump. Rooms on the executive floor of the Hilton Anaheim in Los Angeles offered this Trumpism in October 2006: "As long as you are going to think anyway, think big."

In American society, the image of success carries as much weight as actual success and power. Individuals across the United States build multi-million dollar homes and spend large amounts of money on clothes, cars, and jewelry to acquire social recognition. This indulgence and extravagance are glorified by the global media in shows such as *Lifestyles of the Rich and Famous* of an earlier decade and currently MTV's ostentatious *Cribs*, which displays some of the most luxurious and expensive houses in the world. The desire for wealth and overblown consumerism is also the bread and butter of globalization, which needs expanding markets for its vast array of unnecessary and expensive products.

While the "me" culture fuels the engine of globalization and keeps it working, it also produces some serious "pollutants." By encouraging self-centeredness in the pursuit of economic goals and pleasure, it destroys the capacity to empathize with others. Traditional societies, which are mainly community centered, see the world in a different light, viewing excessive concern with the self as both an aberration and a sign of social breakdown. The rich and powerful in traditional societies usually feel a moral obligation to help care for the poor because the community is defined in holistic terms rather than as a collection of individuals. Some recent scholarship on the sense of entitlement common among Americans indicates that the ethos of hard work and personal independence leads many to argue that those who are less well-off have only themselves to blame and could improve their lives if they changed their attitude. This may well be true in some cases but certainly not all and must not be allowed to bias society against the poor or suppress compassion for the needy.

Another adverse effect of globalization is that the gaps between the rich and poor within and among countries are growing, without any sign of slowing down. Already billions are living in poverty and close to starvation while three of the world's richest individuals are collectively richer than half the earth's inhabitants combined.[4] Globalization and the free market policies of the World Bank and International Monetary Fund, meant to alleviate poverty worldwide, often do not help the disenfranchised in traditional societies. Yet many commentators see no alternative but to accept global-ization and compete under its terms: it is a matter of survival, not choice. If some nations are slower to catch up or share in the benefits, their own sluggishness is to blame, not the system. While America's strong sense of individualism stokes the fires of globalization, the same quality, as already mentioned, discourages responsibility for personal actions, an attitude now spreading around the globe. Americans fail to realize that their rhetoric and actions, particularly consumer behavior, are having a direct impact on the outside world, with increasing criticism. Many observers agree that responsibility and awareness are being abandoned as a result of globaliza-tion, even among political leaders.

Many Americans live in a bubble consisting of the office, the super-market, and their sections of town, where they are not necessarily forced to engage with people who are different from them—racially, ethnically, reli-giously, or economically. Within this bubble, life can be extremely pleasant and remote from the realities of the nation at war, of a drug-related killing in a poor part of the city, or the desperate poverty in another. Bethesda, where I live, is a beautifully maintained suburb of Washington, D.C., and home to largely white, upper-middle-class residents, a striking contrast to the demographic and sociological range of Southeast D.C., composed mainly of blacks. Washington's infant mortality among African Americans is higher than that in the Indian state of Kerala, and throughout the United States, black children are twice as likely to die before their first birthday than white children.[5] Oprah Winfrey featured CNN's Anderson Cooper in "Oprah's Special Report: American Schools in Crisis," a two-part television program broadcast in 2006 that exposed the appalling con-ditions of inner-city high schools including those in Washington. Many of the people I mix with in Washington have little idea of these figures or their social significance because they are so busy with their own lives.

Similarly, few Americans, despite their general wealth, travel outside the United States or possibly Europe and therefore have a very limited per-spective of other nations. American news tends to focus on national events interspersed with stories about the wars in Iraq and Afghanistan. Little is heard of the world outside unless it has a direct impact on the United States.[6] Furthermore, little is done to counteract stereotypes of other coun-tries and peoples. Thus Americans tend to have a narrower vision of the world than one might expect from the sole superpower.

Although individuals appear to be surrounded by noise, color, and movement, they remain isolated from society and even lonely in their daily routines, whether it is in their homes, driving their cars, and or going back and forth to work. This is an age of less and less human contact or reflection upon the state of other human beings. This isolation and emotional desensitization are reflected in the literature of Tom Perotta, for example, or films such as *One Hour Photo, American Beauty,* and *Crash,* which opens with a car crash and a voice saying: "It's the sense of touch. Any real city, you walk, you know? You brush past people. People bump into you. In L.A., nobody touches you. We're always behind this metal and glass. I think we miss that touch so much that we crash into each other just so we can feel something."

Perhaps worst of all is the loneliness of children growing up under globalization, which in some cases is drawing both parents into full-time jobs and in others causing the family unit—both the nuclear and extended family—to break down. The incidence of divorce is so high that every second child in the United States comes from a divided home. According to the U.S. Bureau of the Census, 61 percent of all children will spend all or part of their formative years in households headed by a single parent.[7] These are widely recognized trends with troubling effects: less parental involvement and more independence for children means greater access to adult material and greater reliance on television or video games to keep them company in their environment of solitude. Schools, too, are failing to promote friendship and goodwill. Many have large classrooms and classes that are simply arenas of competitive bullying. From high school onward young men and women are exposed to a culture of permissiveness, hedonism, and self-indulgence.[8]

What a child, and even an adult, sees on the television screen becomes crucial in understanding how average Americans think about a whole range of issues, including race, religion, and society. Many children will acquire their knowledge about the politics of hatred or sex from this source because these subjects are discussed more often on television than by their parents. The perceptions of those who have little knowledge of other ethnic groups can be heavily influenced by violent and ethnically poisonous video games and television shows. Such entities reinforce existing stereotypes through the use of advanced technology. Their profound effect on the young can be seen in the random and senseless violence among high school students documented in Michael Moore's film, *Bowling for Columbine*. Where religion should be guiding societies toward a more inclusive understanding of the world, it is further exacerbating the prejudices. In a modern interpretation of the Bible titled *Left Behind*, of which more than 63 million copies have been sold, authors Tim LaHaye and Jerry Jenkins describe the apocalypse in a setting like a flashy action film, prompting many readers to believe that the end is near and thus to support certain political actions both in the United States and abroad. Prejudices are also being fueled by new video games such as "Eternal Forces" in which players fight on behalf of Christ's army against the anti-Christ's army in places like New York City. Here is the literature that accompanies the game:

> Are guns used by Christians against non-Christians? Why or why not?:
>
> The storyline in the game begins just after the Rapture has occurred—when all adult Christians, all infants, and many children were instantly swept home to Heaven and off the Earth by God. The remaining population—those who were left behind—is then poised to make a decision at some point. They cannot remain neutral. Their choice is to either join the anti-Christ—which is an imposturous one world government seeking peace for all of mankind, or they may join the Tribulation Force—which seeks to expose the truth and defend themselves against the forces of the anti-Christ.[9]

The target audience is "the millions of parents—and many casual players of games—who are looking for entertainment that also offers positive, inspirational content." The only problem is that the video game identifies all non-Christians as the enemy, implying that all non-Christians are villains and that one must either convert them or kill them. Games and books such as these are extremely popular and emphatically discourage their players or readers from accepting those outside the Christian faith. While I believe that all people should follow their own religious beliefs, this exclusivist line of thinking, much like some extreme elements within the Deoband model in Islam, makes it much harder to reach out to other civilizations in friendship and peace.

Military-minded video games in which players, often portraying U.S. soldiers, shoot crazed Muslims with little or no context, have also become popular. These include "Counterstrike," "Close Combat: First to Fight," and the free online game "America's Army" (with more than 7.5 million users), released in 2002 by the U.S. Army to help bolster recruitment. Although Muslims are not the only villains, the games reinforce stereotypes and feed perceptions in the Muslim world that the United States is waging a war against Islam. In response, some companies in Muslim countries are releasing their own games with players killing Americans and Israelis.[10]

The lack of personal responsibility fostered by dynamic individualism affects the future of the planet. Unaware of these wide-reaching consequences, Americans fail to understand that their culture is drawing critical notice in other parts of the world or that the seemingly casual arrogance of their leaders is only making matters worse. Indifference to arguments about the effects of carbon dioxide gases on global warming, excessive military expenditures, the tendency to run up debts in the pursuit of short-term gains, and hastily planned and clumsily executed military adventures abroad may well prove to be a turning point in the fortunes of America and Americanization itself.

Savage Nation

It is far easier to deal with an explosive story like Abu Ghraib by saying that the acts of Lynndie England and her colleagues were simply an aberration of the American way or that Steven Green and his friends who raped a girl in Mahmudiyah did so because they were "under pressure" in Iraq. Even the massacres in Haditha were dismissed as a "mistake," the assumption being that no American would ever commit such atrocious crimes. However reluctant Americans may be to admit them, these barbarous acts correlate with the climate of hate and violence against Muslims that has developed in the United States in the past few years. Furthermore, because of that reluctance, the correlation has been either missed or ignored.

Radio and TV talk show hosts have emerged from this cultural milieu to define and drive it, often prattling on about subjects they claim to have knowledge of. Their xenophobic and shrill appeal to the crudest form of patriotism feeds into and from the mood of insecurity. Fear and anxiety permeates the land. Airports and railway stations, so central to globalization because they symbolize travel, trade, and communications, have now become small armed camps where passengers are delayed and frustrated on almost every trip. Muslims are forced to confront the shame of 9/11 every time at these travel points because of the special attention and humiliation reserved for them. They have become victims of the sense of collective responsibility imposed on them by the media for the actions of the hijackers.

The popular Fox television show *24* mentioned earlier, and described by *Time* magazine as one of the "best television events of the decade," owes much of its popularity to its accurate reflection of the American mood after 9/11.[11] The espionage drama traces the events of a single day in the life of counterterrorism agent Jack Bauer, shown constantly racing against the clock to check assassination attempts, foil germ warfare and terrorist plots, and therefore "save the day." The series presents the highly tense events as they unfold during the day by using split-screen and "real-time" devices, thus moving television in a new direction. But the programs also have a controversial aspect: they tap into the sense of uncertainty and suspicion that pervades society. Muslim villains are never far from the plot, and torture is depicted as necessary to defeat terror in "ticking time-bomb" scenarios. Nonetheless, the show has gained a large American audience. Even Department of Homeland Security head Michael Chertoff commented on the show's relevance to the U.S. war on terror and on the need for perseverance like agent Bauer's to help America defeat terrorism.[12]

Living in the age of globalization means that the Fox programs depicting Muslims as villainous terrorists are discussed in the international Muslim press almost immediately after they are broadcast, as the following report from a leading Pakistani daily illustrates: "A popular TV drama, which opened its sixth season this week, is causing much anxiety to the Muslim-American community because of its portrayal of Muslims as terrorists setting off bombs in major US cities. The current season of Fox's *24* opened with a two-hour episode which pitched the viewer two years in the future, with America being terrorised by Islamic suicide bombers. The African-American president's chief of staff sets up Muslim internment camps, reminiscent of such camps for Japanese-Americans in World War II."[13]

In other words, Islamophobia is undisguised and loud in the media. Another case in point concerns Michael Savage, the television and radio host of "The Savage Nation." Savage, a major radio personality with an audience of 10 million, espouses blatant hatred against Arabs and Muslims, and has called for the United States to "kill thousands of Iraqi prisoners and nuke a random Arab capital."[14] Nor is he alone in expressing these sentiments or even remotely aware of what he is doing to make the world a more dangerous place. At a public appearance in San Francisco in May 2004, Savage said: "I don't give a damn if they [Muslims/Arabs] hide behind their women's skirts—wipe the women out with them! Because it is our women who got killed on 9/11! And it's our women who are gonna get killed tomorrow unless we get rid of the bugs who are destroying us!" Savage successfully creates a climate of crude patriotism and blind emotion in his audience. When he asked, "Does anyone in this crowd care a shit about the Iraqis?" the crowd yelled an uproarious, "NO!"

Savage dismisses George W. Bush's attempt to win Muslim "hearts and minds." To him, being gentle in dealing with the Muslim world has nothing to do with winning hearts and minds; it is being too "soft." When the Abu Ghraib scandals emerged, Savage jokingly said, "These are tough interrogations? My father put me through tougher interrogations when I was 16!" He then went on to argue that Lynndie England was the poster girl for the war on terrorism and that kicking "Muslim ass" can be "fun."

According to this mind-set, the relationship between America and the Muslim world has to be an expression of power. It does not matter what other countries or "bleeding-heart liberals" think about it. Many of this persuasion—Rush Limbaugh is one—insist that what happened in Abu Ghraib was a harmless fraternity prank. James Inhofe, a senator from Oklahoma, insisted that the prisoners got what they deserved. During hearings on the prisoner abuse scandal in 2004, Inhofe said: "I am probably not the only one up at this table who is more outraged by the outrage than we are by the treatment. These prisoners, they are murderers, terrorists, they are insurgents, many of them probably have blood on their hands. And here we are so concerned about the treatment of those individuals."[15] Senator Inhofe went on to say that it is the U.S. troops who deserve sympathy. "I am also outraged that we have so many humanitarian do-gooders right now crawling all over these prisons looking for human rights violations while our troops, our heroes, are fighting and dying." This remark came after the Red Cross alleged that 70–90 percent of Iraqi prisoners were "arrested by mistake."[16] Conservative columnist Ann Coulter also brushed off the incidents as minor errors, if that, in comparison with the overwhelming brutality of the Muslims. She also laid down her no-nonsense "policy" for Muslims, which "prompted a boisterous ovation" in February 2006: "I think our motto should be post-9-11, 'raghead talks tough, raghead faces consequences.'"[17]

On a November 14, 2006, broadcast of his CNN Headline News prime-time TV show, commentator Glenn Beck challenged the first-ever Muslim congressman, Democrat Keith Ellison, to "prove to me that you are not working with our enemies."[18] Beck whips himself up into a frenzy of Islamophobia in almost every show. Anyone who is seen to be sympathetic to a Muslim cause is a potential target—from President Ahmadinejad of Iran, who for some inexplicable reason Beck calls "President Tom," to President Carter for daring to write about the plight of the Palestinians in his latest book, *Palestine: Peace Not Apartheid*.[19] Beck also promotes and is generous with air time to the critics of Islam such as Ayaan Hirsi Ali and Irshad Manji.

As a university professor teaching Islam and a frequent media guest, I receive many responses to my remarks, both positive and negative. Fortunately, the positive outweigh the negative. One letter, written in September 2006, states: "Islam is an evil belief system that seeks to corrupt, dominate and destroy the West. We will never submit to your barbarism and superstition. You will never be able to defeat us. We will NEVER forget September 11th. . . . And WE will destroy this dark evil that has been brought forth into this world by the devil's messenger Mohammed. . . . Stop promoting this evil in the United States of America." Another is from a friend, a prominent media personality, responding to my request for her advice concerning the hate: "Frankly, this guy sounds to me like the dyed-in-the-wool racists I've met a few times in my life. His views sound like they are rooted more in emotion than reason, and many folks like this are not open to change. And the right-wing media like Fox only make it worse. And he probably listens to such networks." She, too, had seen the connection between the person who sent me the hate letter and the climate of fear and hatred being cultivated by the media.[20]

Even before the events of 2001, a climate of hostility and intimidation had been building against Muslims in the United States. Hollywood films and media commentators were depicting Muslims, especially Arabs, as extremists or advocates of violence who were intrinsically hostile to the United States. After 9/11, the hatred and violence grew exponentially.

Since the war in Iraq, it has become even worse. Some people even refer to Arabs as "dot-heads," confusing religion and gender, in that only Hindu women paint dots on their foreheads.

Indeed, as pointed out in the earlier discussion of the Orientalists and the neocons, there is a pattern of anti-Muslim rhetoric in recent American history that has infiltrated the U.S. Army and now translates into action: "You have to understand the Arab mind," one company commander told the *New York Times,* displaying all the self-assurance of Douglas MacArthur discoursing on Orientals in 1945. "The only thing they understand is force—force, pride, and saving face." Far from representing the views of a few underlings, such notions penetrated into the upper echelons of the American command. In their book *Cobra II,* Michael R. Gordon and Bernard E. Trainor offer this ugly comment from a senior officer: "The only thing these sand niggers understand is force and I'm about to introduce them to it."[21] Similarly, well-known Christian leaders have not been living up to their own statements about love and justice for all. The Reverend Franklin Graham, who offered the invocation at President George Bush's inauguration, called Islam "a very wicked and evil religion."[22] Islam's God was not the God of Christianity, he said. The Reverend Jerry Vines denounced the prophet of Islam as "a demon-possessed pedophile."[23] For Jerry Falwell, the Prophet was a "terrorist."[24] In a later controversy, General William Boykin, deputy undersecretary of defense for intelligence and a key figure in the war on terror, declared that Islam was a satanic religion of idol-worshippers.[25]

Matching the mood of these statements, U.S. legislation opened the door for the objectification of Muslims and denial of rights afforded to every other American citizen. The Patriot Act has been regularly challenged for trampling over the civil rights of Muslims and Arab immigrants. Intended to fight terrorism, the law is often used to harass Muslims unnecessarily and in far too many cases persecute them with little or no justification. In one instance, investigators are looking into what they call a credible claim in which a guard at an immigrant detention facility held a loaded gun to a detainee's head. In another case, Muslim prisoners have presented persuasive evidence that they were taunted because of their religion and possibly forced to eat food that Islam prohibits. The base at Guantánamo Bay, too, circumvents U.S. laws to implement illicit policies that the Pentagon and White House feel are necessary. According to the Council on

American-Islamic Relations, attacks on Muslim girls wearing the hijab, on mosques, and on Muslims have gone up dramatically since 9/11.[26]

In this climate of Islamophobia, the appearance of a burning cross outside the Prince George's County Mosque and Islamic School in Maryland in July 2003 was not entirely unexpected. Reminiscent of the Ku Klux Klan's symbols of hatred toward African Americans in the early part of the twentieth century, the burning three-foot-high wooden cross was not large by KKK standards, but its significance was enormous. A videotape from a surveillance camera on the property showed that several white men were involved in what was the first cross burning reported to authorities in Maryland in at least three years. A few days earlier, two young Muslim students were shot to death in the same county. Soon after 9/11, in Arizona, a Sikh male who may have been mistaken for an Arab because of his beard and turban was shot in Phoenix. In Illinois, an explosive device destroyed a Muslim family's van.

In the United States, cross burning and the rhetoric of hate also evoke the struggle for American identity and sense of self. They speak of an ongoing battle for a more just, more tolerant, and more democratic society fought by visionary leaders such as John F. Kennedy and Martin Luther King Jr. The central paradox of the burning cross is that it symbolizes hatred, while the cross itself is an undisputed symbol of Christianity, which by definition carries the message of its founder—Christ. As Muslims know from the high reverence and affection they have for him, Christ embodies love, compassion, and humility. To kill or be violent in Christ's name is a gross distortion of his teachings. Besides, for American leaders who are trying desperately to win the hearts and minds of the Muslim world, such acts undermine their initiatives and credibility. The symbol of a burning cross at a mosque will play into the hands of those in the Muslim world who are arguing that America is on the warpath against Islam itself. Such acts do not help Americans either at home or abroad.

The climate of hostility both before and after 9/11 in the United States is described by a member of our journey team, Hadia Mubarak, who has worn a hijab since her youth:

> Recently, when my husband and I were walking back to our hotel in Hershey, Pennsylvania, after celebrating our one-year wedding anniversary at a nice restaurant, I was startled when a red truck drove

really close up to us and the driver yelled, "You suck!" It was dark and there were no other cars or pedestrians on the street but us and the truck. My heart skipped a beat, as the truck roared past us and its tires skidded as it made a quick turn.

Religious bigotry is nothing new to me. I was only four years old when our next-door neighbor called my mother a "rag head," as she buckled my sister and me into her white station wagon and silently drove us to our day-care in New Brunswick, New Jersey.

I was about twelve years old when two young teenagers fishing at a creek near my parents' house in Panama City, Florida, yelled out to me, "Do you fuck with that on?" in reference to my headscarf.

I was the last one to walk out of the Islamic Center of Tallahassee when Charles Franklin—who was later convicted and jailed—slammed his truck into the front entrance to "let Muslims know they're not safe in this country," as he later admitted to authorities.

Growing up in a country where Islam remains a mysterious, widely misunderstood religion, stereotyped by the images of submissive veiled women and the absurd notion of "Holy War," I have become accustomed to the double takes at my headscarf, the racial slurs at my religion or ethnicity, and the sheer prejudice produced by ignorance. Nevertheless, 9/11 provided a new context for much of the growing tension toward Islam in this country.

The unfathomable images I witnessed on the morning of 9/11, sitting among a large circle of students at Florida State University, as planes crashed through one of the greatest economic symbols of our nation, pierce my mind as if it just happened yesterday. I can still conjure to memory every moment of that chaotic day, every emotion that penetrated my being, and every thought that swam through my consciousness, as if I was in a state of paralysis and as if logic and reason were only products of our imagination.

It was also the first time, however, that I realized my own displacement as an American Muslim in the American public consciousness. Before I was allowed to shed my tears, grieve for the thousands of innocent lives, or try to make sense out of the absurd violence that shook our lives, I was put on the defense seat. American Muslims quickly became the target of hate crimes and discrimination due to sweeping generalizations that associated all Muslims with the terrorists.

Those days, as a junior at Florida State University and the Public Relations Director of the Muslim Students Association, were some of the most testing in my life, as my beliefs were questioned, my religion misunderstood, and my identity as an American Muslim regarded with suspicion. The moments I experienced after 9/11 were the most defining of my life as I began to explore questions of loyalty, identity, and belonging. Where was home? Where did I belong? The double pain I experienced as an American whose country had been attacked and as a Muslim whose religion was now being vilified confirmed my hyphenated identity as an American Muslim.

While Muslims in the United States were plunged into self-reflection, prominent figures in the administration explicitly attacked Islam, and with the hostility against Muslims in the media, it created a negative environment for understanding Islam. Young Americans, like Lynndie England and Steven Green, thus went abroad with an idea of Muslims in their minds as a demonized community that was even less than human. The social and cultural environment in the United States that is unpleasantly aggressive toward Muslims is encouraging Americans in authority to behave in a manner that is far removed from the ideals of the American Founding Fathers and to condone inhumane acts such as torture. In the climate of anger and ignorance toward the "other," Americans are permitting a deeper distortion of American ideals of acceptance and freedom of religion—even if individuals still retain them—once held in such high esteem by the society and its leaders.

When radio host Jerry Klein suggested on his show that all Muslims in the United States should be marked with a crescent-shaped tattoo or an armband, callers jammed his phone lines to present even wilder ideas. Some suggested interment camps like those for the Japanese and Germans during World War II. Others had a simpler solution: "Not only do you tattoo them in the middle of their forehead but you ship them out of this country . . . they are here to kill us."[27] But the joke was on the callers. Klein had deliberately played a hoax. "I can't believe any of you are sick enough to agree for one second with anything I said," he told his audience on November 22, 2006, on AM station 630 WMAL, which covers Washington, Northern Virginia, and Maryland. The responses of his callers had, however, illustrated a deeper truth. The years of hatred and ignorance had taken their toll. The prejudice against Muslims was high and was reaching dangerous levels of intolerance.

Irresponsible Action

During the dinner in Amman and discussion of the Abu Ghraib scandal, I was reminded of the high moral standards Islam expects of those in authority. My hosts were right. Islamic role models like the Prophet, Abu Bakr, Umar, and Ali behaved with magnanimity toward captured prisoners. Abu Bakr had laid down the conduct of war for Muslims, which, as mentioned, forbade them to harm women and children, noncombatants, and even priests and holy men of other religions. Destroying trees or vegetation was strictly forbidden. The bloody massacre in Jerusalem in 1099—when the crusaders, according to Christian accounts, killed thousands and the blood in the streets ran so deep as to reach the stirrups of the horsemen—created an outrage in the Muslim world and a yearning for revenge. Saladin, after capturing Jerusalem from the Crusaders in 1187, demonstrated his generosity and compassion by allowing the well-off to pay their ransom and then covered the ransoms of the poor Christian crusaders from his own estate.

In my presentation in Amman, I pointed out that despite American anger after 9/11, this emotion was out of character. Benjamin Franklin, one of the Founding Fathers, had warned his nation: "Whatever is begun in anger ends in shame."[28] As for the scandals emerging from the American prisons, I shared the story of George Washington during the Revolutionary War against the British. When American soldiers, who were then "insurgents" to the British, were captured, the British threw them, sick and wounded, into dank prisons with no hope of release or justice. In contrast, the American commander-in-chief, who had everything to fight for and to lose, went out of his way to ensure that captured British soldiers were treated with dignity and fairness in spite of the desire for retribution. "Treat them with humanity," Washington instructed his lieutenants, "and let them have no reason to complain of our copying the brutal example of the British army."[29] Washington understood that the mistreatment of British soldiers would only lead to moral degradation of his cause and would sully the character of the new nation. It would also lead to repercussions ten times worse than the mistreatment itself. Thus, for Washington the government and those in authority always had to be held to a higher moral standard, as expressed in words widely attributed to him: "Government is not reason, it is not eloquence, it is force; like fire, a troublesome servant and a fearful master. Never for a moment should it be left to irresponsible action."[30]

The invasion of Iraq and the subsequent developments provide a good case study of how war is being conducted in the age of globalization. For most Americans, the removal of Saddam Hussein meant an instant change in the way Iraq had been run in the past. Free elections, democracy, and free speech would flourish and there would be security and justice for all. With much fanfare, President Bush declared, "Mission Accomplished." In a culture of instant information, high expectations, and simplistic ways of looking at the world, most Americans took that pronouncement literally.

That culture has disconnected thought and consequence, which explains the reckless actions abroad, such as American soldiers indulging in "irresponsible action" with little consideration of the consequences. While many soldiers behave bravely and justly, a few bad apples are staining the name of the army and compromising the ideals of a whole country. Perhaps Donald Rumsfeld's dismissal of the looting of the treasures of the Baghdad Museum indicated the attitude of the Pentagon and White House leaders in a nutshell. When told that priceless antiquities were being carried off openly in spite of the presence of American troops in Baghdad, he shrugged his shoulders and replied, "Stuff happens."[31]

President Bush's own attitude may well have set the tone for his administration. Bob Woodward's third book dealing with the Bush presidency, *State of Denial,* has some startling revelations, perhaps none more illuminating than the president's instructions for the senior general that he was dispatching to Iraq as his chief administrator. When General Jay Garner looked at the list of objectives, he replied that he could not hope to achieve more than four of the items. Presidential clarification came in the form of the crystal-clear response: "Kick ass, Jay."[32]

The inevitable disaster in Iraq was set in motion at the very moment that the Americans were appointing their first viceroy. Historical figures from Alexander, Julius Caesar, and Napoleon Bonaparte to America's Dwight Eisenhower have instructed their subordinates on how to manage territories after fresh conquests, but perhaps never in history has the complexity of tribal, sectarian, and religious identities and politics in one of the most turbulent regions of the world been reduced to one phrase. Bush's ultimate sound bite is as much a reflection of his vocabulary and philosophy as it is of the age of globalization, which demands that even the most complex issues be reduced to simplistic and graphic phrases. Clearly, Americanization and globalization, which reflect each other in so many complex ways, both encourage such reduction.

Even if Americans cannot yet see what they have lost in these debacles, other countries have spoken up, noting that the United States has lost its credibility. After President Bush called on him to implement more democratic measures at the G-8 summit in Moscow in July 2006, Russian President Vladimir Putin replied, "We certainly would not want . . . the same kind of democracy as they have in Iraq."[33] Principles like human rights and the rule of law, once compromised, cannot easily be taken up again with any authority. George Washington understood this well, but unfortunately the United States has now lost its virtue in the eyes of the international community.

One incident contributed significantly to that loss. Steven Green, of the Army's 101st Airborne Division, according to an FBI affidavit, is now charged with raping a fourteen-year-old Iraqi girl, then setting her body on fire to eradicate traces of his guilt, in the village of Mahmudiyah south of Baghdad in March 2006. He is also charged with killing three members of her family, including a five-year-old girl. Unlike the Vietnam war's My Lai incident, an act that came to be recognized as limited to the madness of the moment, Green and three companions from his unit spent several days planning to hunt the girl down and trap her just as a group of hunters in the forest would pursue a prized animal. On March 12, Green, the alleged ringleader, and the other soldiers got drunk, abandoned their checkpoint, and changed clothes to avoid detection, before heading for the victim's house. Eventually tried back in the United States by military court, the perpetrators appeared unrepentant. When asked why they committed the terrible crime one of them answered: "I hated Iraqis, your honor."[34]

The irresponsible actions of Lynndie England and Steven Green are not the only cases of their kind. Others are emerging, indicating something has changed in American society and its high standards have sunk well below those originally established by the Founding Fathers.

The Other Side of the Same Coin

Three short months after the terrible episode in Mahmudiyah, three American soldiers from Green's unit were on patrol with their guns strapped to their chests, helmets on, walking down a dusty road southwest of Baghdad in the town of Youssifiyah. Suddenly they heard gunshots and ducked for cover but were separated from the rest of their battalion. In the skirmish that ensued, two of the soldiers were taken captive and a third killed. A video later released by the Mujahadeen Shura Council, which is linked to al-Qaeda, showed two bloodied bodies lying on the edge of a bridge. An Associated Press report described the 4:39 minute video in gruesome detail: "One of them, partially naked, has been decapitated and his chest cut open. The other's face is bruised, the jaw apparently broken and his leg has long gashes. Fighters are shown turning the bodies over and lifting the head of the decapitated man."[35] According to the Shura Council statement, the video was released as "revenge for our sister who was dishonored by a soldier of the same brigade." The fighters were determined to take this brutal action as soon as they heard of the rape-slaying but "kept their anger to themselves and didn't spread the news. They intended to avenge their sister's honor."

While their anger was rooted in notions of honor and revenge, their violence represented an abandonment of the core values of Islam. The great Caliph Ali, the Prophet's son-in-law and cousin, faced a similar dilemma in a fight with an enemy warrior, when he threw him to the ground and raised his sword to finish him. At this point, Ali's opponent spat on his face, whereupon Ali stood up and walked away, to the amazement of both armies. He later explained that had he killed his foe, he would have done so in anger, rather than in opposition to the forces of tyranny and injustice against which he was fighting. Today's post-9/11 world—with its revenge, dishonor, and gratuitous violence—is far from the ideals of either Ali or George Washington.

It is not only on the battlefield where people are forsaking the ideals. I observed the nuances of the "clash" between Islam and the West from another angle in Cairo in December 2005. Although some leading intellectuals I interviewed in Egypt—Ismail Serageldin at the Alexandria library, Saad Eddin Ibrahim at the Ibn Khaldun Center, and Sallama

Shaker at the Foreign Ministry in Cairo—dismissed the idea of a civilizational clash I saw it manifested in my taxi ride.

At one point during the trip, an Egyptian friend had stopped a taxi for me and explained to the driver in Arabic the name and address of my hotel. As we drove off, the driver increased the volume of the recitation of the Quran that he was listening to. He himself began reciting the Quran loudly while revolving prayer beads in one hand. Dangling from the mirror were verses from the Quran. Egyptian taxis are small with low ceilings, and the space can become claustrophobic, which the volume accentuates.

As a Muslim, I find few things more pleasant than the sound of the recitation of the Quran. The driver saw me, in my Western clothes and speaking English, as someone from the West and therefore probably a non-Muslim. Why should he therefore be playing the Quran so loudly and almost aggressively to a non-Muslim? Was it an attempt to intimidate the passenger? Or to express pride in his identity as a Muslim? Was it cumulative anger at the poverty, hopelessness of life, and vast gap between the lives of the corrupt ruling elite and those of the poor?

When the recitation of the Quran reached a crescendo, I punctured the tense atmosphere by repeating some of the Quranic verses that I knew. Seeing the driver staring at me in his rearview mirror, I announced that I was from Pakistan and a Muslim. His attitude changed completely. Pakistanis were good Muslims, he said with a smile and a *salaam* (greeting of peace), and his hand discreetly moved to the dial and turned down the volume.

One of my female American students who had studied abroad in Cairo—intelligent, blue-eyed, and blond—complained that most drivers would make lewd sexual advances when she was alone in taxis. In both the Quran and Arab society, women are treated with respect, and men will even avoid looking at women directly for fear of violating their modesty. Yet for my student, men masturbating and exposing their penises were hazards. She would remind them that God expected modest behavior in females and males and that they would have to answer to God. This apparently had the effect of inflaming the passions in the heart of the amorous Arab male even further. They saw her as a sex-crazed Western woman like those seen in movies or television shows. Another student of mine, an American from India, dark-haired and dark-eyed, did not face similar problems as people saw her as a "native" and did not attach the same stereotypes to her as to the blond American student.

For me, the taxi ride—and I had several similar experiences in taxis—revealed another side of the complex encounter between the West and Islam. I felt that here was one of the few points of contact in a neutral zone between Muslims and foreigners where the Muslim could express his sentiments away from the security detail and police. If I had been a non-Muslim, the encounter would have left me feeling uncomfortable and even intimidated. The taxi had thus become a front line in the confrontation between Islam and the West. It was the Lynndie England situation in Abu Ghraib in reverse. Like England and her cohorts, the Arab taxi driver was perverting the ideals of his culture and fueling the charged, abrasive, and too often violent encounters between the two civilizations. To understand these developments in the Muslim world, one must look at current society there and the factors that shaped it.

On the political front, for example, Muslims are using local elections to respond to what they see as attacks from the West, voting in Islamic parties, which are more critical of the West than any others. This trend can be seen even in the North-West Frontier Province of Pakistan, which for the past century has maintained a fine balance between several political forces. The religious parties—collectively and somewhat contemptuously called the mullahs by others—never got more than 15 to 20 percent of the seats in the provincial assembly. After September 2001—with the increasing attacks on Islam begun in the United States, led by prominent religious figures such as Franklin Graham, Pat Robertson, Jerry Vines, and Jerry Falwell—the mullahs saw their chance. In the next elections they entered the political fray by declaring that they would fight for the honor of Islam whereas everyone else had compromised. Anti-American sentiments were so strong that this time the mullahs won almost every seat in the assembly, sweeping away what were once unbeatable tribal chiefs and princely figures. As a result, the critical Tribal Areas of the province, stretching along the Afghan border, began consorting with the Taliban, rumored to be in the area in growing numbers along with Osama bin Laden and al-Qaeda. Before long, large parts of the province were directly under the control of those openly sympathetic to the Taliban. With this strategic advantage, the Taliban became a serious threat to Western forces in Afghanistan. These events trail back to insensitive attacks on Islam and its Prophet, which thus may have placed American lives and interests abroad in jeopardy.

The confrontation between Islam and the West was soon spreading to other arenas as well. International tourism in Bali, Indonesia, for example, became a target of attack, intensifying social tensions in an already strained community of Muslims living on the Hindu-majority island. The invasion of global tourism had been the last straw for the culturally and religiously threatened Muslims, particularly with the announcement that *Playboy* was about to launch an Indonesian version of its magazine. An intense debate ensued over how to handle the crisis and how far an outside culture should be allowed to affect Indonesian values.

Just as our team was leaving Bali, it came across a *Time* magazine containing a two-page article on Indonesia's pornography laws.[36] The Muslims in Indonesia were seeing almost naked men and women on the beaches or dancing and drinking in discos, which violated their sense of Islamic propriety. This clash of cultures was behind the 2002 bombing of the discotheque in Bali that left several hundred people dead. "We could be going the way of the Taliban," lamented Leo Batubara, a member of the Indonesian Press Council, in the *Time* article.

The tensions between the demands of ideal Islam and the irresistible tidal wave of globalization, with its powerful stereotypes, were observed by Amineh, the young Muslim anthropologist on a tour of Bali to "get a real anthropological feel" of its culture.

We took a tour guide from our hotel to see a traditional Hindu dance illustrating the story of Rama and Sita. Our guide was Hindu and eager to express his knowledge of Bali in his English. . . . I asked the guide to explain from his perspective the Balinese bombing and his reply was that Bali was a peaceful place dominated by Hindu and Buddhist ideas of harmonious existence until, he paused, frowned disapprovingly and pointed to his clean-shaven chin, gesturing the shape of a beard and a turban on his head, i.e., implying Muslims.

To me, trained as an anthropologist, I found the Hindu guide's comment striking and one that possibly reflected a widely held perception about Muslims in Bali. Bali is a "Paradise Island"—the type one sees in Hollywood movies or reads about in novels. Its

A Hindu religious procession passes by in Bali, where Hindus are in a majority, although Indonesia itself, the world's largest Muslim nation, has a Muslim majority population. Traditionally peaceful, Bali has recently seen acts of terrorism aimed at encroaching western culture.

beaches and bikini-clad bodies, palm trees and orchids, sunshine and tropical weather, night clubs and expensive up-to-date modern hotels arouse the human senses and give the holiday-maker a sense that he or she has here all the self-gratifying comforts of this world. Yet it is this worldly paradise that seems to offend some groups of people who see themselves as battling hard in a temporary world to avoid wastrel superficiality, sensual pleasures, and carnal desires. Muslims make up the majority of the population of Indonesia, but are a minority in the Indonesian island of Bali, where the population is largely Hindu and Buddhist. Amongst this diverse population of Indonesian Muslims are more stringent groups who would go literally to the extreme end to blow themselves and many others up in night clubs and discothéques as a form of protest to the way of life described in the Balinese "Paradise Island" scenario.

An even more dramatic flashpoint between the West and Islam concerns the theological aspect of Islam, particularly since the publication of Salman Rushdie's controversial *The Satanic Verses* in 1988, the depiction of the Prophet in Danish cartoons, and questionable remarks by Pope Benedict XVI. To the West—and those who value free speech and freedom of expression—the right of an individual to say and write what he or she wishes is fundamental to civilization itself. For Muslims, any form of criticism of the Prophet is a serious transgression. Because the Prophet embodies the divine word of God, the Quran, an insult or a perceived insult to the Prophet is an attack both on the faith and on the person. Moreover, because the Prophet is known and loved as a father, husband, and leader in times of hardship, Muslims think of him in highly personal ways, even as a part of their own family. It is this intense love and personalization that largely explains the emotional response to perceived attacks, which are thought to indicate that the West is denouncing the core of their religious, cultural, and personal identity, and in turn their notions of honor and pride.

Akbar Ahmed (left), Amineh Ahmed (center), his eldest daughter and fellow anthropologist, and Hailey Woldt (right) with traditional Hindu dancers in Bali, who performed the monkey dance based on classic religious texts.

In Bali, Jonathan Hayden gets acquainted with a denizen of a sacred monkey temple. Hindus revere monkeys, as well as other creatures, which are featured positively in classic religious texts.

While Muslims have desired free speech, they have also underlined the need to respect people's beliefs and traditions. Muslims are aware of limitations to free speech because in their multicultural and multireligious societies, careless and disrespectful comments would degenerate into confrontation. Even in the United States, Mel Gibson's anti-Semitic comments, and those of comic actor Michael Richards (also known as "Kramer" from the *Seinfeld* series) shouting the objectionable word "nigger" repeatedly at young African Americans at a comedy club in 2006, caused understandable outrage. Such hateful remarks remind all of us of the nature of intolerance and prejudice. The African American and Jewish communities have faced terrible suffering and persecution in the past in different ways and in different historical contexts. The compassion, wisdom, dignity, and humor associated with their communities are therefore nothing short of the triumph of the human spirit and its refusal to be crushed.

Muslims note that no such outrage follows in the United States when there are equivalent slurs about Islam. The feeling that Muslims are being isolated and victimized has grown and has created resentment in many individuals. The violent response in some parts of the Muslim world is due primarily to a combination of the perception that Islam is under attack from the West and the emergence of the Deoband model, which emphasizes Islamic pride and stimulates Muslim emotions. In contrast, the enfeebled Ajmer model, which advocates calm discussion, and the Aligarh model, which urges the building of modern institutions such as free speech and allegiance to the nation-state, are becoming marginalized. Had the Aligarh model been dominant, the Muslim responses to the Danish cartoons and the Pope's remarks would have been to engage in debate and write letters. Because the Aligarh model has failed to provide a forum for expression or to represent Muslims, the nation-state and the Aligarh model are not a viable alternative in the Muslim world at present.

The Taj Syndrome

Muslim fury and despair arise not only from the perception that U.S. policies are misguided. There are also inner demons. Muslims today, especially those living in what were once the famed capitals of Islam such as Istanbul, Damascus, Cairo, and Delhi, suffer from what I call the "Taj Syndrome." A building like the Taj Mahal evokes the glittering past for Muslims. Its physical splendor juxtaposed with the painful and wretched present triggers a mixture of emotions—pride, anguish, and anger: pride at the splendor of the past, anguish at the reality of the present, and anger at the uncertainty of the bleak future. This is the Taj Syndrome, and Muslims of every kind are in one way or another affected by it: looking at the Taj Mahal, those of the Ajmer model see a timeless ethereal beauty that confirms for them the universal message of love; followers of the Deoband type are inspired to renew the struggle to revive the past and restore its glory; while those who subscribed to the Aligarh form see the splendor of Islamic civilization, long capable of synthesis and excellence, and hope it can once again be at the cutting edge of art, architecture, and knowledge.

The Taj, the very symbol of the power and compassion of Muslim rulers, now sits forlornly amidst a sea of squalid dwellings inhabited by impoverished Muslim artisans claiming descent from its builders. Visiting the Taj Mahal in Agra with my team, I experienced again the sophistication of concept, beauty of execution, and depth of spiritual thought of the architecture, symbolizing a civilization at its zenith. It reflects the most magnificent synthesis of both the Islamic and the Indic traditions. The Taj evokes the passions that move human beings—love, compassion, and sorrow—yet it also reaches out to concepts of the hereafter and forces visitors to confront themselves.

Islam once gave the world a rich civilization that included powerful empires such as the Abbasid, Ottoman, Safavid, and Mughal. Muslim rulers welcomed people of all faiths and were among the most benevolent and enlightened of history. Driven by the spirit of ijtihad, Muslims adapted the traditions of Islam to the changes taking place around them. Tradesmen created new caravan routes, moving goods and products between Asia, Africa, and Europe. The legendary "silk road" through central Asia, which linked China with the Muslim world, was a testimony to their thriving civilization. Ever since the time of the Prophet, who was also a merchant, Islam has held the trader at a certain level of respectability.

Knowledge, too, has always been held in high esteem. At the peak of Islamic civilization about 1,000 years ago, the court library in Córdoba contained some 400,000 books, while the largest library in Europe at the time had only about 600. Acknowledging the debt the West owes to Islam for retrieving Greek thought, which had laid the foundations for the European Renaissance, historian Philip Hitti notes that "had the researches of Aristotle, Galen, and Ptolemy been lost to posterity, the world would have been as poor as if they had never been produced."[37] Religious scholarship was encouraged along with the growth of literature, which explored new expressions of verse. Emphasis was placed on dialogue and understanding between those who believed in the Ajmer, Deoband, or Aligarh models. The great Islamic philosophers such as Imam al-Ghazzali reflect the balance between these three models. It is little wonder that Islamic civilization was the light and glory of the world in its day.

The Taj Syndrome is further reinforced by the state of the media in the Muslim world. On our journey, as mentioned in an earlier chapter, we saw satellite antennas and dishes everywhere, even in the poorest neighborhoods. In the midst of these crowded and depressing neighborhoods, Muslims see glamorous and seductive images from the West that challenge their traditional values—some of naked women in provocative poses, some

The Taj Mahal, built by the emperor Shah Jehan, reminds Muslims of the splendors of the past. The struggle between the emperor's sons, Dara Shikoh, the mystic, and Aurangzeb, the orthodox, resulted in Dara's death and reflects current debates concerning Islam.

of wars against fellow Muslims, and some of grandiose luxuries, all of which serve to disillusion Muslims with the outside world or with their own society.

The Taj Syndrome is symptomatic of the crisis in the Muslim world. Leadership, authority figures, relations with the state, the economy, how people view their neighbors and treat the women in their families, and religion itself are all caught up in the mixture of emotions engendered by the syndrome. This crisis is not a direct consequence of the events set in motion after September 11, as some commentators in the West believe, but has been under way for the past two centuries. The mounting anger and perception of injustice among Muslims in the wake of that fateful September day is but a further flare-up of the Muslim fire of unrest. One college student at Fatih University in Istanbul aptly described the Muslim world as "a sleeping bear that has been awakened. It is difficult to put that bear back to sleep."

That unrest, as we saw on our travels—especially in the great cities of the Muslim world—is rooted in the gaps between the rich elite and the poor, now reaching dangerous proportions. Large estates with magnificent houses similar to those in America's wealthiest communities sit amidst poverty and squalor. New office buildings and international hotels rise above a sea of makeshift homes and shops. The two sides are separated by watchdogs and armed security guards who check everyone entering the expensive homes and hotels to guard against suicide bombings. The poor feel not only left out but also angry at the realization that they have little chance of sharing the economic cake the elite seem to be consuming so greedily. As for the elite, their primary concern seems to be to protect the money that has come with international contracts and deals, in some cases from a lucky venture in globalization with a swift payback, much like the "dot-com" phenomenon in the United States. The Islamic injunction of giving to charity and providing for the community is sidestepped with excuses such as the "trickle-down theory," suggesting that if the wealthy spend enough money, eventually the poor will see some of it. Globalization is successfully injecting such communities with one of its more toxic characteristics—greed.

Meanwhile, the small apartments and shantytowns of the poor are becoming more crowded and rundown. In most of the cities I visited, the infrastructure was collapsing under the weight of the population explosion and constant influx of migrants from the rural areas. Water supplies, transportation, electricity, and public health facilities were erratic at best, sometimes not even available. Karachi and Jakarta are urban nightmares with large populations living in poverty. In Cairo, the poor live in such desperate circumstances that they have become squatters in cemeteries.

This is not to say that we saw no beneficial effects of globalization on our journey. Living standards were certainly higher in some places, Delhi being one, and the gap between rich and poor showed some signs of decreasing. In general, however, I saw only the rich growing richer from globalization. The elite of the oil-producing Muslim countries are perhaps the worst culprits, leading lives far removed from the majority of the ummah and in many respects from the ideals of Islam itself. The vulgar "conspicuous consumption" of the elite is apparent in the way they live, dress, and move physically. Their girths would suggest poverty must not exist in the Muslim world. The fact is that they are guzzling the honey of globalization all by themselves.

The ordinary Muslims who are watching the elite are not as willing to "ride the wave" of globalization. One fifty-year-old man in Indonesia said that he had recently seen "more dependency on technology, materialism, and selfishness" with a resulting "lack of good deeds, no sincerity, and the contamination of Western civilization." The danger is real as many are watching television several hours a day, surfing the Internet, and buying the latest technological products like iPods. Even a thirteen-year-old in Indonesia told us that technology had made "young people lazy and irresponsible" and dependent upon an "instant culture." Although a middle class is emerging in many places, its focus is not necessarily on re-creating Islamic values. What Muslims see on television both repels and attracts them, and this is the dilemma afflicting the Aligarh model.

While each Muslim country we visited could boast a few excellent centers of learning, the overall picture of education in the Muslim world is depressing. Comparative figures published by the United Nations Development Program and the World Bank consistently put Muslim countries at the bottom of the ladder. Their dismal educational performance is a particularly sore point because the pursuit of knowledge is the highest calling in Islam, some would say even higher than prayer itself, yet the number of educational or intellectual prizes won by Muslims on the international stage is small in proportion to their world population. In desperation, Muslim parents send their children to madrassahs with limited facilities and even more limited syllabi. In most Muslim societies, the few elite schools are too expensive and out of reach for the majority of the population and free public education offered by the state limited.

The education of the elite who study abroad unfortunately does not help Muslims resolve social ills. They return with a few Western phrases and clichés on their lips, and they make no serious attempt to relate the rich legacy of their own Islamic traditions to the great Western minds they study. A tradition of critical thinking has been missing for the past few decades in the Muslim world. Indeed, some Muslims appear blissfully unaware of the need to provide hard and sometimes painful answers to the difficult questions relating to the disconnect between the West and Muslim world. Their understanding of both worlds is often superficial, compartmentalized, and even manufactured by the West. When I asked a prominent Arab minister in Doha who his favorite author was, he replied with a broad grin, "Professor Bernard Lewis." He was clearly oblivious to the irony that an Arab might quote with such relish the quintessential Orientalist, accused by Arabs themselves of contributing to the Western misunderstanding of their culture and history. I wondered whether the seminal work of Edward Said on Orientalism had made any impact on the Muslim elite.

As someone who grew up in the mainstream of the Aligarh model, I am amazed at its slow but steady decline over the last decades. It is difficult to imagine now that Muslims were actively engaged in relating the traditions of their past with the conditions of the present, and doing so within the frame of ijtihad, or "innovative thinking" encouraged in Islam. These Muslims were at the cutting edge of change and were truly towering figures, with admirers both in the East and the West. Today their names redound in glory—Muhammad Abduh and Jamal Ad-Din Al-Afghani in the Middle East; Sir Sayyed, Jinnah, and Iqbal in South Asia. These thinkers were not isolated scholars living in ivory towers. Their ideas were a catalyst for change affecting the lives of millions of people.

What is evident is that the Aligarh form of leadership became corrupt and distorted during the second half of the twentieth century. While those who followed the Aligarh model strove for a modern democratic Muslim polity based on Western legal systems, they found the pressures of the cold war forced them to choose between either socialist or capitalist camps. Joining one or the other camp brought aid, weapons, and international standing but also led to a dependence on the source of this support and a lack of accountability to the state's citizenry. The resulting repressive regimes precluded the development of genuinely modernist Muslim societies. Gamal Abdel Nasser, for example, was a hero of Arab nationalism in the 1950s and 1960s, but he resorted to torture and executions to deal with orthodox Muslims such as Syed Qutb, who became a martyr for orthodox Islam after he was executed in 1966. Such acts of repression radicalized a large segment of the population and would reverberate during the next decades with each misstep taken by so-called democratic leaders, who were compromising the Aligarh model.

Another factor that hinders the development of democracy in most Muslim countries is that the army is by far better organized and trained than any other part of the establishment, to the exclusion of democratic systems of governance. There is a more sinister aspect to the lack of democracy, too. The intelligence services are now being widely used to persuade politicians and critics of the government to fall in line. Tactics can range from assassinations to straightforward blackmail or the abduction of family members. The army's anticorruption or antiterrorism agencies have become the most coercive authority to win over wavering politicians, poisoning the atmosphere almost as much as in the time of Saddam in Iraq. Ultimately, dictators rule through fear. When people are too frightened to stand up and speak their mind because of what happens to critics, democracy is further discouraged. Even if a democracy is present, political parties tend to be opportunistic and disorganized, and to easily shift alliances, abandoning their leaders when offered a better deal. When the military hanged Pakistan's most popular elected political leader, Zulfiqar Ali Bhutto, in 1979, people expected a storm of reaction, but nothing very much happened and life went on as normal. The new military dictator was hailed as a savior, and he ruled with an iron fist for over a decade, until his plane exploded mysteriously in midair.

The failure of the world powers and the helplessness of Muslim leaders to solve the long-standing problems of the Palestinians, Kashmiris, Chechens, and now Iraqis, Afghans, and Lebanese, have further angered Muslims. Political developments over the past century have left millions of Muslims displaced from their homes, surrounded by despair and uncertainty. The stagnation and lack of moral leadership have only added to Muslim anger and frustration, feeding directly into the Deoband model.

Most Muslims whom our team talked to felt dissatisfied with the state of affairs and desperately wanted change. Whatever misgivings Muslim commentators may have had about the American-led invasions of Afghanistan and Iraq, they were tempered with the hope that perhaps a new era of democracy would be introduced to these nations, and people would lead better lives. There was heady rhetoric about democracy, human rights, and civil liberties following the invasions. Unfortunately, the biggest challenge for both Kabul and Baghdad has been to maintain law and order. The rapid collapse of society into tribal and sectarian rivalries and killing dissipated whatever goodwill remained for the experiment in democracy, especially after scandals emerged of the almost casual cruelty inflicted on local people by American troops. The uncertainty of life for most people turned to despair and then anger. However loathed the Taliban in Afghanistan and Saddam in Iraq, people looked back with nostalgia to recent times that offered some semblance of stability. Thus in its attempts to improve its image, the United States was now in lower esteem than even the harshest of religious governments or the worst dictator.

"Fool Me Once, Shame on You—Fool Me Twice, Shame on Me"

While Dick Cheney and Donald Rumsfeld helped President Ronald Reagan—with advice from Henry Kissinger and Lewis—to change the world for the better by hastening the demise of the Soviet Union a quarter of a century ago, they also set in motion contradictory policies involving the Muslim world that plague us today. Even with the end of the cold war, cold war–era policies toward the Muslim world remained in place, partly because of the durability of some of the same players, with the same worldview.

Cheney, Rumsfeld, Paul Wolfowitz, and Kissinger still dominate and define American foreign policy, which continues to be directed at the "problem nations": the Palestinian territories, Iraq, Syria, and Iran.[38] The U.S. relationship with these countries remains problematic even after decades of American intervention. The same policies and tactics that failed with these Muslim nations earlier are again being employed for them by the same U.S. leaders. The chances of a different outcome this time are not high.

Broadly, U.S. policies toward the Muslim world are based on the assumption that Muslim leaders can be divided into two camps: the "moderate Muslims" and the "radical Islamists." The former are believed to want close ties with the West and make large defense purchases from it or agreements of mutual interest; the latter are the bearded clerics in black robes who make radical anti-American statements, take American hostages, and are inherently evil. The "good guys" are thus separated from the "bad guys." Washington's policy has been to see the world in this simplistic binary frame and act upon it.

The American public has yet to recognize the irony that the leaders they are looking to for safety are the same ones who brought today's "evildoers" to power and are again keeping them there with their flawed policies. A quarter of a century after U.S. policies, directly or indirectly, helped bring Khomeini to power in Iran, they have precipitated another sequence of events that inflated the prominence of anti-American Shia leaders: Mahmoud Ahmadinejad in Iran, Muqtada al Sadr in Iraq, and Hasan Nasrallah in Lebanon. The popularity of these leaders is a direct consequence of their defiance and ability to bait the United States and Israel. U.S. policies, aiming to check these very "extremist" Islamic leaders, instead created an arc of revivalist Shia charismatic leadership in the heart of the Muslim world, thus upsetting the delicate ethnic and sectarian balances in the region. The emergence of the Shia leaders, who tower like giants even on the Sunni horizon, may be a temporary phenomenon, and ethnic and sectarian instincts may soon reassert themselves, but for the present time, ill-conceived Western policies have succeeded in bridging the deepest divide in Islam in some parts of the Middle East. Throughout our journey, many Sunni quoted Shia leaders as their role models. And despite the severe sectarian violence in Iraq, the larger perception that Islam is under attack still guides Muslim emotions.

Two commentators from the Muslim world provide valuable perspectives here: a Pakistani journalist and an Egyptian scholar, each from an important capital in a Muslim nation that is a key ally of the United States. They provide us with a fairly clear picture of how Muslims are viewing current events. The first, widely read Pakistani columnist Ayaz Amir, had this comment to make about the situation in the Muslim world after the Israeli invasion of Lebanon:

> Hezbollah already is a symbol of defiance far beyond the confines of Lebanon, its leader, Sheikh Hasan Nasrallah, arguably the most popular figure in the Islamic world today. So what will the Israeli aggression against Lebanon, and American policy supporting it, achieve? Hezbollah will still be around. But with the one big difference that more young men and women will be ready to join the Islamist cause, more people holding up Hasan Nasrallah as an icon of resistance.
>
> Personally I find myself in a strange position. I am as secular in my thinking, if not more than most other people. . . . My secularism, however, collides with an unpleasant reality: the picture of the Islamic world in thrall to American power, Muslim elites dancing to America's tune, Muslim countries little better than satellites orbiting around the U.S. I see this in my own country where there is too much American

influence, much of it of the wrong kind. If the Muslim world is to progress, this bondage has to be broken.

Even democracy won't come to the Muslim world unless this influence is overthrown. It's one of the biggest myths of our time that America wants democracy to flourish in the lands of Islam. How can it when democracy doesn't suit its interests? If we have popular governments in Muslim countries the first thing they will demand is an end to American hegemony.

The Americans were happy with the shah, they can't abide democratic Iran. They can't abide Hamas which is the elected representative of the Palestinian people. They can't abide Hezbollah which has a representative status in Lebanese politics. Democracy in the Muslim world and the interests of American foreign policy just do not mix. That is why any kind of popular movement in the Muslim world finds itself on a collision course with U.S. interests.

Now if we take it as correct that American domination of the Islamic world is not a good thing and deserves to be resisted, it becomes hard for so-called secularists like myself to close their eyes to the uncomfortable fact that the only forces resisting this domination, often successfully, are those which, in some form or the other, draw their inspiration from Islam.

Savour then the irony of it. The "war on terror" was meant to fight and contain radical Islam. Instead, the Bush administration has turned out to be its biggest supporter, through its arrogance, lies and blind support of Israel giving radical Islam an impetus it could never have hoped to achieve on its own.[39]

Second, Egyptian scholar Saad Eddin Ibrahim traces the rise of Nasrallah and correlates it with the lackluster standing of the Arab establishment leaders:

In more than four weeks of fighting against the strongest military machine in the region, Hezbollah held its own and won the admiration of millions of Arabs and Muslims. People in the region have compared its steadfastness with the swift defeat of three large Arab armies in the Six-Day War of 1967. Hasan Nasrallah, its current leader, spoke several times to a wide regional audience through his own al-Manar network as well as the more popular al-Jazeera. Nasrallah has become a household name in my own country, Egypt.

According to the preliminary results of a recent public opinion survey of 1,700 Egyptians by the Cairo-based Ibn Khaldun Center, Hezbollah's action garnered 75 percent approval, and Nasrallah led a list of 30 regional public figures ranked by perceived importance. He appears on 82 percent of responses, followed by Iranian President Mahmoud Ahmadinejad (73 percent), Khaled Meshal of Hamas (60 percent), Osama bin Laden (52 percent) and Mohammed Mahdi Akef of Egypt's Muslim Brotherhood (45 percent).

The pattern here is clear, and it is Islamic. And among the few secular public figures who made it into the top 10 are Palestinian Marwan Barghouti (31 percent) and Egypt's Ayman Nour (29 percent), both of whom are prisoners of conscience in Israeli and Egyptian jails, respectively.

None of the current heads of Arab states made the list of the 10 most popular public figures. While subject to future fluctuations, these Egyptian findings suggest the direction in which the region is moving. The Arab people do not respect the ruling regimes, perceiving them to be autocratic, corrupt and inept. They are, at best, ambivalent about the fanatical Islamists of the bin Laden variety. More mainstream Islamists with broad support, developed civic dispositions and services to provide are the most likely actors in building a new Middle East. In fact, they are already doing so through the Justice and Development Party in Turkey, the similarly named PJD in Morocco, the Muslim Brotherhood in Egypt, Hamas in Palestine and, yes, Hezbollah in Lebanon.[40]

Even before the Lebanese-Israeli conflict erupted in 2006, authoritative American voices were questioning whether certain U.S. policies in relation to Israel were detrimental to both countries. Clayton E. Swisher, director of programs for the Middle East Institute, for example, has argued: "If we are ever to repair our relations with the Arab and Muslim world, we must have an honest and open examination regarding our role in the Arab-Israeli conflict. Too many American, Israeli, and Arab lives depend on it. Considering all the threats facing our country in the Middle East, the time for petty politics and mythification has passed. There are many sides to this complex story, yet the one-sided mantra of Arab blame is still all-pervasive."[41] A highly controversial article on this subject by John Mearsheimer and Stephen Walt, "The Israel Lobby," triggered a national debate among intellectuals, one of whom, Scott Ritter, an expert on the geopolitics of nuclear weapons, linked Israeli policies to the neocons in Washington.[42] In Ritter's view, the war in Iraq, however great a disaster it was, and the talk of attacking Iran were part of the same nexus between Israel and the neocons.

A debate was also emerging around the role and position of dictators and the support they have received from the United States for decades in the struggle against communism. Since 9/11 the rhetoric and role of dictators have changed subtly, although their relationship with their people remains the same. They, too, talk of democracy while continuing to suppress their people. Having learned to exploit their distant masters in Washington, they have turned the situation to their own advantage by crushing any opposition to their power and labeling it as "terrorist," with Washington then giving them a blank check to continue committing human rights violations and accumulating unchecked power and wealth.

David Wallechinsky of the *Washington Post* recently defined a dictator as "a head of state who exercises arbitrary authority over the lives of its citizens and who cannot be removed from power through legal means. The worst commit terrible human-rights abuses."[43] Drawing on information from global human rights organizations, including Human Rights Watch, Freedom House, Reporters without Borders, and Amnesty International, Wallechinsky finds that five of the world's top ten dictators and eight out of the top twenty are Muslim. In 2005 and 2006, a Muslim ranked number one—Omar al-Bashir, the president of Sudan. Both Moammar Gaddafi of Libya and Pervez Musharraf of Pakistan were in the top ten in 2005 but then dropped to the top twenty, "not because their conduct has improved, but because other dictators have gotten worse."[44]

It should also be pointed out that at least three of the Muslim dictators are closely allied to and supported by the United States: King Abdullah of Saudi Arabia, Islam Karimov of Uzbekistan, and Pervez Musharraf of Pakistan, facts that are not widely reported in the U.S. media. The United States, convinced that it had to choose between a Muslim dictator and a Muslim religious leader, invariably found the former more attractive than the latter when it saw a rising tide of Islamic fanaticism. As President

Franklin D. Roosevelt once put it when making similar choices in the South American context: "He may be a son of a bitch, but he's our son of a bitch."

Iran provides a good example of how the United States has gotten into difficulties by supporting autocratic leaders. The story goes back at least half a century. In the early 1950s, the democratically elected prime minister of Iran, Mohammad Mossadegh, upset the United Kingdom by nationalizing the Anglo-Iranian Oil Company. With the help of the United States, the United Kingdom deposed Mossadegh and brought the shah of Iran, Mohammad Reza Pahlavi, back to power. The United States justified its support under its policy of containment, which sought to safeguard U.S. economic interests and stop the spread of communism.

Beginning with the Kennedy administration, the United States worked to improve Iran's infrastructure through massive loans to the country's development bank. Funds went into agricultural and industrial projects such as textile and cement plants, pest and water control projects, and the creation of agricultural cooperatives. They helped establish health programs in Iranian universities, created a network of rural health care centers, and set up programs in the United States to train qualified Iranians as doctors and public health care officials.[45] When Richard Nixon assumed office in the early 1970s, however, U.S. emphasis turned from developing Iran to doing business there. Meanwhile, the shah made increasingly outlandish attempts to safeguard American aid by demonstrating the power of the "new Iran," in the grand tradition of earlier Persian empires under Darius and Cyrus the Great. He staged spectacular events, including a theatrical coronation for himself in 1967. An even greater event in 1971 in honor of Cyrus featured the best the West had to offer, ranging from Parisian chefs to the finest Western china. Fine ceremonies were presented for the benefit of Western diplomats, and businessmen found Iran to be a gold mine for their operations and a viable market for services and technology. The shah's displays may have worked to his advantage in securing Western support, but they alienated the Muslim population.

In the wake of the Vietnam war, U.S. foreign policy sought to deal with regional crises through proxies rather than direct military involvement, a policy that became known as the Nixon Doctrine. Both the Nixon and Ford administrations, convinced that Iran was an effective cold war ally, readily endorsed the shah's concept of Iran's policing the Persian Gulf area.

They permitted the shah to acquire virtually unlimited quantities of any non-nuclear weapons the United States could produce. Within a few years, he had built up what was the fifth or sixth largest army in the world. By 1976 it had an estimated 3,000 tanks, 890 helicopter gunships, more than 200 advanced fighter aircraft, the largest fleet of hovercraft in any country, 9,000 anti-tank missiles, and much more equipment either on hand or on order from the United States and its allies.[46]

For its part, the United States sought to develop Iran's nuclear program. In 1975 Secretary of State Henry Kissinger signed a national security document, U.S.-Iran Nuclear Co-operation, laying out the details of the sale of nuclear energy equipment to Iran. In 1976 President Gerald Ford signed a directive offering Tehran the opportunity to buy and operate a U.S.-built reprocessing facility for extracting plutonium nuclear reactor fuel. President Ford's team—which included Dick Cheney, who had succeeded Donald Rumsfeld as chief of staff, and Paul Wolfowitz, who oversaw nonproliferation issues at the Arms Control and Disarmament Agency—not only endorsed Iranian plans to build a massive nuclear energy industry but also worked hard to complete a multibillion-dollar deal that would have given Tehran control of large quantities of plutonium and enriched uranium, the two pathways to a nuclear bomb. In addition, it continued efforts to supply Iran with nuclear technology. U.S. companies, led by Westinghouse, stood to gain $6.4 billion from the sale of six to eight nuclear reactors and parts.[47]

The increasing influence of the United States, through billions of dollars intended for business purposes and oil deals, served to widen the gap between the rich and poor at an alarming rate. As the shah and his Western corporate backers enjoyed lavish celebrations, millions languished in poverty. When a tangible backlash to the shah's obsessively pro-Western stance began to grow in the early 1960s, the shah became increasingly authoritarian, unleashing his notorious secret police, SAVAK, to deal with the dissent. The regime's opponents ranged from socialists and Marxists to conservative Muslims, some "moderate Muslims," and elements of both the rich and poor. Anti-Americanism also grew.

One of the only figures able to stand up to the shah's government and SAVAK was Ayatollah Ruhollah Khomeini, a cleric teaching Islamic ethics at the Fayziyah Madrassah in Qum. Believing that Islam was under attack in Iran by the United States, Khomeini had no scruples about saying this publicly and in 1963 took the first step in what became a sustained attack on the shah, whom he portrayed as an enemy of Islam. Khomeini protested the cruelty and injustice of the shah's rule, torture, and wicked suppression of all opposition, with denouncements of the United States and Israel as well. He spoke loudly and passionately on behalf of the poor, calling on the shah to leave his palaces and visit the shantytowns of south Tehran. The shah, alleged Khomeini, wanted to destroy Islam itself: "Our country, our Islam are in danger," he said in 1963, "we are worried and saddened by the situation of this ruined country. We hope to God it can be reformed."[48] He further declared Iran an American colony, asking, "What nation would submit to such indignity?" and lamented that he expected many would die in the coming winter, "God forbid, from cold and starvation."[49]

Khomeini also railed against the immunity the shah had granted U.S. forces, declaring the shah had "sold" Iran's independence: "If some American's servant, some American's cook assassinates your *marja* [inspiring religious figure, ayatollah] in the middle of the bazaar or runs over him, the Iranian police do not have the right to apprehend him! Iranian courts do not have the right to judge him! . . . [T]hey have reduced the Iranian people to a level lower than that of an American dog. If someone runs over a dog belonging to an American, he will be prosecuted. But if an American cook runs over the shah, the head of state, no one will have the right to interfere with him."[50] In a society still defined by tribal notions of honor, these actions inflamed the national pride of ordinary Iranians and their sense of public indignation.

Following this speech, Khomeini was forced into exile in Iraq, and the government launched another crackdown on dissent. It targeted the madrassahs for supposedly teaching hate against the government, torturing to death Ayatollah Riza Saidi for objecting to a conference to promote American investment in Iran and for denouncing the regime as a "tyrannical agent of imperialism."[51] Tension mounted in the late 1960s and early 1970s as hundreds were killed amid the crackdowns, and inflation began running rampant, while many villages remained desperately poor. These are the very conditions in which the Deoband model thrives and rejects the "democracy" and "free trade" promoted by the United States.

Recognizing that it was only infuriating the masses by effectively trying to erase aspects of Islamic culture, the government tried a different approach. Islam was to be "modernized" and dubbed "civil Islam." To facilitate this transition and show that the government in fact honored Islam, it formed a new agency that would rely on "mullahs of moderation" to go out to the masses and promote literacy, build infrastructure, and vaccinate livestock, thereby showing that Islam was compatible with the modern age. This was the Aligarh model. To the shah's once loyal subjects, however, the friendly hand reaching out seemed too little too late. By then Iranians were filled with such resentment and anger that not even these positive reforms could erase the memory of his arrogance, lack of compassion, and unwillingness to work with different groups issuing legitimate demands for democratic participation. Compounding their anger was the perception that Americans were the real power behind the throne.

The public then turned to Khomeini as a credible and promising alternative to the shah, using modern technology such as cassette tapes to spread his defiant messages from his home in exile. He gained further credibility with the ordinary Muslims when a son who was with him in exile died suddenly, and it was assumed SAVAK was involved.

Like other Iranian figures of the time, such as Ali Shariati, Khomeini believed that Shia Islam carried a very modern message in an age plagued by inequality, misery, and uncertainty: "Islam is the religion of militant individuals who are committed to faith and justice. It is the religion of those who desire freedom and independence. It is the school of those who struggle against imperialism." Islam, he said, championed the modern ideals of liberty that the West claimed to have, and he urged Iranians to reject Western culture and to rediscover their own heritage: "We have forgotten our identity, and replaced it with a Western identity, . . . becoming enslaved to alien ideals."[52]

As social conditions worsened and disenchantment with the government increased, all sections of society, including the artistic community and business leaders, joined the clerics in a chorus of protest against the government. By now, the upper classes, the lower classes, and everyone in between despised the United States, and violent protests picked up. From 1971 to 1975 there were thirty-one bombings and bomb threats against American organizations and facilities, including two bombings of the embassy itself.[53]

In strongly anti-American rhetoric echoing the sentiments of all sections of Iranian society, Khomeini painted the United States as a source of evil in the world. Apparently unable to understand the situation,

Americans clung to the view that Iran was central to U.S. business interests and strategic geopolitical goals—the elite of Tehran were people they could work with. In 1977 President Jimmy Carter arrived in Tehran on a state visit and toasted the shah with the extraordinarily ill-timed observation that Iran was an "island of stability in a turbulent corner of the world," which it owed to the shah's "enlightened leadership," and was "a tribute to the respect, admiration and love" the Iranian people had for him. Little more than a week after Carter left Iran, the revolution was in full swing at the behest of Khomeini from Paris, and riots broke out across Iran.

While the United States continued to insist that a revolution was not imminent and to express its loyalty to the shah, graffiti appeared on the streets of Tehran casting Jimmy Carter as Yazid, the ruler who martyred the Prophet's grandson Hussein in 680 C.E., and the shah as Shimr, the general Yazid dispatched to massacre Hussein and his army. It is important to understand just how powerfully evocative the names of Hussein and Yazid are for the Shia: the former is the ultimate symbol of heroism in the face of tyranny and the latter that of evil itself. This perception was reinforced by SAVAK's brutal crackdown on demonstrators, which left many dead in Qum and elsewhere, encouraging Iranians to see themselves as martyrs rising up against the tyranny they had withstood for far too many years.

Although the United States expressed steadfast support for the shah, it was wary of a bloodbath. It had invested so much in Iran and so many of its citizens were living in Iran and Iranians in America that it was reluctant to do anything that could jeopardize their position. Yet it could not escape the realization that the shah was rapidly losing influence, especially when demonstrators turned out in the hundreds of thousands in August 1978 to protest the introduction of martial law. On September 8 SAVAK opened fire into a crowd in Jaleh square, a practice that had become routine whenever and wherever large crowds gathered in 1978, and killed hundreds of protesters. Nevertheless, President Carter called the shah after the Jaleh incident to express America's unwavering support, which pleased the shah so much that he published their conversation. To many Iranians, it appeared as though the shah were being congratulated by Carter on the massacre.[54]

As the crisis spiraled out of control, the United States grew increasingly impatient with the shah. Realizing its interests in Iran were in grave danger, the administration implored him to act in any way he could to stabilize the country, even if it meant stepping down in favor of an appointed successor. Khomeini then returned to Iran, greeted at the airport by a million people, and the shah's regime collapsed like a house of cards.

In October 1979 the hated shah was admitted to the United States for medical treatment but was subsequently refused asylum and asked to find refuge elsewhere. This refusal, perhaps intended to show Muslims that the Americans were distancing themselves from the shah, backfired—merely confirming for Muslims that Americans had no sense of honor or loyalty even toward an ally who had been so faithful to them. Honor and loyalty, as explained in chapter 3, are central to Muslim culture, and this action highlighted the dramatic differences between the two societies. In the chaos after the revolution, students overran the American embassy and seized hostages, refusing to relinquish them until the shah returned to Iran for trial. While still in exile, Khomeini had opposed an earlier takeover attempt by Marxists but lent this new action by a disorganized group of angry student revolutionaries his support. Remembering the 1953 coup, they were convinced that the U.S. Central Intelligence Agency (CIA) was heavily involved in Iran and would soon act to reinstate the shah. The students stormed the embassy both to forestall a new coup and to avenge the 1953 overthrow.

Radicals now seized control of the revolution, sidelining those who did not fall in step and labeling them supporters of America and thus enemies of the revolution. The hostage standoff lasted 444 days and poisoned relations between the United States and Iran. The students grew frustrated when it seemed that more Americans were not taking notice of the revolution, a key motive for seizing the hostages in the first place. As the crisis wore on and relations with the United States worsened, the students and Khomeini shored up their position inside Iran.

In early 1980 the United States approached the UN Security Council for assistance, hoping sanctions would be imposed on Iran. This idea was opposed by the Soviet Union, however, which had just launched an invasion of Afghanistan, fundamentally altering the geopolitical landscape. The U.S. National Security Council discussed many other strategies for getting the hostages back, including military strikes and blockades. It even considered launching a coup against the revolutionary government but ultimately decided against such a move.

Instead, a group from the U.S. Army Delta Force went into Iran to rescue the hostages with helicopters. The mission, dubbed Operation Eagle's Claw, was a complete failure. Poor weather conditions, which the army had overlooked, caused one helicopter to drop out of the mission with mechanical failure and another to collide with a C-130 transport plane, killing eight crew members. For the Carter administration, the military option was now permanently off the table, forcing the most powerful nation in the world to simply wait until the Iranians were ready to release the hostages. Although they showed some signs in this direction in mid-1980, Khomeini decided to wait until January 1981, on the eve of Ronald Reagan's inauguration, to prove, it is said, that he could unseat an American president just as the CIA had unseated Mossadegh in 1953.

Almost overnight, the United States not only lost its key ally in the region but also inadvertently put into power an extreme Deoband-model leadership that saw the United States as the "Great Satan." Matters could have taken a far different course—if the United States had restored diplomatic relations with Iran immediately after Khomeini's revolution and underlined its respect for Islam as a religion that could accommodate democracy; if it had helped strengthen the new Iranian democracy by assisting with elections, developing civil services, and engaging with educational institutions; if it had not launched what Iranians perceived to be a media onslaught on their culture and religion; and if it had addressed the *people* of the nation through some strong gestures of goodwill to signify a change from the dictatorship of the years past. Although there would have been a residue of anti-American feeling, the aftermath of the hostage crisis and the subsequent steps along the path to the present confrontation could have been avoided. Yet the United States seemed unfazed by its experience in Iran: it soon became the patron of another dictator, Saddam Hussein, also another future enemy.

Following the revolution, Iran took growing interest in the Shia of Iraq, who were being persecuted under the government of Saddam Hussein, and urged them to launch a jihad against the Iraqi dictator. The Iranians frequently referred to Saddam as a "puppet of Satan" and accused him of being "mentally ill."[55] For his part, Saddam had been watching the Iranian situation through the 1970s with a concerned eye, especially after Khomeini threatened to export the revolution to Iraq, notably to the holy city of Karbala. Seeing what Khomeini had already accomplished against the shah, Saddam thought his fears were justified. Many figures from the shah's military fled in droves to Iraq, where they attempted to persuade Baghdad to help them regain their country. Some said that the Iranian army had been plagued by desertions and purges (hundreds of political dissidents had been executed). Convinced that the Iranian revolution could be reversed in favor of a more friendly government to Baghdad, Saddam decided to launch a surprise invasion of Iran. More to the point, Iraq would gain oil revenue, and Saddam would become the undisputed master of the Arab world. So, on September 22, 1980, Saddam began a long and bloody war that would claim more than a million lives.

The United States began giving significant support to Iraq. In February 1982 it removed Iraq from its list of states supporting international terrorism, thus paving the way for a significant boost in U.S.-Iraqi trade relations. In December 1984, merely a month after the reestablishment of diplomatic relations, the newly opened U.S. embassy in Baghdad began supplying the Iraqi army with important military intelligence. At the same time, Washington nearly doubled Iraq's credits for food products and agricultural equipment, from $345 million in 1984 to $675 million in 1985. In late 1987 Iraq was promised $1 billion credit for fiscal year 1988, the largest such credit given to any single country in the world.[56] The U.S. military also intervened in the war directly, sinking Iranian ships in the Persian Gulf.

With the war progressing toward a stalemate, Iraq grew frustrated by its inability to score decisive victories and decided to try using chemical weapons. By late 1983 Baghdad had stockpiled enough mustard gas for the purpose, soon followed by choking agents such as phosgene, and then nerve agents such as tabun, soman, and sarin. Saddam's chemical attacks on Iran inflicted horrific damage mainly on unprotected civilians. Iranians scrambled to purchase gas masks, but these offered little protection against the more advanced nerve agents, lethal on exposed skin. Many Iranian men who had grown beards could not wear the masks properly and died. In all, Iraq's chemical agents probably killed about 50,000 Iranians during the war.[57] In the closing months of the Iran-Iraq war in 1988, Saddam launched his worst chemical attack on Kurds and their Iranian backers in Halabja, massacring at least 5,000 people.[58] The Kurdish areas of Iraq were not only subjected to chemical weapons, but their villages were also destroyed and their populations transferred to labor camps. Almost certainly aware of these operations, the United States, in violation of the 1925 Geneva protocols and in defiance of the United Nations, had authorized the sale to Iraq of poisonous chemicals and deadly biological viruses, such as anthrax and bubonic plague. The U.S. Department of Commerce also approved the export of insecticides to Iraq, despite widespread suspicions that they were being used for chemical warfare. In February 1984, an Iraqi military spokesman issued this chilling warning to Iran: "The invaders should know that for every harmful insect, there is an insecticide capable of annihilating it . . . and Iraq possesses this annihilation insecticide."[59]

The previous year a senior State Department official, Jonathan T. Howe, told Secretary of State George P. Shultz that intelligence reports showed Iraqi troops were resorting to "almost daily use of chemical weapons" against the Iranians. But the Reagan administration had already committed itself to a large-scale diplomatic and political overture to Baghdad, culminating in several visits by Donald Rumsfeld, the president's recently appointed special envoy to the Middle East. Iraq was supplied by a multitude of Western corporations, including Bechtel, Union Carbide, and Honeywell. CIA director William Casey used a Chilean company, Cardoen, to supply Iraq with cluster bombs intended to disrupt Iranian human-wave attacks, where thousands of martyrs would rush the Iraqi lines.[60]

The United States was determined to do anything it could to stop Iran, which included supporting Saddam, an authoritarian dictator, and was creating another "shah of Iran" situation for itself. Had the United States respected international laws and continued to observe its highest ideals, Americans would not have the stain of this Middle East blood on their hands, which has not been forgotten in that part of the world. Nor would it have waged two wars with Saddam that have resulted in so many thousands of lives being lost.

Not only have lessons from the spectacular collapse of the shah of Iran and the equally spectacular rise of Khomeini been ignored, but policies from that debacle have once again been activated. The pundits and politicians who misled the American people then appear on a similar track once again with regard to the threat of Syria and Iran, even while problems in Iraq and Afghanistan remain unresolved. Indeed, it seems Americans have run into a dead end with Ahmadinejad. Foreign policy experts who counseled the shah to ignore the Islamic voices are now advising the U.S.

administration to ignore them. This is only creating resentment and agitation against the United States. Moreover, whereas before Americans had an alternative "secular" government to work with, there are only Islamic parties to deal with now, all of which require different and nuanced approaches. As it is, Americans are ignoring too many Muslim governments and genuine popular movements, instead misunderstanding and labeling them "terrorists." Thus Americans are losing and alienating vast populations and making enemies of them, rather than forging a working relationship that could develop into support and friendship.

When Mahmoud Ahmadinejad, backed by hard-line clerics, became president of Iran in the summer of 2005, it ended the sporadic but steady talk of dialogue between civilizations that his predecessor Khatami had initiated.[61] Already unstable with the entrenchment of Western troops in two bloody wars in Iraq and Afghanistan, the world now lurched toward an even more dangerous level of confrontation.

Nasty rhetoric, broadcast in the media, has painted Ahmadinejad as a Hitler in the United States and Bush as the great Satan in Iran. Yet Ahmadinejad's worldview has been directly shaped by U.S. policy toward Iran in the 1970s and 1980s, when he was a student leader during the revolution and later fought in the Iran-Iraq war. Ahmadinejad's highly provocative statements calculated to infuriate the United States and Israel need to be seen in this light. I suspect he believes that American troops are now so helplessly trapped in the quicksand of Iraq that the United States has been reduced to a toothless tiger. What is undeniable, though, is that Ahmadinejad's extreme statements have gained him popularity with ordinary Muslims, even among the Sunni as we saw on our journey.

Lebanon, too, fits neatly into the Iranian worldview. When the newly formed, anti-American government of Ayatollah Khomeini looked out at the world to find similar instances in which Muslims were being dominated and oppressed, particularly fellow Shia, it quickly focused its attention on Lebanon. Israel had invaded Lebanon in 1978 to stop the Palestine Liberation Organization (PLO) from attacking northern Israel with rockets. In 1982 the Israelis pushed all the way to Beirut and occupied the city, seeking to establish a buffer zone in Southern Lebanon. The Israeli occupation of Lebanon was often brutal and led to widespread dissent, especially among the Shia. To fight the occupation, the new government in

Iran took money and weapons to Lebanon, which it used to form a militant organization that could struggle not only against the Israelis but also against America. Countering both the United States and Israel, Hezbollah embraced suicide bombings during its 1983 attack on the U.S. Marine barracks in Beirut, a new maneuver introduced in 1981 when an Islamic Shia group attacked the Iraqi embassy in Beirut. Hezbollah and Iran viewed these as missions of "self-martyrdom," not suicide, which is forbidden in the Quran.[62] When Hamas among the Palestinians began the use of suicide bombings, it spread from Shia Islam to Sunni Islam to become the militants' weapon of choice against the West. After the American invasion of Afghanistan and Iraq, Sunni and Shia were both employing suicide bombing to battle each other, challenge the establishment, and fight Western troops. Soon the suicide bomber was making his—and even her—impact felt in other Sunni-dominated countries like Saudi Arabia, Jordan, and Pakistan. Muslim outrage at tyranny and injustice had combined with tribal notions of revenge and honor to create new, controversial, and apocalyptic interpretations among scholars of the Quranic notion of suicide.

With this context in mind, one can more readily compare the perspectives of the September 19, 2006, speeches of Presidents Bush and Ahmadinejad before the United Nations. Directing his remarks to the Iranian people, President Bush said that although "your rulers have chosen to deny you liberty and to use your nation's resources to fund terrorism and fuel extremism and pursue nuclear weapons," he was hopeful for "the day when you can live in freedom, and America and Iran can be good friends and close partners in the cause of peace." Ahmadinejad presented several criticisms, noting the UN Security Council had failed to call for an immediate cease-fire after war broke out between Israel and Hezbollah in Lebanon in 2006. It took thirty-four days to arrive at a truce to end the conflict: "The Security Council sat idly by for so many days, witnessing the cruel scenes of atrocities against the Lebanese . . . Why?" asked Ahmadinejad. He also stated defiantly: "I am against the policies chosen by the U.S. government to run the world because these policies are moving the world toward war."[63]

Although different on the surface, the remarks by Bush and Ahmadinejad are quite similar in their understanding of what the Abrahamic faiths call the end of time. It is this understanding that shapes their view of the world. Both believe in a final once-and-for-all battle between good and evil and each thinks that he represents good as much as his opponent embodies evil. Both also believe that Jesus will return to earth and join them against their opponents—and here the paradox that both Christianity and Islam belong to the Abrahamic family overwhelms the argument and reduces it to absurdity. Most striking, each believes he was specifically chosen to lead his nation by a divine power and actively propagates his eschatological vision. Bush believes that Jesus is on his side—when asked to name his favorite book, he invariably replies the Bible—while Ahmadinejad believes in exactly the same thing, that is, God is on his side. According to Muslim tradition, the end of time will be marked by the return of Jesus Christ, who will fight the evil forces of the *Dajjal*, who is the Muslim version of the anti-Christ. For devout Shia Muslims like Ahmadenijad, this moment is of added significance because it will pave the way for the return of the Hidden Imam, a direct descendant of the Prophet, who will fight alongside Jesus Christ against the anti-Christ.

Bush's Christian belief demands that he secure Jerusalem in preparation for Jesus's return, just as Ahmadinejad's Muslim belief requires him to welcome the return of the Hidden Imam, whose arrival would herald the coming of Jesus. Both are committed to hastening the process that would bring Jesus back to earth. As legitimately elected leaders of two major nations, these men are actually reflecting the beliefs of a large segment of their population.

The American campaign to prevent Iran from developing a uranium-enrichment program and Iran's determination to do so needs to be seen within this context. Each country's foreign policy was based on the vilification and abuse of the other's president and culture. That helps explain why, at the World Affairs Council conference in Philadelphia in 2006 (see chapter 4), Henry Kissinger laid down an outline for a nuclear assault on Iran. Only a few weeks later, the Middle East erupted in war when Israel invaded Lebanon and American commentators openly clamored for a nuclear strike against Iran to prevent it from acquiring nuclear technology. Iran was not Iraq or Afghanistan, which were smaller, more impoverished, and less homogeneous nations. A nuclear strike on Iran would not only inflame the world's Muslim Shia population but also destabilize Iran's important neighbors Pakistan and Saudi Arabia, key American allies. The complicated interplay between confused foreign policy and theology was driving the world to the brink of a global war.

These policies are making the Ajmer model irrelevant and the Aligarh model little more than an excuse to compromise with the West. Muslims who consider themselves under attack from the West, not only militarily but also culturally, see little point in talking about Ajmer universal humanism and, given the established track record of U.S. foreign policy, have little hope of support for democratic leaders of the Aligarh model unless they are prepared to surrender national interests. That is why so many Muslims rally to the Deoband model. But because the United States refuses to talk to them, communications break down, the same old arguments of the past few decades resurface, the same old policies are implemented, and the same disasters take shape.

As Americans struggle to either help the Muslim world or to control it, the situation only seems to grow more chaotic and to continually echo the past. The Muslim world notices this and is not fooled by U.S. talk of democracy. Instead it awaits the predictable—and avoidable—disasters that loom on the horizon.

Even now, a radical shift in policies toward the Muslim world could avert those disasters, both in the long and short term. A giant step in the way of creating trust and goodwill would be to reach out to the Muslim world and emphasize respect for its culture and religion. The United States should also match its rhetoric about democracy with genuine support for the democratic process irrespective of the need for convenient allies. Similarly, rather than giving military aid to Muslim countries, it should develop educational programs and facilities that would change the thinking of the young Muslims now schooled by radical madrassahs. The Muslims' hateful view of the Americans comes from being at the receiving end of American weapons used by either their dictators or American soldiers to the point where they attribute these brutal actions to the United States as a whole. If these policy shifts were implemented in the war on terror, it would change the relationship dramatically and reduce the number of current and future enemies. None of these initiatives are expensive or require anything more than applying sensible thinking to the complicated issues that have U.S. policymakers in a quandary following the backlash against the neocon enterprise and the "Bush Doctrine," reflected in the 2006 midterm election results: the Democrats won control of both the House and Senate (the Senate by a narrow margin), widely seen as a referendum on the war in Iraq and the war on terror.

As the cycle of violence that now embraces the planet continues in its seemingly uncontrollable orbit, Western and Islamic civilizations are moving further and further away from their cherished ideals of justice, compassion, and wisdom. It is essential for all humankind to understand this complicated relationship, whatever one's political perspective or religious beliefs. Without the universal will to halt this momentum, the violence and uncertainty will eventually progress into an unending global nightmare. Societies need to return to those ideas that have nourished them over the millennia and created in them compassion and empathy for others. In sum, the current crisis is nothing short of a challenge to the very identity of humankind as a caring and thinking species.

SIX

Lifting the Veil

Sir,

Assalamu Alaikum wa Rahamtullah [peace be with you, blessings of God be with you]. I hope your good self will be OK.

I received your email and so pleased that I can't describe in words. Alhamdulillah [thanks be to God], the translation of your book is going fast and it will be published less than three months according to promise, Insha Allah [God willing].

Where [are] you sir these days and how is your journey? I had learned many things in your short company. I hope in future your guidelines [may be followed]. Jazakumullah, may Allah Almighty bless you.

> With regards
> Aijaz Arshad Qasmi
> General Secretary, Islamic Peace Foundation New Delhi
> Ex. Online Mufti, Darul Uloom Deoband

WHO CANNOT MARVEL at the capacity of the human spirit to expand and change? When I first met Aijaz, he seemed fully set in his opinions, one whose world consisted of simple, clear-cut categories that differentiated friends from foes and good religion from bad religion. Author of *Jihad and Terrorism*, he seemed obsessed with "American barbarism" and "Israeli barbarism." There were no shades of gray in his worldview. Although intensely religious in a formal and orthodox manner, he had yet to develop a spiritual expansiveness that would coincide with the Quranic vision of a common humanity. Now, before me, was his e-mail, which had arrived only a few days after the team returned from the field trip in mid-April, expressing the glimmering of a new vision or, as he put it, "guidelines."

After our visit to Deoband, Aijaz accompanied us for the next week as we met with various Muslims in Delhi in gatherings large and small. He had arranged some of the meetings himself, such as a visit to the head-quarters of the Jamat-i-Islami, the orthodox Islamic party of South Asia. Throughout the week, he listened carefully to my speeches about my American friends—both Christians and Jews—which stressed that Americans are not all alike.

At every forum, he would hear me emphasize the need for dialogue and understanding as a Quranic duty, especially in view of the globalizing forces impinging on the ummah today. At times, Aijaz showed growing territorial pride when introducing me at my lectures. Initially, at Deoband a week before, he had introduced me as a somewhat remote and distant "great scholar." Now, with some defiance in his voice and more than a hint of South Asian hyperbole, he was calling me the best model for the Islamic faith—indeed, for all faiths.

I believe we were the first Americans Aijaz had met and certainly spent so much time with. He had long conversations with Hailey, Frankie, and, later, Hadia about serious issues that had been agitating him regarding world affairs. Although he was initially reserved about speaking directly with Hailey and Hadia, he later opened up to them after spending a few days in the field with us, at last able to put a human face to what he had earlier called "American barbarians." These Americans were actually listening to his opinions and willing to discuss them seriously, in contrast to the stereotypical media commentators who labeled people like him "Islamic extremists" without any engagement or acknowledgment of their common humanity.

Toward the end of our visit in India, Aijaz said that he would like to translate my book *Islam under Siege* into Urdu. The book explores the idea of common humanity, especially after 9/11, explaining that today all societies feel under siege and off balance. It is vital for them to learn to trust each other, which can only be accomplished through dialogue and under-standing. Later, as he began the translation, he seemed grateful beyond words that at last someone was actually trying to "explain the Islamic

Concept in [the] contemporary world. May Allah Bless you, I pray to Allah Almighty for your good health and good serving of Islam."

How clear it seemed that the principle of dialogue and understanding could indeed have an effect. Through the translation of *Islam under Siege* over Deoband's vast network of madrassahs and mosques, Aijaz would spread these ideas to thousands of young readers, and hopefully my message of dialogue with other world civilizations would take root. Instead of interpreting jihad as violence, young men might now think of it as a peaceful movement aimed at creating better understanding; maybe now they would think of the place of Islam in the twenty-first century in a more balanced and compassionate manner, prepared to reach out to other civilizations, or at least attempt to understand them.

If Aijaz could change his hard-line position, so could others taking similar stances, including Americans and even Israelis. Like Aijaz, other individuals might finally abandon their "us" versus "them" dialectic for one that encompasses all of humanity. For me, Aijaz's conversion was as momentous as an oil tanker reversing course in mid-ocean.

I had not heard from Aijaz for several months and began to wonder what happened to the plans to translate *Islam under Siege* into Urdu. Then, in mid-December, he wrote to explain where he had been and how the project stood:

> I am so sorry on disconnect since a long times, actually I was out of India last three months on South Africa and Doha (Qatar) tours. now I have come back to India 2 weeks ago. Alhamdulillha, translation of the book was completed in August but unfortunately its not published till date [because] I was not here. Insha Allah, after Idul Azaha the urdu version of your book will be released by Mrs Sonia Gandhi [wife of late Prime Minister Rajiv Gandhi]."

I noted that Aijaz was showing his primary title as general secretary of the Islamic Peace Foundation of India based in New Delhi. His titles also included a reference to his former position with Deoband as the "ex spokesperson Darul Uloom Deoband." Aijaz was clearly involved in his new commitment to build bridges and foster peace.

Aijaz's new awareness promised hope in an otherwise bleak landscape. He had done what the Buddha had recommended—challenged the poisons in himself. With his anger at and ignorance of Americans now in check, he had begun a journey of immense importance not only to the ummah but also to the world at large, though he was probably little aware of it.

"In Me, Where It Mattered"

Aijaz's spiritual progress did not entirely surprise me; life consists of a journey for all human beings, and they have the capacity to change as they progress through it. Religions and sages provide them with guidance or markers to signal its different phases. The trajectory of my own life has been marked by such change, without my being aware of it.

As a young man, I admired Aurangzeb because he seemed to embody the ideal Islamic ruler. He appealed to my youthful loyalty and passion for my religion, and I saw him as a champion of the faith. He would not compromise on matters that exposed Muslims to threat. Having grown up in an environment of large-scale religious riots, the memories of which have haunted me throughout my life, I felt that no Muslim could fail to be moved by Aurangzeb, the champion of Islam and the personification of the Deoband model.

Later in life, I discovered another Muslim hero in Jinnah. All the issues that my colleagues and I debated as undergraduates had been tackled by Jinnah when he led the Pakistan movement. Unlike Aurangzeb, Jinnah was prepared to interact with and even absorb foreign ideas about democracy and voting rights for women and minorities. Yet Jinnah would not compromise on the rights and security of his community either. I was thrilled to see him on the same level as Mahatma Gandhi and Jawaharlal Nehru, the Indian icons. As a Muslim, I took great pride in Jinnah's successful wresting of a Muslim Pakistan from the powerful grip of the British and the Indian National Congress. That he achieved this success within constitutional limits further enhanced his stature in my eyes.

As I grew older, I became more and more interested in the mystic and universalist Islam to which my father, who worked first in the government and later in the United Nations, had introduced me when I was a student at Lahore. He would ask me to accompany him to the shrine of Dahta Sahib, the famous saint of Lahore—Lahore is also known as the Nagri or city of Dahta Sahib—which I would agree to do more to humor him than out of personal desire. He never insisted that I go with him or lectured me about his ideas of Islam. It was only toward the end of his life that he pressed me to spread the universalist message of sulh-i-kul, or "peace with all," as embodied by Dahta Sahib.[1] But something in those visits had touched a spiritual part of me I did not even know I possessed. Later, after completing my studies at Cambridge University, I returned to Lahore to attend the elite Civil Service Academy, the embodiment of the Aligarh model. I was still convinced of the merits of the Aligarh way of thinking and admired Jinnah and Aurangzeb as heroes of Islam, although I had begun to have doubts about the latter. Yet even then, something drew me to Dahta Sahib, and when I visited his shrine, in the old section of the city, one evening in the winter of 1966, I wrote a poem, "Walking the Streets with the Dahta," to describe the experience, not even aware of how it would reflect my inner soul later in life:

> They were all there:
> love remains love
> however crudely exhibited
> faith turns to love
> however clumsily expressed
> love creates faith
> from whatever quarter coming
> I came back that evening
> levitated on the horns that tossed me
> acute-feeling the goodness and
> friendship
> of the Dahta
> flowing in the streets of his Nagri
> and in me
> where it mattered.[2]

The young entrants to the Civil Service Academy in Lahore saw themselves as the personification of a modernist Islam—a true product of Aligarh—and were inclined to snigger at the ways of Ajmer and Deoband. To them, the mystics were too otherworldly, unrealistic, and confused, while the orthodox seemed fanatical, backward, and irrelevant. The former were sneeringly dismissed as "Sufis" and the latter as "damned mullahs." After all, the Aligarh model had successfully led the nation to independence from the British and would safeguard that independence into the future.

Akbar Ahmed as a young civil service officer with his mother in the late 1960s. The Civil Service of Pakistan was an elite service based on a confident modern Islam, the Aligarh model, but Ahmed was also exposed to more traditional and mystic influences during this period.

Thus, my peers at the academy, who suspected I went to Dahta's shrine, were unsure of my motives. There was conjecture and debate about why I really disappeared from time to time. They saw Ajmer and Aligarh as mutually exclusive. It was one or the other.

Looking back from the vantage point of four decades, I am mortified and amused in equal measure at that brash, cocky young man bursting with energy, ideas, and self-worth. One part of me said, "I have made it to the top. I am the best, the smartest, the greatest." The rest of me rejected that part, and the whole was easily able to contain it. My trips to the Dahta helped to check the intoxication of the academy. When I entered the shrine and began taking off my shoes and covering my head, the arrogance and self-importance induced by the academy evaporated.

When I accompanied my father to the shrine of the saint in Ajmer, who has a spiritual relationship with the saint in Lahore, I discovered the enduring beauty of the mystic message. Even in the midst of a swirling mass of humanity, a feeling of calmness would descend on me, erasing any traces of anger, arrogance, and ambition, and fill my soul with a sense of divine spirit, making me feel that I was at one with everyone around me and that they, too, were experiencing the same connection to the divine through their acceptance of the other pilgrims, whether rich or poor, Muslim or non-Muslim. Although we all had arrived as strangers, we had become brothers and sisters in goodwill, recognizing our common humanity in this place of worship. There was no past or future, only the peaceful present. I could see clearly, as if a curtain had been removed from my eyes, how truly close humans are to each other and how ugly the barriers they have erected that prevent them from seeing the beauty in the world's diverse souls.

On our journey into Islam, my young assistants observed firsthand the impact that Ajmer had come to have on me, as described by Hadia:

In Ajmer, I suddenly saw our dear professor, Dr. Akbar, transform from the seasoned diplomat and the analytical researcher to a calm, peaceful mystic, overtaken by the spirituality around him. He quietly followed our guide to the burial site of the twelfth-century Sufi saint, chanting hymns and prayers under his breath. When we entered the shrine of Moin-uddin Chisti, Dr. Akbar's face completely changed. It was the most emotional I had ever seen him. Perhaps he remembered his father, who accompanied him in previous visits to the shrine in Ajmer. Dr. Akbar reminded me to recite the opening chapter of the Quran, Al-Fatiha, for the soul of the deceased saint. "Every time I've prayed here, great blessings have come my way," Dr. Akbar confided to me. He then proceeded to hold his palms in supplication towards the heavens and say his own prayer. He looked enveloped by an aura of peace and connection to His Creator. He just sat there silently for some time, eyes closed and head tilted forward, as if unaware of anything else around him.

When we sat down in the open courtyard between the mosque and the shrine, Dr. Akbar seemed to slowly come out of his trance-like state as if returning from a different world. We could all see that Dr. Akbar was completely moved by the visit. He sat cross-legged and listened to the words of the Muslim devotees singing praise to God. "Open your heart," he told me. "Find room for everyone in your heart."

We can only see into each other's souls if we take the trouble—and sometimes the risk—to visit each other. Unfortunately, few Americans in the Muslim world venture out from behind the high security walls of their compounds to meet the ordinary merchant or cab driver on the street. Imagine the impact if a diplomat from the U.S. embassy in Damascus visited the house of a well-known sheikh for a casual conversation. Imagine the cultural and psychological barriers that would be crossed.

Our team did just that. We traveled to Damascus, where we visited Sheikh Hussam Al-Din Farfour, the head of Fatah Institute, a well-known Islamic university. Looking stern in a white turban and well-trimmed white beard with the black robe covering his large frame, the sheikh was waiting for us in his dimly lit office with over a dozen of his senior department and faculty heads, all seated on outdated furniture. They were talking nostalgically of their visits to universities in the United States and the United Kingdom. During the meeting, the sheikh's students came in with trays of juices for us to sip.

Although I began with some questions about Islam, the conversation eventually lapsed into another tedious and somewhat meandering description of the troubles with the United States. We had been treated to essentially the same lecture for the last few days, and I braced myself for a long and sterile afternoon. As the discussion wore on, my impression of the sheikh was that of a bureaucrat who had adapted Islam to the socialist rhetoric and system in which he operated. The official portrait of President Bashar al-Assad in the office and the sheikh's glowing acknowledgment of the president's services to the cause of the nation and Islam only confirmed this feeling. As we prepared to leave, the sheikh invited us for dinner at his home. I promised to let him know if I could come, leaving myself time to think of a good excuse because I was not sure I could take another session of this kind.

Despite my concern that we would be in for another wearying session, we turned up at the sheikh's home the next night. In characteristic Arab style, it was situated in a crowded alley with an obscure-looking entrance that led into a nondescript courtyard followed by a hallway and another courtyard, this one structured and elegant, which opened into a spacious and comfortable home with distinct quarters for men and women to preserve modesty, according to local tradition. We were ushered into the

Guests assemble before a formal dinner at the Damascus residence of noted Islamic scholar Sheikh Farfour. The nature of the evening was transformed when the sheikh began to hum mystic songs of love and compassion in praise of the Prophet of Islam.

owner's grand study, filled with leather-bound books on Islam of the kind one would find in the home of any affluent and educated senior official in the Muslim world. Present were some of the same professors we had met at the university as well as some new faces, which included leading religious figures and disciples of the sheikh.

The sheikh seated me in the place of honor in his main living room with Hailey, the only woman present, next to me. Soon more guests arrived, many in long black robes and white turbans signifying their high religious status. Some of them were the most distinguished religious figures of Damascus. In the midst of these arrivals, an unusual group of persons appeared. Instead of saying salaam accompanied by a handshake, each would touch his heart—a traditional Sufi greeting. The hint of Sufism awakened my curiosity.

As the guests responded to us with obvious warmth and hospitality, the evening took on a new feeling. After a conversation that thankfully went beyond politics to the scholars of the past, the sheikh invited his guests into his dining room. The dinner, laid out on a wide table, consisted of a variety of delicious Arab dishes that must have taken days to prepare. We sat down with our plates, and the introduction of food made the guests more relaxed. In order to make Hailey feel more comfortable, the sheikh had invited his daughter-in-law, who was from Spain, to sit with her, as normally men and women are segregated. Hailey spoke Spanish so the two began to chat about the daughter-in-law's conversion to Islam after her marriage.

Enjoying the food and the warm company, the sheikh no longer looked like the formal head of an Arab household but a man at peace with himself. He began to hum with his eyes closed, gently swaying back and forth to the rhythm that he had begun to tap on his knees. His disciples whispered to us that he loved to sing verses in praise of the Prophet. They encouraged him to sing louder, and in his soothing yet powerful voice, he filled the dining room with his passion and love. He sang about the nobility, beauty, and compassion of the Prophet, and soon the others in the room had the same look of serenity on their faces.

The gathering began to reveal a complex interplay between the models identified in this book. What had seemed to be the Aligarh model, which calls for a synthesis with non-Muslim systems, in this case socialism, appeared to dissolve into the Ajmer model, with its traditional mystic expressions of peace, compassion, and universal humanism. The change in rhetoric matched the body language of Sheikh Farfour, who had transformed from a formal, prickly, even slightly hostile-looking bureaucrat to a gentle, smiling, and welcoming Sufi master.

After dinner, the sheikh escorted us to the main entrance of his home, where we waited for our car to arrive. The February wind had picked up a bit, and Hailey shivered slightly. In an instant, on some words from the sheikh, his son was in and out of the house and handing him a camel-colored scarf. The sheikh lifted it above his head, closed his eyes, and recited a blessing in Arabic. Our translator later told us that he had said, "A blessing for peace and good travels. May you be protected and live a happy life." Hailey wrapped the scarf around herself with a smile and has since treasured it as a reminder of a spontaneous moment of genuine kindness and connection between cultures.

The day before I left Damascus, I had several urgent messages from

Sheikh Farfour stating he wanted to see me. He was to be a guest at the Pakistani ambassador's dinner later, and I suggested he travel in my car so we could save time by talking along the way. But he insisted that we meet alone. When he arrived at the hotel and stepped aside to speak privately, he explained that he wanted to give us all presents and wished to make this gesture with quiet dignity. He gave me one of the most exquisite Qurans I have ever seen, a special edition made for President al-Assad. In it, he inscribed Arabic words of beauty and encouragement. He gave presents to each member of my team as well, writing messages of peace and spiritual blessing. Hailey was particularly moved:

> He had specially selected each book for different members of our group, choosing mine in Spanish rather than Arabic. Inside of the front cover he wrote and had translated a message of hope for the future of the world and the work we were doing. He wrote that our love for God and humanity is the only hope and that he would pray for me to continue to work for peace. Sheikh Farfour, Aijaz, and countless others we met along the way proved that the only way to battle the intolerance and hatred in our world is with compassion and love as our intention rather than exclusion and hatred. Thus we must approach the world, not from the position of fear as I had done before this trip, but from that of love and friendship that I see the world in terms of now. It is possible, but it requires a dramatic shift in our manner of thinking and acting as a world power. Think—if three Americans with their professor can make such a difference, what can a whole government and nation do with the power of compassion and dialogue?

A Muslim may reflect Ajmer, Deoband, and Aligarh in different ways at different or even simultaneous moments in life. Progress from one model to another depends on personal growth, circumstances, and opportunities. In my case, the movement was part of the trajectory of my life; in Aijaz's case, it was a distinct shift in direction. Extrinsic factors and general societal attitudes influence the flow and popularity of these models within individuals. That makes it all the more important to understand what influences Muslims around the world and to reach out to the model of acceptance and love.

Using the Knowledge of the Sages in the Age of Globalization

As I moved through life traveling the world and developing spiritually, I gained some insight into the best path forward for those interested in peace. Along the way, I met more and more people who were not of my faith and culture but whom I grew to respect and admire. These relationships brought me to yet another new perspective: I found that my heroes, Aurangzeb and Jinnah, embodied forms of Islam that still acted as barriers to understanding. Aurangzeb was too much of an "Islamic" exclusivist, and Jinnah, while accepting the influence of Westminster on his politics, failed to appreciate the spiritual dimension and character of other cultures.

In my effort to encourage peace and dialogue between cultures, I thought the Ajmer model was so amorphous and its interpretation so personal that it was too idiosyncratic to stand up to the pressures of this age of rampant consumerism. I assumed that the only way forward lay in promoting the Aligarh model. At least it had the merit of being practical, and its frame of reference could be understood by both Muslims and the West. I believed that ultimately the Aligarh model, like that of Jinnah, could help to create a sense of modern nationalism. While Aligarh may promote the language of international commerce and politics, nationalism by definition creates boundaries that exclude neighbors and thereby prevents true understanding and lasting peace between cultures. Faced with globalization, the Aligarh model clearly has the potential to produce wisdom and justice, but it falls short of producing compassion, which is the only sure way to bring civilizations together in friendship. The young students of Aligarh our team met may well have spoken English and read Thomas Friedman, but few had gone deeper into the civilization they are at odds with to read the prose of Aquinas, the poetry of St. Francis, or even the plays of Shakespeare. They were unable to connect spiritually or culturally. As applied nowadays, the Aligarh model has been reduced to kowtowing to mainly superficial commercial transactions and consumer products of ephemeral value. In other words, the Aligarh model fails to make the all-too-necessary spiritual connection between cultures.

If the Aligarh model has its shortcomings, so does the Deoband, which is too easily inflamed into anger and emotion. It cannot function effectively in the age of globalization either, unless it begins to change. Muslims cannot remain an island of isolated believers in a sea of different cultures and faiths. As members of a world civilization, people are now too close to and dependent on each other to afford the luxury of ignoring and excluding others. Deoband must approach different beliefs with acceptance and compassion if it is to move forward. One of its most faithful sons, Aijaz, showed that this was possible.

Just as Aligarh creates political boundaries, Deoband creates religious ones. All those—Muslims or non-Muslims—who create boundaries around themselves on the basis of either nationalism or religion invariably exclude those on the other side. This exclusion easily degenerates into indifference to the pain of others and too often into violence against them. It is only Ajmer followers—whether Muslims or non-Muslims—who believe in a common humanity and thus are able to live comfortably with others and to adapt to them and learn from them. This is the great lesson that world history and the current impasse teaches. How else is civilization to live in peace and harmony in the future?

That brings one to the idea and practice of acceptance provided by the universalist Ajmer model. This is not to say that the looming problems of the planet will be readily solved by the dreamy and mystic side of the Ajmer model, which is sometimes dangerously tempted to withdraw from society altogether. Clearly, the accepting nature of the Ajmer model must be buttressed by the commitment and fervor that Deoband can provide, along with the skill and dexterity to negotiate with governments, organizations, and political parties that is characteristic of Aligarh.

The strength of the Ajmer worldview is that it has the same spirit of acceptance inherent in other traditions. The Judaic texts, the Bible, the Quran, the Gita, and the Granth Sahib, the sayings of Confucius and Buddha—all have taught something more than how to intone prayer and observe external ritual. They have taught how to penetrate deep into their message and look for the one underlying and common theme in each: the importance of justice, compassion, and knowledge as the sure antidotes to the poisons that plague and pervert human society. It is but a matter of looking for and understanding the true spirit of faith.

The dire problems of poverty, population explosion, global warming, and religious and ethnic killings around the globe seem inexplicable at this point in history, when world civilization has inherited such a rich legacy of spiritual thought. One may well ask whether the three abstract philosophic precepts outlined in this book are able to help. The answer, I believe, is that not only can they help in a direct and personal way to uplift souls, but they can also elevate both national and international debate on precisely these global problems. But hard work will be required, in both the long term and the short term.

The solutions must take into consideration the interconnectedness of the world, the fact that everything happening in the United States is making an almost immediate impact in the Muslim world, and vice versa. Unless societies receive and are seen to receive justice, anger will continue spreading its poison throughout the world. The events of September 11 symbolized the anger of the Muslims, which provoked the anger of the Americans. So great was the outrage at the scale of the tragedy and loss of human life that it was unlikely and unreasonable to expect compassion and understanding from Americans at that time. It would have defied human nature itself. If cool thinking had prevailed, however, the first task at hand would have been to capture the perpetrators and then to consolidate the worldwide sympathy that had spontaneously expressed itself for America—even in anti-American countries like Iran—into a movement for a better common future for the planet. But this was not to be.

George Bush reacted to the tragedy on September 11 in anger rather than with compassion or understanding. "Our grief has turned to anger, and anger to resolution," he said a few days later, addressing the joint session of Congress to thunderous applause. By doing so, Bush violated more than the Buddhist warning against the poison of anger. He publicly rejected two of Christianity's central commandments: one inherited from Moses, "Thou shalt not kill," the other from Christ himself, "Thou shalt love one another." Henceforth, Bush's anger would be directed at anyone he wished to label a "terrorist." This line of thinking would become the foreign policy of the United States, which would itself be reduced to the simple aphorism: "You are with us or you are with the terrorists." Bush's arguments that he was involved in a Christian "just war"—he even used the word "crusade" early on—are rejected even by some Christians themselves. Pope John Paul II had publicly said that Iraq was not a just war: neither the people of Afghanistan nor Iraq were involved in a war against the United States. Instead, the United States should have targeted al-Qaeda and brought it to justice.

Bush was to launch one of the most asymmetrical wars in history, using the most advanced technology known to man against two small, deeply divided, and impoverished Muslim nations, Afghanistan and Iraq. Torn by ethnic and political strife, their people, millions on the verge of starvation, looked to the United States for assistance and friendship. They were stunned when it launched an onslaught on them, which has resulted in many thousands of deaths. In addition, too many people have been tortured and sexually humiliated. The nightmare Bush had created for these Muslim societies very quickly involved large parts of the world, including his own society. Although Americans took time to realize it, they eventually saw that they were on a slippery slope that could lead to the suspension of civil liberties, universal surveillance, and mindless neurosis and hatred of others, with open discussions of "interning" Muslims in the United States. Torture was supported, with the vice president leading a campaign on its behalf, notably for water-boarding, but general criticism was muted.[3] The argument that terrorists must be defeated whatever the cost prevailed. The mood of anger that Bush had articulated fed directly and powerfully into the actions of the administration and the larger media, inciting fear and insecurity in people.

For several years after 9/11, opinion leaders in the United States, including television talk show hosts, parading under the mantle of punditry, blindly echoed the administration's fears that another strike on U.S. soil was imminent. Americans grew increasingly fearful that they were in immediate danger and angry because their lives had changed so much. It was left to the comedians to introduce some perspective and point out notably after the invasion of Iraq what was incorrect, unjust, and absurd in the developments taking place around them. Their voices grew in volume after the disastrous news from Iraq became unstoppable, and soon people were tuning in to Jon Stewart and Stephen Colbert on Comedy Central for the news. I was personally grateful to know that Americans still retained their famed ironic humor, sharp intelligence, and feeling for the underdog.

None of us can predict how we would react to personal tragedy—the unexpected death of a spouse or a child or even a relative. When such a tragedy involves an entire community, it tends to be magnified, and if it is caused by traditional antagonists, then the overriding reaction is as much anger as it is hatred. Human beings are capable, however, of responding to the worst kind of attack with compassion and nobility of spirit. For writers such expressions of human graciousness are "saintly acts" and for poets they are "divine sparks." The events that took place on September 11 produced many such examples of these sparks. "Our Voices Together," headed by the indefatigable Marianne Scott, was organized by those who lost relatives on that day (see the website www.ourvoicestogether.org). One of the group's projects was to build educational centers in Afghanistan. Aware that al-Qaeda and bin Laden had lived among the people of Afghanistan, Our Voices Together wished to convert strangers into friends. Judea Pearl too made a similar gesture when he reached out in dialogue and then friendship to me with my Pakistani background. While his beloved son had been murdered in Pakistan, he overcame a natural revulsion for those who had committed this crime to reach out to those from the very nation that had produced the killers. The dialogues he and I have conducted from 2003 onward have helped to promote Jewish-Muslim understanding and to create bridges between communities.

Politicians too have shown that they can rise above common human emotions and attain an almost superhuman moral plane by insisting on compassion and justice in the face of massive death and destruction. Gandhi, Nehru, and Jinnah are three such statesmen. In the summer of 1947, Hindus, Muslims, and Sikhs slaughtered each other in South Asia; up to two million people may have been killed and up to 15 million displaced from their homes to find a new one in a new land.[4] Yet each one of these three leaders stood firm against communal violence even if it meant challenging their own community. On several occasions, Gandhi began a fast unto death until Hindus stopped rioting against Muslims in India; Nehru declared that his nation had gone "mad" and ordered his entire administration to check the violence as its top priority; and Jinnah, on the other side of the border in Pakistan, seeing an angry Muslim mob surrounding a group of Hindus in Karachi, threw himself into the crowd to stop the violence and declared, "I am going to constitute myself the Protector-General of the Hindu minority in Pakistan."[5] As a consequence, these leaders were threatened by their own communities. Gandhi eventually lost his life to an assassin who had complained of Gandhi's support for Muslims.

Jews, Christians, Muslims, Hindus, young and old, men and women, Americans, Pakistanis and Indians—countless examples from among them illustrate the capacity of human beings to attain moral heights in the most difficult circumstances. Thus, ordinary individuals become extraordinary ones, and those already recognized as extraordinary pass into the realm of folklore and legend.

Alas, no extraordinary and selfless leader was present to lead the United States after September 11. The great anger felt after that catastrophic day has not abated and continues to cloud the judgment of U.S. leaders and citizens. As a result, the institutions, so valued by many societies today, of democracy, human rights, and civil liberties, are endangered and weakened. To compromise the American Founding Fathers' high ideals on the pretext of war is to betray not only their vision but also the future of the union.

The United States, especially, because it is relatively young and powerful, must construct a new philosophy toward other civilizations. Because it is dealing with Muslim nations of diverse social and political character, it needs to quickly appreciate the nuances of these societies. Muslims widely complain of the lack of justice, widespread corruption, and collapse of law and order. Too frequently the United States backs strong military intervention, unaware of how this support encourages turmoil or how negatively this support is seen within a country.

Perhaps one reason for the U.S. response is that its policymakers tend to focus less on long-term objectives and more on immediate emergency situations, which encourages a more visceral approach. In addition, current foreign policy may be influenced by the desire to win another election in four years. Both factors deter American leaders from talking to Deoband representatives, even if they are democratically elected, as in the case of the Hamas party or Mahmoud Ahmadinejad, the president of Iran. By avoiding such dialogue, the United States is not only ignoring voices that speak for large sections of Muslim society but also enhancing their prestige above and beyond their real worth. By refusing to engage with them, it is making Muslims in the Deoband model who genuinely wish to work with the United States more frustrated and angry and, therefore, more inclined to join the ranks of those who support more aggressive action. There are many others like Aijaz from Deoband, who can be persuaded through dialogue to adjust their view of Americans, as illustrated by an e-mail from the head of the Department of English Language and Literature at Deoband, sent June 2006: "i met u when u came to visit Darul Uloom Deoband. . . . it was one of the happiest moments in our life. we [were] very much impressed by all of u."

American policymakers and diplomats can work with Deoband model regimes to promote U.S. standards of justice, equality, and human rights, but it can only happen through dialogue. Visits to mosques and madrassahs and serious attempts at dialogue by American scholars and diplomats can make an impact. Dialogue does not preclude U.S. action against those guilty of violence, but a finer distinction must be made between those who are actually guilty and those who happen to be part of their community. There needs to be much more research and truth seeking before issuing accusations of the doings of "terrorist regimes" or announcements of "terror plots," which are later proven hollow. Even in the case of individual "enemy combatants," it is essential to respect the due process of law, which must operate swiftly and visibly so that the world knows that American justice is above reproach.

Truth and justice are American ideals. Television cannot be a substitute for reality, and Americans should not complacently distance themselves from the injustices of the world. Questions all Americans should ask are: What does it mean to be the most powerful nation on earth? Does it mean possessing and using weapons that can destroy large numbers of people living in villages in distant parts of the world? Building a fortress mentality for themselves? Or does it mean developing social and political institutions to enlighten and benefit all of humanity? As moral and political leaders of the planet, Americans must try to move other world civilizations to tackle the common global problems. No other power can play this role.

In dealing with the Muslim world, the West's commentators and policy planners need to understand the influence of the three models on Muslim politics. As noted throughout this book, leadership of many Muslim societies has been captured by the Deoband model, gaining the upper hand because the modern Muslim state has been unable to provide security to its people, or so much security, it terrorizes them, or to provide ordinary services such as proper health care and education. In times of national crisis, some states have failed even to ensure the integrity of national borders. Equally important, some Muslim states have not instilled a sense of national pride and identity that energized Muslims when achieving independence from Western colonial powers half a century ago. When a people feel their government no longer relates to their aspirations, they are alienated from it and sense it has become an illegitimate and artificial reflection of the West's will. To take one example, Musharraf's Pakistan, at best, has been turned into a distorted version of Aligarh as would be seen by a disenchanted Ajmer follower and an indignant Deoband adherent.

The Deoband leadership has stepped neatly into the vacuum created by the failure of the state. It has not only provided health and education facilities, for example, but in many cases has also become the only champion of the nation itself against foreign forces—as Hezbollah has done in repelling the Israeli onslaught in Lebanon in 2006 and the Iraqis and Afghan Taliban have done in slowing the American war machine. These accomplishments against the most powerful army in the Middle East and the most powerful army in the world have only added to the luster and credibility of the Deoband model. In contrast, Aligarh-inclined governments have appeared weak and uncertain, almost to the point of being irrelevant.

As modern information technology made clear to ordinary Muslims, President Musharraf, heading one of the most powerful military armies in the Muslim world and armed with nuclear weapons, immediately capitulated to American anger after 9/11, whereas the so-called insurgent and suicide bomber was ready to sacrifice everything for his land and people. Though many may not condone the violence of their fellow Muslims, because it kills more innocent people than soldiers in combat, they would applaud and recognize the courage and commitment of those prepared to give the ultimate sacrifice. Rudyard Kipling's lines, "Two thousand pounds of education/Drops to a ten-rupee jezail," about British soldiers felled by Muslim tribesmen, find an echo in the cheaply made and easily available improvised explosive device (IED) proving so deadly against American soldiers.

Americans have made the fatal mistake of fighting the war against terror by resurrecting a strategy used in the cold war against the Soviet Union. This approach, however, fails to consider the complexity of Muslim society. All Muslims, whichever model they may follow, are committed to their faith, and all will defend it, and by extension their own homeland, in different ways against what they see as attacks from the outside. By contrast, Soviet citizens, terrorized and disillusioned by the entire state system and structure, lost their belief in the ideology of the state, whose collapse seemed not only inevitable but brought relief. Those hoping for a similar outcome from military campaigns in the Muslim world after 9/11 failed to recognize that Muslim society, buoyed by Islam, would rise to meet the challenge of what seems a global campaign against it. That is to say, Islam is a holistic and integrated system, and its different parts come into play at different times in history to preserve the larger whole.

Western policy, relegated to condemning those inclined toward Deoband as terrorists and refusing to talk to them has led to an unrealistic and inevitably failed policy. Because so many Muslims are influenced by Deoband, the West needs to seriously devise ways in which to engage with its leadership. And the West also needs to vigorously encourage and support the genuine forms of Aligarh—meaning unfettered democracy and not a form that comes under the guise of military dictators posing as benefactors. The West must also look for and strengthen the Ajmer model, as it provides an authentic and permanent platform for global understanding.

For their part, Muslims need to review the three models with a view to adapting them for the present times, living as we are in the age of globalization. Islam encourages every individual to struggle to attain a higher spiritual plane. That endeavor, as mentioned earlier, is called jihad, which literally means "striving." Muslims therefore need to rediscover the struggle, to improve life in a spiritual sense, which is the "greatest jihad," while actively discouraging the interpretation that equates it with violent acts, even if committed in self-defense or the "lesser jihad." Muslims need to recognize that the most effective "weapons" for addressing their grievances are knowledge and reason, rather than brute force. They must revive the ideals of ijtihad, which allows for innovative thinking to accommodate new conditions and needs of modern societies, such as the rights of women, minorities, and the less privileged. The deep loyalties to tribalism must be pushed aside in order to cooperate in a more integrated world. Educational centers of excellence need to be opened and supported by governments to revive the ideals of Islam.

Equally important, there should be no excuse for setting Quranic ideals of justice, compassion, and wisdom aside. Muslim leaders must strive to live up to their own vision of the ideal society. Too many Arab rulers use the crutch of Israel directly or indirectly to avoid working toward a democracy until that "problem" is resolved. For Pakistan's politicians and army generals, the crutch is Kashmir and the "threat" from India, which they use to delay introducing genuine democracy, human rights, and civil liberties. Too often Muslim leaders evoke an "enemy" to justify the suspension of civil law and to impose draconian regulations and brutal police methods. Even leaders in the United States and the United Kingdom have begun relying on crutches such as threats of terrorism and to security. Unless all societies live up to their own high standards and do not look for excuses to abandon them, they will ultimately descend into a world of legitimized terror.

What if the Muslim world had responded in the Ajmer way—or even the Aligarh one—after the American invasion of Afghanistan and Iraq? The Muslim restraint would have impressed people in the West and created sympathy for Muslim causes. As it happened, the beheadings, the suicide bombings, and the hyperbolic rhetoric of violence—all veering away from the Ajmer and Aligarh models—confirmed already existing stereotypes of Muslims. Very soon, people in the West began to equate violence and terrorism with Islam itself. Worse yet, they began to see all Muslims as inherently bloodthirsty creatures, a view that fed into the growing Islamophobia around the world, escalating its pejorative overtones. Even President Bush took to using the word "Islamofascism," perhaps not realizing its implications and how much offense it has caused many Muslims, including his own allies.

Though the age-old poisons of greed, anger, and ignorance continue to afflict humankind, a far greater legacy is the wisdom of the sages. Their advocacy for compassion can today be the most effective tool for squelching the greed that drives powerful multinational corporations and even governments that ruthlessly exploit the natural resources of poorer countries and disregard the genuine needs of millions. This epidemic coming in the wake of globalization has led to the gap between a few individuals who live isolated lives of extravagance and millions who struggle for their daily food—what social scientists have called "global pillaging."[6] As the Ajmer model urges, nations must learn to live on less as a philosophy of life. They must use less power, less water, and less food if any of them, let alone the planet, is to survive. Each one of us must accept the invitation and challenge issued by Sir Jonathan Sacks, one of the truly outstanding religious sages of our age, to heal our fractured world.[7]

So too we must apply the sages' urge for knowledge. Without this, each human being is reduced to a world consisting of his or her own cell. Each of us needs to be much more sensitive to what is sacred or highly symbolic of a culture in other civilizations. Just as Muslims are—and will always be—sensitive to abuse of their Prophet and holy book, so Americans are sensitive to any desecration of their flag, which they see as the very embodiment of their nationhood and identity. Ignorance of other cultures leads to serious policy mistakes, whether conducting warfare or peace negotiations. With knowledge of other peoples and cultures, societies are less likely to see those others as disconnected from themselves. Once they recognize how closely dependent on each other they actually are, they will stop responding to provocation with more provocation.

To this equation must be added justice, which will prevent anger from consistently begetting crude force. Together, compassion and justice will stamp out the causes of violence, and I would encourage all nations to include this philosophy in their policymaking. The ongoing violent confrontations of our times can be resolved if worked out within such a framework. One of the most tragic and bloody of these conflicts has been taking place in the Middle East for half a century with little hope of resolution because of the perception on both sides that compassion and justice are missing. The milestones that create further hatred and violence are as fresh as the morning news in the minds of the combatants: the Muslim anger early in 2007 at the excavation alongside the Noble Sanctuary in Jerusalem (which reflects the Muslim feeling discussed in the last chapter that there is a sinister plot to demolish the mosque); the Israeli invasion of Lebanon in the summer of 2006, when Israel retaliated with overwhelming force against Hezbollah for the kidnapping of Israeli soldiers; the deaths and destruction caused by Israeli bombardment in Gaza and the West Bank; and the stirring of the Arabs to find more recruits for their crude and murderous suicide missions, killing passengers on buses and clients at pizzerias. The list is long. It is time for the two sides to come together as equals, working within each other's cultural and religious frameworks, and—with full consideration for each other's grievances—forge a lasting peace. Without compassion and justice, the cycle of death will only accelerate and involve more and more people in its path.

However, friendship and love must be present on both sides before the cycle can be broken. The Quran repeatedly asserts that when an individual has reached a certain stage of spiritual enlightenment, a veil or curtain is lifted from the eyes and the individual is able to see the world and its truths clearly, free from attachment to worldly pleasures, pains, or selfish needs. If the poisons of globalization are overcome, then truth and reality may emerge and the benefits of globalization safely reaped without toxic effect.

If asked to distill what I learned during my journey into Islam into a few words, it would be this: Be true to your own ideals. For the United States, this would mean staying focused on the practice of democracy and the promotion of education and justice, and using "diplomatic strings" to achieve those ends. For instance, U.S. foreign policy could dictate that its support for Pakistan would be guaranteed only if a freely elected government were established within a specific time frame. The United States has given Pakistan about $5 billion since 9/11 alone (and it is estimated about the same outside the budget for security and terror-related activities) and could have demanded that this support be spent on building schools, training teachers, and translating books for Pakistanis, and in turn, making Pakistani literature available to Americans, not on defense purchases. Pakistanis would benefit from the wisdom and elegance of the prose of Franklin and Jefferson, and Americans would appreciate the democratic character of Jinnah and the poetic vision of Iqbal. This simple change in policy and direction would ensure what the present course has failed to accomplish: it would create a genuine appreciation of American involvement in Pakistan among ordinary people and thereby lessen the security threat to Americans.

My recommendation to the Muslim leaders would be the same. Stay as close to your ideals as possible. Emphasize *ilm*, knowledge; *ihsan*, balance and compassion; and *adl*, or justice in your societies. At this time, your people groan under your rule because they see little of these attributes. Neither you nor the surrounding world can afford to keep the Muslim ummah from playing its full role on the world stage. That role will be positive and beneficial to everyone when it is defined by these great Islamic ideals. You need to keep in mind—just as Western leaders must—that according to current demographic estimates 25 percent of the world population of about 11 billion will be living in the fifty-seven Muslim majority nations by 2050.[8]

It was in the spirit of dialogue and compassion that I traveled the world to discover the answers to the problems of our age. I spoke with presidents and prime ministers and questioned scholars and students. I searched in synagogues, churches, mosques, and temples. I had set out to seek wisdom in the sayings and doings of the sages, and I glimpsed the glory of the divine in the hearts of the innocent and the pure. I saw love in the prayers of the pilgrims at the shrine, the kindness of a stranger, and the welcome of our hosts. I was not distracted by the strutting and bellowing of men who, like boys in a school play, convince no one but themselves. I have seen ignorant souls shout down those who spoke of peace and compassion. I heard voices loud and hoarse shouting "not now" and "not here." But I also heard the sweet sounds of other voices through the noisy din, which said, "If not now, then when?. . . It is time, it is time." I heard the echo in the houses of worship, in the cities and villages, in the valleys and mountains: it *is* time.

EPILOGUE

The Hope of the World

AS SEEMS FITTING, our journey to the Muslim world ends at the National Cathedral in Washington, D.C., the city where it began. One of Washington's most recognizable and renowned monuments, the National Cathedral sits atop the highest hill in Washington, its towers visible across the Potomac in Virginia. Built of white and grey stone in the Gothic style, this magnificent and awe-inspiring structure houses dazzling stained glass windows and elaborate chapels. The windows depict American scenes, one of which displays a rock brought back from the moon.

It was a cold February afternoon, with high clouds blocking the sunlight. Inside the cathedral, conditions were much the same, but I felt aglow. The bishop of Washington was dedicating a special evensong in honor of my being named the Washington, D.C., Professor of the Year 2004 in an unprecedented interfaith event.

Together a Jewish rabbi, a Christian bishop, and an Islamic scholar read from their holy texts, delivered sermons from the pulpit, and talked of their friendship and outreach to each other in these difficult and troubled times. I surveyed the audience from the pulpit and felt the triumph of the generosity of the human spirit and my heart soared:

> This event itself is so highly symbolic to me. There are others at my university far more deserving of this unprecedented honor. Its symbolism alone is a landmark in interfaith dialogue. Imagine a

reversal of the event: the central mosque in Cairo or Lahore or Kuala Lumpur inviting a leading Jewish or Christian scholar at the Friday prayer and dedicating a sermon to the scholar. It is a great gesture and I hope will be reciprocated by Muslim religious leaders.

Therefore I wish to point out my friends, John and Bruce, that you are the true leaders of dialogue, compassion, and understanding in our world and I know while I have been involved in this dialogue I have often received negative, even hate mail from others who do not believe in it. Equally I know that you two have had similar negative responses from your own people. Indeed I have seen the attacks on the Bishop under the banner "Washington's first openly Jewish and Muslim Bishop." My friends, these are titles of honor and I am sure that those great Biblical figures that inspire us from the time of Abraham would commend you for recognizing our common humanity in very difficult and dangerous times. Indeed I wish to place on record that I have seen and heard both the Bishop and the Senior Rabbi stand up and speak boldly against the human rights violations and loss of civil liberties that Muslims often have to endure. This is true faith and friendship.

That Sunday evening, some 700 people had gathered to share in this powerful and special moment of interfaith dialogue. Participants included students, ambassadors, and former prime ministers. Guests came from outside Washington—from Palm Beach, Los Angeles, and Boston. A Zoroastrian friend, Jimmy Engineer, the Pakistani painter, had arrived from Karachi to join the event. Notable among the attendees were Muslim ambassadors, imams—including Imam Magid, head of the largest Islamic center in the Washington area—the directors of the Council on American-Islamic Relations (CAIR) and the Islamic Society of North America (ISNA), and the secretary general of the Pakistan American Congress. They were all aware that they were participating in an extraordinary experience. Emotions ran high, and there were many moist eyes—even a BBC journalist had tears in her eyes.

The symbolism was powerful. This was, after all, the National Cathedral, one of the largest churches in the world, and situated in the heart of the capital city of the only superpower in the early part of the twenty-first century. This is where the president of the United States has prayed and state events are held such as the recent funeral service for President Ronald Reagan and even more recently for Gerald Ford.[1]

Bishop John Chane of the National Cathedral hosts an unprecedented evensong in honor of Akbar Ahmed at the cathedral in Washington, D.C., in February 2005. The bishop and Rabbi Bruce Lustig of Washington Hebrew Congregation had made Ahmed and his family feel welcome after September 11, when anger against and distrust of Muslims were widespread.

This unprecedented event for the three Abrahamic faiths—Judaism, Christianity, and Islam—came as a result of my friendship with two remarkable souls: Episcopal Bishop John Chane, with his hearty laugh, open heart, and kind words, and Senior Rabbi Bruce Lustig, head of the Washington Hebrew Congregation, the youngest of the three of us and yet always wise and caring. Both the bishop and rabbi greeted people with wide friendly smiles and a twinkle in their eyes. Their hearts were as pure as their thoughts. For me, the two embody the best of their respective faiths.

I first met Rabbi Lustig through his wife, Amy, at a big annual dinner not long after September 11, 2001. Sensing that I looked lost because I did not know anyone there, she introduced me to her husband, Bruce. Not long afterward, he invited Zeenat and me for dinner to meet the newly arrived Bishop John Chane and his wife, Karen. We met that night and stayed up late discovering that we shared a passion for finding common themes in different faith traditions, and from it grew a strong friendship. Together, we launched several important initiatives, including the First Abraham Summit hosted by Bruce and the now nationally known Unity Walk held annually on September 11. The walk is led by the three of us, beginning at the Washington Hebrew Congregation, stopping at the National Cathedral, and ending at the Islamic Center of Washington with members of every faith joining us.

At the ceremony, Rabbi Lustig ascended to the pulpit of the cathedral to give his passionate Abrahamic invocation, called "Dr. Akbar Ahmed: A God Seeker":

> To find such an individual is rare. In a post-9/11 world when the common becomes suspect, when fear and indifference prevail, rather than look for others we too often shun them; we build walls to protect ourselves and we become more fearful and more isolated. We are unable to look for others or for God. . . . As a descendant of Abraham, when others choose to build walls of fear he chooses to build bridges of understanding. Akbar does this not by denying the harsh realities of our day, but by, in spite of them, meeting others in "I–thou" encounters. He has stood in front of the open Torah on the *bimah* of our synagogue; he has brought religious leaders from Pakistan's Islamic community to participate in an interfaith seder; he has been on countless panels and TV broadcasts. From church basements in folding chairs to the White House next to the President's chair, he never misses the opportunity to teach so that we may understand that true Islam is a religion of peace. Amidst the voices of extremism on all sides, we are grateful that we have found another voice—it is Akbar's voice; it is calm, it is gentle, it is filled with wisdom and truth. Indeed, Akbar has that courage, to say no to hate and violence, and no to fear and isolation. It is true courage, for even in times of personal risk, he continues to say no to injustice and yes to dialogue and faith in God.

Bishop John Chane, then closing with his Sunday sermon, filled the nave with his warm spirituality and moral clarity:

> Bruce, Akbar and I represent the dreamers and visionaries of our global community. . . . Our times together sharing food and conver-

sation at a common table with our families have filled my heart with joy and hopefulness. It is a hopefulness that the world, too often divided by those who presume to possess exclusive claims to the true and inerrant knowledge of the God of all creation, will become a world where all can live together in peace and harmony. . . . We gather in this great cathedral tonight, a sacred space for a sacred journey; a Jew, a Christian, and a Muslim, to remind one another and each of you that with God, all things are possible. And with God we believe with all our hearts that there will come a time on this earth when all of God's children will all be able to celebrate that peace which passes all understanding.

We are living in times where the world is dangerously imbalanced. We simply cannot go on as we are. I believe the world is becoming more aware than ever before of our shared human destiny. For we are brothers on a journey who share the same God and in many ways the same ancient, holy stories that both mystically bind us together and yet define each of our religious traditions as being distinctly different. For many this may seem a radical statement—for me it is the hope of the world!

The bishop is right: this is the hope of the world. When I look at other human beings, I may notice their ethnicity or their different religion, but I know that each and every one of us is destined to go through the same cycle of birth, growth, and eventual death; that we all feel pain, happiness, and grief; I know that our hearts cry when a child is in pain or someone old and helpless is suffering. I know how deeply our destinies are now linked on this already overpopulated and increasingly impoverished planet. I feel the loneliness that is at the heart of the human predicament and the deep sorrow at the greed, anger, and ignorance that encroach on us.

I also know of the goodness and vitality in individuals of every race and religion. I know that although the planet's societies are running against time, there is hope for them as a world community; but that they must embrace love in the spirit of those who have spoken of it—and sometimes suffered for it—as an expression of humanity's all-inclusiveness. To transcend race, tribe, and religion and cherish our common humanity, every individual must become the message, conveyed by one simple word: that is the hope of the world.

Analysis of the Questionnaires

Hadia Mubarak

with the "Islam in the Age of Globalization" Team

Questionnaires were distributed in universities, hotels, cafés, mosques, and homes in Turkey, Qatar, Syria, Jordan, Pakistan, India, Malaysia, and Indonesia. Responses averaged 120 per country and provide a sampling of contemporary and historical role models, as follows.

Demographics

Most respondents ranged in age from the teens (high school age) to late twenties. Therefore, our data generally reflect the perceptions and views of youth in the countries we visited. Since we usually started our project by visiting universities and high schools, we continued this approach throughout our trip. Despite this bias toward educated youth (those enrolled in school), we sought a balance between male and female respondents and between low and high socioeconomic backgrounds. For example, in Jordan we visited an elite, Western-oriented high school, the Amman Baccalaureate School, and a similar school in Pakistan, Karachi Grammar School. Both schools are attended by the children of diplomats, government officials, and the upper class. At madrassahs, respondents reflected a lower socioeconomic class. We also included middle-class universities, such as Quaid-i-Azam University, University of Jordan, Abu Nour Institute, Islamic University of Malaysia, and Qatar University.

One interesting finding is that although our sampling represents a variety of elite, upper-class, middle-class, and lower-class professionals and youth, respondents were consistent in their selections of religious figures. Those mentioned by one set of students in a religious school were also mentioned in the secular schools. Hence the responses reflect a strong sense of religious identification.

Contemporary Role Models

Responses showed no consensus on a contemporary role model. Furthermore, most of the contemporary role models are region-specific: most selected in the Arab world do not coincide with those selected in South Asia or Southeast Asia, with some exceptions. Contemporary figures as a whole fall into three categories:

1. Nongovernmental figures from the Deoband model. Some represent a modernist Islamic approach that is politically pragmatic, encouraging political participation and recognizing the legitimacy of the modern nation-state system in order to advance its Islamic cause. Examples of such figures identified in nearly all of the countries were Yousef al-Qaradawi, a charismatic preacher, Abu A'la Maududi, an influential Muslim theologian, and Hassan Al-Banna, founder of the Islamic Brotherhood. Respondents who identified other popular Deoband figures, such as Osama bin Laden, were opposed to participation in any electoral process.

2. Deoband figures involved in government, either heads of state or other political figures who are perceived as revolutionary and who have stood up to the West or Israel at some point in their political career. Some examples are Mahmoud Ahmadinejad, Yasser Arafat, Hasan Nasrallah, and Ayatollah Ruhollah Khomeini.

3. Muslims from the Ajmer and Aligarh models. Many are icons of a newly emerging Islamic pop culture or are leaders of an interpretation of Islam that seeks to "modernize" Islam in a traditional context or attempt to synthesize Islam and the West. Examples are Sami Yusuf, an Iranian-British singer and songwriter, Yusuf Islam (Cat Stevens), and Hamza Yusuf, an American convert to Islam. Amr Khaled stands out as the top contemporary role model in every country we visited in the Arab world. He was selected by 45 percent to 60 percent of the populations in each Arab country. There is a sense among the respondents that the image of

Islam, and hence of all those who follow Islam, is being defined and nego-tiated by current political events. Thus they are looking to role models who can either undo the damage or at least impose some damage control by presenting the "proper image of Islam." Amr Khaled's presentation of Islam resonated loudest with Jordanian, Syrian, and Qatari youth. Where most Muslim youth in all countries surveyed believe that the West's "incorrect image of Islam" is the number one problem facing the Muslim world, there is an attempt to restore the "authenticity" or true image of Islam. Thus one of the most common reasons cited for Amr Khaled's pop-ularity is his proper representation or love of the religion and his strength, determination, and sacrifice for Islam. Other more politically active names associated with the Aligarh model included Mahathir bin Mohamad, the former prime minister of Malaysia.

Turkey

Turkey's top role models are predominantly Islamic thinkers and lead-ers who represent the Ajmer and Aligarh models. The leading two are Fethullah Gülen (45 percent) and Said Nursi (18 percent). Gülen is an Islamic Sufi intellectual known for his promotion of interfaith dialogue in different communities, nations, and cultures. He has millions of followers and is considered one of the most influential Turkish Islamic figures of his generation. His movement, the Gülen movement, has founded hundreds of schools, primarily in Turkey and Central Asia. The author of thirty books, Gülen currently resides in Pennsylvania. Said Nursi, an Islamic intellectual named by 18 percent of respondents, sought to combine reli-gious and secular education. Nearly 30 percent of respondents said they did not have a contemporary role model, which reflects a level of disenchant-ment among Turkish youth.

Qatar

Respondents in Qatar revealed a strong sense of religious identification. Young Qataris overwhelmingly selected two religious scholars as role mod-els: Sheikh Yousef al-Qaradawi (45 percent), identified with the Deoband model, and the young charismatic preacher Amr Khaled (45 percent) of the Aligarh model. Qaradawi is an influential scholar and preacher best known for his popular Al-Jazeera program, *Al-Shariah wal-Hayat* (Shariah and Life), and his website IslamOnline, launched in 1997. He has also published some fifty books, including *The Lawful and the Prohibited in Islam* and *Islam: The Future Civilization*. More popular than Oprah Winfrey is in the United States, Khaled is the world's first Islamic television evangelist with millions of followers. The person next in popularity was Sheikha Moza bint Nasser al-Misnad, the first lady of Qatar, owing to her manifestation of religious symbols. One student at Education City wrote, "She's improving things and keeping traditions, even the hijab. She makes us proud." Another young female from Qatar's Ministry of Foreign Affairs admired Sheikha Moza for her "dawah for Islam ["invitation" to Islam] and love to guide others and benefit society." The next top two role models are also religious scholars or figures: Tariq Sweidan (13.2 percent) and Sheikh Al-Sudais (10.5 percent), the imam of the Grand Mosque of Saudi Arabia. Hasan Nasrallah, Hezbollah's leader, was also chosen by 10.5 percent of respondents as their contemporary role model.

Syria

As in the other Arab countries visited, Amr Khaled was the number one contemporary role model in Syria. As in Jordan, Khaled is the only contemporary model to receive a majority of the respondents' votes. With the exception of Mahathir bin Mohamad, all of the role models selected in Syria are religious figures, either scholars, preachers, or authors who explore religious issues. One possible reason for the former prime minister of Malaysia's popularity in Syria is his outspoken criticism of the United States and Israel during and after his term. Second and third on the list were Ahmed Kuftaro, the former Grand Mufti of Syria, and parliamentarian and imam Muhammad Habash. However, since a significant proportion of our respondents were students of Ahmad Kuftaro's academic institution, Abu Noor, or attended Az-Zahra's Mosque, where Muhammad Habash preaches, these results need to be viewed in the light of the respondents' affiliation to either scholar in some way. A fifth of respondents mentioned Yousef al-Qaradawi as their top contemporary role model. Qaradawi is one of the few regional figures whose name emerges in nearly every country we visited.

Jordan

The majority of respondents in Jordan (60.5 percent) selected Amr Khaled as their contemporary role model. Fewer than 20 percent of respondents chose contemporary role models. One young female wrote she would consult Amr Khaled and Yusuf Qaradawi if she had a religious question "because they are not too strict or too loose, but moderate. Their approach is easy and makes one love religion; it is not hateful or repugnant." The second most popular figure in Jordan is Tariq Al-Sweidan, who is renowned for his lectures and shows on Islam and character development. He is also the founder of Al-Resala satellite channel. His message is not too different from Khaled's. He also emphasizes the need to relay the message of Islam with competence and perfection. He stresses the importance of representing the lifestyle of Islam in a way that is compatible with contemporary social needs. As in Qatar, 10.5 percent of the respondents in Jordan chose Hasan Nasrallah, Hezbollah's leader, as their contemporary role model. While this may not be a huge share, it is still significant. He was considered more popular than Jordan's current ruler, King Abdullah II. Christian and Muslim students alike chose Nasrallah as a role model. For example, a Christian Jordanian female (nineteen years old) indicated that Nasrallah is her role model because of "justice, courage, and [protecting] the rights of individuals." One twenty-year-old Jordanian female wrote: "I feel proud that such strong authority figures can shine unselfishly doing charitable acts and not abusing their religion." About 9.9 percent chose Ahmed Yassin, the spiritual adviser of Hamas who was assassinated by Israel in 2004. At least 10 percent in Qatar also saw Yassin as a role model.

Pakistan

Pakistani respondents' top role models, unlike their Turkish and Arab counterparts whose choices were regional, were not confined to South Asia. And while at least one major figure emerges as the role model for over 50 percent of the population in the Arab states, there is no such consensus in Pakistan. About a quarter of those interviewed did select Mahathir bin Mohamad, the former prime minister of Malaysia (1981–2003), as their top choice as role model. As in Turkey, 16 percent of Pakistani youth said they had no role model. Again, this reflects a mood of disenchantment and disappointment among the youth. Fourteen percent of the youth interviewed selected Yasser Arafat, former president of the Palestine Liberation Organization (PLO), and Mahmoud Ahmadinejad, the current president of Iran. Both of these figures reflect an inclination toward figures seen as "revolutionary," "strong," and able to stand up to the West.

Interestingly, the three kings of Saudi Arabia made it as top role models for Pakistani youth, with 7.1 percent selecting King Fahad and King Abdullah, and 4.8 percent King Faisal. Ironically, Arab respondents made no mention of Saudi Arabia whatsoever. The fact that all three kings were mentioned by various youth in diverse locations (Quaid-i-Azam University, Aga Khan University, and Karachi Grammar School) illustrates a level of admiration for or affinity with the Kingdom of Saudi Arabia among educated youth in Pakistan. Some of the reasons cited for King Abdullah bin Abdul Aziz's selection were "we always found him a friend" or "his services for the Muslim ummah" or "he has the best foreign policy with Islamic states." Some reasons cited for selecting King Fahad were that he "played a vital role in the prosperity of Muslims" or "fought against Jews for the spiritual freedom of Muslims." Ten percent of Pakistani youth selected Abdul Sattar Edhi, a major philanthropist in Pakistan, as a role model. As the founder of the Edhi Foundation, he has established hospitals, ambulance services, clinics, maternity homes, mental asylums, homes for the physically handicapped, blood banks, orphanages, adoption centers, mortuaries, shelters for runaway children and battered women, schools, nursing courses, and soup kitchens. According to the *Guinness Book of World Records,* as of 1997 the Edhi Foundation's ambulance service is the largest volunteer ambulance service in the world.

India

The top role models selected in India were Sir Sayyed Ahmad Khan of the Aligarh model and Sayyed Abu A'la Maududi of the Deoband model, both favored by nearly 18 percent of respondents. Sir Sayyed Ahmad Khan (1817–98), most commonly known as Sir Sayyed, was the most influential Muslim statesman of his time. He pioneered modern education for the Muslim community in India by founding the Muhammedan Anglo-Oriental College, which later developed into the Aligarh Muslim University. His work gave rise to a new generation of Muslim intellectuals and politicians known as the Aligarh movement, which sought to secure the political future of Muslims in India. Believing that the future of Muslims was threatened by their orthodox nature and outlook, Sir Sayyed began promoting Western education by founding modern schools, journals, and organizations.

Sayyed Abu A'la Maududi (1903–79), often referred to as Maulana Maududi, was one of the most influential Muslim theologians of the twentieth century and the founder of Jamaat-e-Islami (Islamic party) political party in Pakistan. Maulana Maududi's philosophy, literary productivity, and untiring activism contributed immensely to the development of Islamic political and social movements around the world. Maulana Maududi's ideas profoundly influenced Syed Qutb, another leading Muslim philosopher of the twentieth century, of Egypt's Jamiat al-Ikhwan al-Muslimun (Muslim Brotherhood). Qutb was the fourth top contemporary role model in India, favored by 10 percent of the youth. Together, Maududi, Qutb, and Hassan Al-Banna are considered the founding fathers of the global Islamic revival movement and represent the appeal of the Deoband model in India today

Zakir Naik (1965–) has emerged as a new popular religious figure in South Asia. He was selected by approximately 12 percent of the Indian youth we surveyed and was the third top contemporary role model. Naik speaks extensively on the subject of Islam and comparative religion. He has delivered more than 600 lectures on Islam throughout the world. A medical doctor by training, Naik appears regularly on many international television channels in more than 100 countries. He is the president of the Islamic Research Foundation (IRF) and has written books on Islam.

Malaysia

As in South Asia, the role models selected in Malaysia represent a variety of regions. Aside from some respondents who named the scholars Tariq Ramadan of Switzerland, and Ismail Faruqi of Palestine, most people expressed support for Deoband figures such as Maulana Maududi, Syed Qutb, and Rachid Ghanouchi, the leader of Al-Nahda, a major Tunisian Islamic party banned by the Tunisian government. The heads of state named as role models are primarily those that have stood up to the West or Israel at some point in time: Ayatollah Khomeini, Mahathir bin Mohamad, Yasser Arafat of the PLO, and Ahmadinejad of Iran. As was the case in Pakistan, the top role model selected in Malaysia is Mahathir bin Mohamad, the former prime minister of Malaysia, selected by 35 percent. The second top role model is Sheikh Yousef al-Qaradawi (favored by 25 percent), the world-renowned Islamic scholar. Qaradawi's name emerged as a top role model in every country in which we conducted surveys. Third on the list is Abdullah bin Haji Ahmad Badawi, who succeeded Mahathir as prime minister in 2003.

Indonesia

Most Indonesian respondents voiced strong support for the Deoband model, but the Aligarh model does make a notable appearance in Abdullah Gymanster (also known as A. A. Gym), a popular Islamic televangelist who has an audience of 80 million. A. A. Gym wants to build professionalism and entrepreneurship through Islam. He has set up a service called al-Quran Seluler, which sends text messages or voice mail of his commentary on the Quran. He reaches at least 60 million people weekly through television and radio, not including his books, cassettes, videos, newspaper, management training seminars, and aphorisms printed on the red cans of the soft drink he markets. A. A. Gym is also one of the only Indonesian Muslim leaders to publicly speak at a Christian church and has been one of the country's most prominent promoters of peace and tolerance. A minority of respondents also listed liberal Muslim intellectuals as their contemporary role models. For example, Nasr Hamid Abu Zayd, who is living in exile in the Netherlands due to his critical, nontraditional hermeneutics of the Quran, was selected by 4.5 percent of respondents. A small number of respondents also selected feminists or progressive scholars like Aminah Wadud, Hassan Hanafi, Fatima Mernissi, and Nawal El-Sadawi. Still, support for the Deoband model was extremely strong in Indonesia. While bin Laden came up as a role model in every country surveyed, in Indonesia he was cited as a role model by 25 percent of respondents. Other figures who "stood up" to the West, including Ayatollah Khomeini, Saddam Hussein, Moammar Gaddafi, and Mahmoud Ahmadinejad, were also extremely popular.

Historical Role Models

There is much more of a consensus on historical role models in the Muslim world. The Prophet Muhammad was by far the top historic role model in every country except for Syria, where the second caliph, Umar, and Saladin headed the list. Nevertheless, more than a majority of the respondents selected the Prophet in each country, with the largest margins in Qatar (87 percent) and Pakistan (82 percent).

Apart from the Prophet, the most frequently mentioned historical role models are the four caliphs in Islam: Abu Bakr (632–634 C.E.), Umar bin Al-Khattab (634–644 C.E.), Uthman bin Affan (644–656 C.E.), and Ali ibn Talib (656–661 C.E.), who are often known as the "four righteous caliphs." Umar is the most popular of the four caliphs, often admired for his justice, strength, courage, and sacrifice for Islam. Muslims look upon the period of the four caliphs as the epitome of an authentic and righteous Islamic government, which the Muslim community never experienced thereafter. These figures reflect young people's reverence for the first Muslim community and those who helped sustain it. For the youth, these figures are larger than life.

There is a strong inclination in all the countries polled toward historical Islamic figures, especially those who represent military conquest. This matches with the present appeal of the Deoband model and the naming of contemporary role models who "stood up" to the West.

Turkey

In contrast to the other countries, many Sufi figures emerge, as they did in the respondents' contemporary role models, including Persian poet and mystic Maulana Jalaluddin Rumi, Turkish poet Yunus Emre, and Islamic scholar Abdul-Qadir Jaylani. Interestingly, Saladin and Khalid bin Al-Waleed do not make an appearance in Turkey, whereas they are extremely popular in all the other countries. However, Turkish respondents inclined more toward other political figures who represent victory and strength for the Muslims, specifically in that region. For example, 12 percent considered Sultan Mehmet (Mohammad) Al-Fatih a role model. He was responsible for the defeat of the Byzantine Empire through his conquest of their capital, Constantinople. Another role model, Imam Shamil (1797–1871), an Avar political and religious leader of the Muslim tribes of the Northern Caucasus, led Caucasian tribes in a resistance against Russian rule in what was known as the Caucasian War and was the third imam of Dagestan and Chechnya (1834–59).

Qatar

Qatar's two most popular figures besides the Prophet and four righteous caliphs are Khalid bin Al-Waleed, the commander-in-chief of the Muslim army during the time of the Prophet up to the second caliphate, and Saladin, the commander-in-chief of the Muslim army that defeated the Crusaders and conquered Jerusalem in 1187 C.E. Named by 45 percent of the respondents, Khalid bin Al-Waleed was more popular than the last two caliphs, Uthman and Ali. Saladin ranked sixth in popularity, after the Prophet, the four caliphs, and Khalid.

The top reasons for selecting Khalid and Saladin were their strength, their sacrifice for Islam, and their ability to bring victory to Muslims. One young woman from Education City said, "They were great leaders in Islamic history who influenced and changed the history of the Muslim world. They achieved great victories for Muslims." Another student wrote, "They left all of life's luxury and stood up in the face of their opponents; they sacrificed their life and soul for the sake of God and Islam." Still another mentioned Saladin and Khalid bin Al-Waleed because of their "perseverance and firmness during difficult times, and for defending the religion despite the obstacles they faced."

Syria

The highest-ranked historical role models in Syria were the second caliph, Umar (67 percent), and Saladin Al-Ayyubi (57 percent), who were selected by more respondents than even the Prophet. This is not an indication of less reverence for the Prophet, however, especially considering the religious nature of the institutions we visited, but more a product of Syria's political circumstances. Anti-American sentiment runs very deep in Syria, as evidenced by the fact that some students refused to fill out our questionnaires. With Syria bearing a considerable amount of U.S. rhetoric against dictatorial regimes and terrorism, the youth are looking to historical role models that signal or represent a military victory for Muslims. Both Umar and Saladin represent strength, justice, and dignity in the minds of the Syrian respondents—precisely the concepts they are seeking to restore today. A similar figure, Khalid bin Al-Waleed, was selected by nearly a quarter of the youth we interviewed. Like Umar and Saladin, Khalid represents strength and victory in Muslim historical consciousness.

Jordan

In Jordan, the Prophet Muhammad ranked the highest, as in every country but Syria. Again, the second caliph, Umar, and Saladin came in second and third as historical role models. Immediately after the Prophet, Umar was selected by a clear majority of Jordanians. As in the other Arab countries, Caliph Abu Bakr and Khalid bin Al-Waleed ranked highest after the Prophet, Umar, and Saladin, with a slight variation.

Pakistan

Pakistan and the Arab states we surveyed differ in two important respects. First, Ali, the fourth caliph, is far more popular in Pakistan than in the Arab states. This is primarily due to Pakistan's large Shia community, which constitutes 20 percent of the population. Second, Mohammed Ali Jinnah, the founder of the Islamic Republic of Pakistan, was the top historical role model, after the Prophet and three of the "righteous" caliphs.

India

As in most of the countries we surveyed, the Prophet Muhammad and Umar Al-Khattab, the second caliph, were the most popular historical role models. In addition to the four "righteous" caliphs, other popular historical figures that emerge are Hassan Al-Banna, Muhammad Ibn Abdul Wahhab, and Ibn Taymiyya of the Deoband model, Sir Sayyed Ahmad Khan of the Aligarh model, and Mohammad Iqbal, the Islamic poet-philosopher of Pakistan, whose thinking reflects all three models.

Malaysia

In Malaysia, the Prophet Muhammad and the four caliphs were the most popular historical role models. Besides the top five, we found a strong inclination toward intellectual figures in Islamic history, from Ibn Khaldun, Ibn Sina, and Al-Khawarizmi to Imam Ghazzali and Imam Al-Shafi'i. Not coincidentally, Malaysia showed a strong intellectual leaning, in that Malaysian respondents relied more on books as primary sources of information than respondents in any other country.

Indonesia

As in Malaysia, the Prophet and the four caliphs were the most popular historical role models in Indonesia. There is a great prevalence of historical Deoband figures in Indonesia, including Ibn Taymiyya, Ibn Qayyim Al-Jawzi, and Hassan Al-Banna. Like Malaysians, however, Indonesian respondents showed a strong preference for intellectual figures such as Imam Ghazzali, Imam Shafi'i, Ibn Khaldun, Ibn Rushd, and, nearer to our own times, Muhammad Abduh.

NOTES

Chapter One

1. See Frankie Martin and Hailey Woldt, "Frankie and Hailey Go to the Muslim World with the Leading Islamic Scholar 'Our Favorite Professor,'" *Pakistan Link* (www.pakistanlink.com/Comunity [May 26, 2006]): "Frequently on the journey we would turn to each other and ask, 'Is this really happening?' Only one year ago exactly we had been sitting in an honors lecture class taught by Professor Akbar Ahmed on the 'Clash or Dialogue of Civilizations' as virtual strangers, but as the three of us were together in a car in India for hours, hot, hungry, and tired, it seemed like we had been family for ages. . . . In taking this trip, we put our complete trust in Dr. Ahmed, and during the course of our journey he became a father to us, always making sure he knew where we were at all times and sometimes correcting our every move like a 'father hen' to make sure we were behaving respectfully so as not to be in harm's way by inadvertently offending local culture. Along the journey, we got to know our professor so well that Frankie and I would often bet on his next moves. On a PIA flight from Lahore to Delhi, Frankie and I bet on whether or not he would eat his sandwich when he came back from the restroom; as usual, Hailey guessed it right."

2. Aijaz Qasmi, *Jihad and Terrorism,* in Urdu (India, 2005).

3. Muslim scholars who followed him, such as Ibn Taymiyya, adapted the saying. See www.mpacuk.org/content/view/2203/34/.

4. Samuel P. Huntington, *The Clash of Civilizations and the Remaking of the World Order* (New York: Simon & Schuster, 2003).

5. For an accessible textbook, see Conrad Phillip Kottak, *Cultural Anthropology* (New York: McGraw-Hill, 2000).

6. Bronislaw Malinowski, *Argonauts of the Western Pacific* (New York: Dutton, 1961), p. 20.

7. Clyde Kluckhohn, *Mirror for Man: A Survey of Human Behavior and Social Attitudes* (Greenwich, Conn.: Fawcett, 1944), p. 9.

8. Clifford Geetz, *Islam Observed: Religious Development in Morocco and Indonesia* (University of Chicago Press, 1968); Ernest Gellner, *Muslim Society* (Cambridge University Press, 1981).

9. See www.pewglobal.org.

10. See, for example, David Ray Griffin, *The New Pearl Harbor: Disturbing Questions about the Bush Administration and 9/11* (Northampton, Mass.: Interlink, 2004); and Griffin, *Christian Faith and the Truth behind 9/11: A Call to Reflection and Action* (Louisville, Ky.: Westminster John Knox Press, 2006).

11. Jonathan Sacks, *The Dignity of Difference: How to Avoid the Clash of Civilizations* (London: Continuum, 2002).

12. Karen Armstrong, *The Battle for God: Fundamentalism in Judaism, Christianity and Islam* (London: HarperCollins, 2000).

13. Akbar S. Ahmed, *Islam under Siege: Living Dangerously in a Post-Honor World* (Cambridge, U.K.: Polity, 2003).

14. Jonathan Hayden, "The Challenge of the Moderates" (www.beliefnet.com [April 24, 2006]).

15. See Hailey Woldt, "A Young American in the Muslim World" (www.beliefnet.com [April 12, 2006]); Martin and Woldt, "Frankie and Hailey Go to the Muslim World"; Hayden, "The Challenge of the Moderates"; and Amineh Ahmed Hoti, "A Journey to Understanding: Reflections from Indonesia," *Pakistan Link* (www.pakistanlink.com/Community [June 9, 2006]).

16. For comments of team members, see Martin and Woldt, "Frankie and Hailey Go to the Muslim World": "Traveling with Dr. Ahmed opened more doors for us than we ever would have imagined possible, and were very surprised at the warm welcomes we received from everyone we encountered, regardless of their ideologies or political positions. Even those who[m] Americans would deem 'Islamic extremists,' like those traditional and orthodox scholars in Deoband, welcomed us because of our relationship to Professor Ahmed and engaged us in discussions. High-profile politicians we met also greeted Dr. Ahmed with great respect, including President Musharraf, who referred to him as 'Akbar Sahib,' a term of high esteem in Pakistan. We were shocked when, after a speech at a hotel in Islamabad, Dr. Ahmed was mobbed by a throng of people wanting to speak to him, as if our favorite professor were some kind of rock star. We began to realize that Dr. Ahmed had a global reach that we were unaware of sitting on campus in Washington, which was integral to connecting us with people across the political spectrum and cultural disparities in such different parts of the world."

17. Thomas L. Friedman, *The Lexus and the Olive Tree: Understanding Globalization* (New York: Farrar, Straus and Giroux, 1999) p. xix; and Friedman, *The World Is Flat: A Brief History of the Twenty-First Century* (New York: Farrar, Straus and Giroux, 2005).

18. See, for example, John Baylis and Steve Smith, eds., *The Globalization of*

World Politics: An Introduction to International Relations, 3rd ed. (Oxford University Press, 2005).

19. Ulrich Beck, *Risk Society: Towards a New Modernity*, translated by Mark Ritter (London: Sage, 1992; originally published 1986).

20. Anthony Giddens, *Runaway World: How Globalization Is Reshaping Our Lives* (New York: Routledge, 2000), p. 33.

21. Ibid., p. 34.

22. Giddens borrowed the title *Runaway World* from another series of Reith lectures delivered by the renowned anthropologist Edmund Leach in 1968.

23. Giddens, *Runaway World*, p. 37.

24. Daisaku Ikeda, "Foreword," in *Subverting Greed: Religious Perspectives on the Global Economy*, edited by Paul Knitter and Chandra Muzaffar (New York: Orbis Books, Maryknoll, 2002), p. xii; see also the study of Buddha and Buddhist thought by Karen Armstrong, *Buddha* (New York: Penguin Books, 2001).

25. Armstrong, *Buddha*. See also Mary Pat Fisher's authoritative *Living Religions*, 6th ed. (Englewood Cliffs, N.J.: Prentice-Hall, 2005); and T. N. Madan, ed., *India's Religions: Perspectives from Sociology and History* (Oxford University Press, 2004). For fuller explanations of these very features in the context of Islamic society and history, see Akbar S. Ahmed, *Discovering Islam: Making Sense of Muslim History and Society* (London: Routledge, 2002; originally published in 1988), and Ahmed, *Islam under Siege*. For an excellent discussion of these values in Judaism, see Jonathan Sacks, *To Heal a Fractured World* (London: Continuum, 2005).

26. See, for example, Al Gore, *An Inconvenient Truth: The Planetary Emergency of Global Warming and What We Can Do about It* (New York: Rodale Press, 2006), and his accompanying Oscar-winning documentary.

27. Sacks, *The Dignity of Difference*, pp. 106–07.

28. See United Nations Population Division, *World Population "Prospects": The 2004 Revision* (http://esa.un.org/unpp/index.asp).

29. Amy Chua, *World on Fire: How Exporting Free Market Democracy Breeds Ethnic Hatred and Global Instability* (New York: Doubleday, 2003); Thérèse Delpech, *Savage Century: Back to Barbarism* (Washington, D.C.: Carnegie Endowment for International Peace, 2007).

30. See, for example, Philip Pan, "Civil Unrest Challenges China's Party Leadership," *Washington Post*, November 4, 2004.

31. Ahmed, *Islam under Siege*.

32. Ahmed, *Discovering Islam*.

33. For an illuminating discussion, see Armstrong, *The Battle for God*; Sacks, *To Heal a Fractured World*.

34. Sharon Marcus, *Sufi: A Commentary* (Toronto: Sufi Press, 2006), p. 362.

35. Ibid., p. 97.

36. Shaykh Fadhlalla Haeri, *The Thoughtful Guide to Sufism* (Alresford, U.K.: O Books, 2004; originally published 1990), pp. 7–9.

37. Ibid., p. 8.

38. Norman Gershman, personal communication. For a groundbreaking study of Arabs who saved Jews during World War II, see Robert B. Satloff, *Among the Righteous: Lost Stories from the Holocaust's Long Reach into Arab Lands* (New York: Public Affairs, 2006).

39. For a perceptive comment on Shia society and history, see Michael J. Fischer, *Iran: From Religious Dispute to Revolution* (Harvard University Press, 1980). For a more contemporary insider's view, see Vali Nasr, *The Shia Revival: How Conflicts within Islam Will Shape the Future* (New York: W. W. Norton, 2006); Vali Nasr, *Democracy in Iran: History and the Quest for Liberty* (Oxford University Press, 2006); and Reza Aslan, *No God but God: The Origins, Evolution, and Future of Islam* (New York: Random House, 2005).

40. Richard Ashby Wilson, ed., *Human Rights in the "War on Terror"* (Cambridge University Press, 2005).

41. Giddens, *Runaway World*, p. 22.

Chapter Two

1. Rajmohan Gandhi, *Revenge and Reconciliation: Understanding South Asian History* (New Delhi: Penguin Books India, 1999), p. 97.

2. Gordon Johnson, *Cultural Atlas of India: India, Pakistan, Nepal, Bhutan, Bangladesh and Sri Lanka* (New York: Facts on File, 1996), p. 108.

3. See Yoginder Sikand, "Beyond 'Hindu' and 'Muslim': Dara Shikoh's Quest for Spiritual Unity" (www.svabhinava.org/MeccaBenares/YoginderSikand/Dara Shikoh.htm [2004]).

4. Akbar S. Ahmed, *Discovering Islam: Making Sense of Muslim History and Society* (London: Routledge, 2002; originally published 1988), p. 80.

5. Amartya Sen, *Identity and Violence: The Illusion of Destiny* (New York: W. W. Norton, 2006), p. 64.

6. Stanley Wolpert, *A New History of India* (Oxford University Press, 2000), pp. 157–58.

7. Michael H. Fisher, *Visions of Mughal India: An Anthology of European Travel Writing* (London: I. B. Tauris, 2007).

8. See prose and letters of the renowned Urdu poet of Delhi, Mirza Ghalib.

9. Tridivesh Singh Maini, *South Asian Cooperation and the Role of the Punjabs* (New Delhi: Siddharth Publications, 2007). Even before writing his book, Tridivesh had shown his capacity to reach out in affectionate generosity to those of other faiths. In a note, he wrote: "Dr. Ahmed is the pride of every South Asian—Sikh, Muslim or Hindu ... rationality, serenity and humility are the great qualities which Dr. Ahmed has." He wished "important people" adopted these virtues as well.

10. Daniel Ladinsky, *Love Poems from God: Twelve Sacred Voices from the East and West* (New York: Penguin Compass, 2002), p. 2.

11. Ibid., p. 9.

12. Coleman Barks, *The Essential Rumi* (San Franciso: Harper, 1995), pp. 201, 204.

13. These words are from the Deoband official website, edited by Aijaz.

14. Barbara Daly Metcalf, *Islamic Contestations: Essays on Muslims in India and Pakistan* (Oxford University Press, 2004), p. 35; see also Metcalf, *Islamic Revival in British India: Deoband, 1860–1900* (Oxford University Press, 2002).

15. See www.DarulUloom-Deoband.com/english.

16. Jawaharlal Nehru, *The Discovery of India* (London: Meridian Books, 1960).

17. See Christina Lamb, *The Sewing Circles of Herat: A Personal Voyage through Afghanistan* (London: HarperCollins, 2002); and William Dalrymple, "Inside the Madrasas," *New York Review of Books* 52, no. 19 (2005).

18. Dalrymple, "Inside the Madrasas."

19. Ibid.

20. For penetrating contemporary comment on Muslims in India, see *Islam and Muslim Societies: A Social Science Journal* 2, no. 1 (2006).

21. These grim statistics are confirmed by articles such as Ayub Khan's "Are Indian Muslims Destined to Become a Permanent Underclass?" (www.markpersaud.ca [June 6, 2006]).

22. See Somini Sengupta, "Report Shows Muslims near Bottom of Social Ladder," *New York Times*, November 29, 2006; and Khalid Hasan, "Report Finds Indian Muslims Lagging Behind," (Lahore) *Daily Times*, November 30, 2006.

23. See Sir Sayyed, *An Essay on the Causes of the Indian Revolt*, translated from Urdu (Allahabad, 1873); and *Loyal Muhammadans of India* (London: 1860).

24. Metcalf, *Islamic Revival in British India*, p. 315.

25. Mohammed Ali Jinnah, *Speeches of Quaid-i-Azam Mohammed Ali Jinnah as Governor General of Pakistan* (Karachi: Sind Observer Press, 1948), pp. 9–10.

Chapter Three

1. Thomas L. Friedman, *The World is Flat: A Brief History of the Twenty-First Century* (New York: Farrar, Straus and Giroux, 2005).

2. Amy Chua, *World on Fire: How Exporting Free Market Democracy Breeds Ethnic Hatred and Global Instability* (New York: Doubleday, 2003).

3. Evelyn Howell, *Mizh: A Monograph on Government's Relations with the Mashud Tribe* (Oxford University Press, 1979), p. xii.

4. For an insightful insider's analysis of the complex politics of Pakistan dominated by the military, see Husain Haqqani, *Pakistan: Between Mosque and Military* (Washington, D.C.: Carnegie Endowment for International Peace, 2005); for an authoritative outsider's view, see Stephen Philip Cohen, *The Idea of Pakistan* (Brookings, 2004).

5. Ali Waqar, "Pakistan Recognises Islamic Emirate of Waziristan?" (Lahore) *Daily Times*, September 19, 2006.

6. John Masters, *Bugles and a Tiger: My Life in the Gurkhas* (New York: Viking, 1956), p. 161.

7. Madeleine Albright, *Madame Secretary: A Memoir* (New York: Hyperion, 2003), p. 469.

8. Nicholas Schmidle, "Migration Season: The Taliban and Their Expanding Influence in Pakistan," NES-4 Pakistan (Hanover, N.H.: Institute of Current World Affairs, June 2006).

9. Ibid.

10. BBC, January 21, 2003.

11. Amineh Ahmed, *Sorrow and Joy among Muslim Women: The Pukhtuns of Northern Pakistan* (Cambridge University Press, 2006), pp. 27–29.

12. For detailed case studies, see Akbar S. Ahmed, *Resistance and Control in Pakistan*, rev. ed. (London: Routledge, 2004; originally published 1991).

13. Muhammad Al-Bukhari, *The Translation of the Meanings of Sahih Al-Bukhari*, translated by Muhammad Muhsin Khan, vol. 8 (Egyptian Press and U.S.C-MSA Compendium of Muslim Texts, 1959), bk. 73, no. 2.

14. Ibid.

15. Shaykh Muhammad al-Ghazali, *A Thematic Commentary on the Qur'an*, translated by Ashur Shamis (London: International Institute of Islamic Thought, 2000), p. 58.

16. Glenn Kessler, "Musharraf Denies Rape Comments: Recording Shows *Post* Article Correctly Quoted Pakistani President," *Washington Post*, September 19, 2005.

17. Mukhtaran Mai, *In the Name of Honor: A Memoir* (New York: Simon & Schuster, 2006).

18. For an account of the nawab and the Bugti tribe, see Akbar S. Ahmed, "Trial by Ordeal among Bugtis: Ritual as a Diacritical Factor in Baloch Ethnicity," in *Marginality and Modernity: Ethnicity and Change in Post-Colonial Balochistan*, edited by Paul Titus (Oxford University Press, 1996).

19. Sylvia Matheson, *The Tigers of Baluchistan* (Oxford University Press, 1975; repr. 1999).

20. (Lahore) *Daily Times*, August 29, 2006.

21. United Nations Development Program Report, "Nigeria 2006" (www.ng.undp.org/documents/nigeria-delta-hdr.pdf).

22. United Nations High Commissioner for Refugees, "Profile of Internal Displacement: Nigeria 2004" (www.unhcr.org).

23. For excellent studies of Somalia, see I. M. Lewis, *A Modern History of the Somali: Nation and State in the Horn of Africa* (Ohio University Press, 2002), and I. M. Lewis, *Saints and Somalis: Popular Islam in a Clan-Based Society* (Lawrenceville, N.J.: Red Sea Press, 1998). Lewis was writing about Somalia in general, not the Islamic courts. On warlords in Afghanistan, see Christina Lamb, *The Sewing Circles of Herat: A Personal Voyage through Afghanistan* (London: HarperCollins, 2002).

24. See, for example, BBC News, July 11, 2006.

25. Anne Penketh and Steve Bloomfield, "U.S. Strikes on al-Qaida Chiefs Kill Nomads," (London) *Independent*, January 13, 2007.

26. Ahmed, *Sorrow and Joy among Muslim Women*, pp. 27–29.

Chapter Four

1. For details, see Sandra Salmans, "The Muslim Awakening of the West," *Trust* (Pew Charitable Trusts) 9, no. 2 (2006).

2. Kissinger came to advise and guide the White House "at least once a month," confessed Cheney to Bob Woodward, "and I probably talk to Henry Kissinger more than I talk to anybody else." Bob Woodward, *State of Denial: Bush at War, Part III* (New York: Simon & Schuster, 2006), p. 406.

3. See, for example, Helen Caldicott, *The New Nuclear Danger: George W. Bush's Military-Industrial Complex* (New York: New Press, 2004). For an insider's perspective, see John Dean, *Conservatives without Conscience* (New York: Viking Adult, Penguin Group, 2006).

4. Coleman/Bartlett's, "Washington Focus," September 29, 2006.

5. For background on the neocons, see "Neoconservatism: Empire Builders," *Christian Science Monitor* (www.csmonitor.com/specials/neocon [June 2005]).

6. Francis Fukuyama, "The End of History?" *National Interest*, Summer 1989.

7. For a penetrating examination of the neoconservative ideology and other strains of U.S. foreign policy thinking since the end of the cold war, see Robert Merry, *Sands of Empire: Missionary Zeal, American Foreign Policy, and the Hazards of Global Ambition* (New York: Simon & Schuster, 2005).

8. Thomas L. Friedman, *The Lexus and the Olive Tree: Understanding Globalization* (New York: Farrar, Straus and Giroux, 1999); Friedman, *The World Is Flat: A Brief History of the Twenty-First Century* (New York: Farrar, Straus and Giroux, 2005).

9. Paul Wolfowitz, speech at Army/Navy Club, Washington, D.C., November 15, 2004 (www.worldsecuritynetwork.com).

10. Bill Kristol, "It's Our War," *Weekly Standard*, July 24, 2006.

11. David Frum and Richard Perle, *An End to Evil: How to Win the War on Terror* (New York: Random House, 2003) p. 9.

12. Thomas H. Etzold and John Lewis Gaddis, eds., "PPS/1: Policy with Respect to American Aid to Western Europe," *Containment: Documents on American Policy and Strategy, 1945–1950* (Columbia University Press, 1978), p. 103.

13. NSC-68, 1950 (www.fas.org).

14. For more on the construction of American security after World War II, see David Campbell, *Writing Security: United States Foreign Policy and the Politics of Identity* (University of Minnesota Press, 1998).

15. National Security Strategy of the United States (www.whitehouse.gov [2002]).

16. Wolfowitz, speech at Army/Navy Club.

17. Edward W. Said, *Orientalism* (New York: Penguin Books, 1978).

18. See, for example, M. Shahid Alam, *Challenging the New Orientalism: Dissenting Essays on the "War against Islam"* (North Haledon, N.J.: Islamic Publications International, 2006). Alam's first chapter, "Bernard Lewis: Scholarship or

Sophistry?" is a vigorous assault on contemporary Orientalists, whom he links to the prominent neocons.

19. Michael Hirsh, "Bernard Lewis Revisited," *Washington Monthly*, November 2004.

20. Ibid. See also Peter Waldman, "A Historian's Take on Islam Steers U.S. in Terrorism Fight," *Wall Street Journal*, February 4, 2004.

21. Cheney's shared view with Lewis and his power over world events leading to the Iraq war and after were uncovered as early as 2003. See cover story, "How Dick Cheney Sold the War," *Newsweek*, November 17, 2003.

22. Frum and Perle, *An End to Evil*, p. 273.

23. Francis Fukuyama, *America at the Crossroads: Democracy, Power, and the Neoconservative Legacy* (Yale University Press, 2006).

24. Francis Fukuyama, "After Neoconservatism," *New York Times Magazine*, February 19, 2006.

25. Marghoob Quraishi, "Neocons in Washington," *Geopolitics Review*, Fall 2003.

26. Charles Krauthammer, "The Truth about Torture," *Weekly Standard*, December 5, 2005.

27. Daniel Pipes, "Fighting Militant Islam, without Bias," *City Journal*, Autumn 2001.

28. Daniel Pipes, Associated Press, October 18, 2001. See also Robert Spencer, "Dr. Daniel Pipes and CAIR's Lynch Mob" (FrontPageMagazine.com [July 23, 2003]).

29. Charles Krauthammer, "The Truth about Daniel Pipes," *Washington Post*, August 15, 2003.

30. Pipes, Associated Press, October 18, 2001.

31. See Ian Buruma, "Tariq Ramadan Has an Identity Issue," *New York Times Magazine*, February 4, 2007, and Deborah Solomon, "Singing a New Song," interview with Yusuf Islam, *New York Times Magazine*, January 7, 2007.

32. Angel Rabasa, Cheryl Benard, Peter Chalk, C. Christine Fair, Theodore Karasik, Rollie Lal, Ian Lesser, and David Thaler, *The Muslim World after 9/11* (Santa Monica, Calif.: RAND, 2004).

33. Ayaan Hirsi Ali, *The Caged Virgin* (New York: Simon & Schuster, 2006); Irshad Manji, *The Trouble with Islam Today: A Muslim's Call for Reform in Her Faith* (New York: St. Martin's Press, 2005); Asra Q. Nomani, *Standing Alone in Mecca: An American Woman's Struggle for the Soul of Islam* (San Francisco: HarperSanFrancisco, 2005).

34. Andrew Bostom (FrontPage Magazine.com [July 5, 2006]).

35. See www.isufirock.com.

36. See www.muslimsforamerica.us and www.muslimsforbush.com.

37. Asma Gull Hasan, *Why I Am a Muslim: An American Odyssey* (Canada: HarperCollins Thorsons/Element, 2004).

38. See Roger Hardy's series, "Europe's Angry Young Muslims," BBC World Service, broadcast in March 2006 and available online.

39. Akbar S. Ahmed, *Postmodernism and Islam: Predicament and Promise*, rev. ed. (London: Routledge, 2004; originally published 1992), p. 157.

40. Ibid., pp. 155–57.

41. One of the first steps we took as commissioners was to define our subject by coining the term "Islamophobia," which since has gained international currency. On the unfolding of these trends, see Akbar S. Ahmed, "Postmodernist Perceptions of Islam: Observing the Observer," *Asian Survey* 31 (March 1991); Ahmed, "World without Honor?" *World Today* (London: Royal Institute of World Affairs, 1998); Ahmed, "Islam's Crossroads," Cross Current, *History Today* (London, 1999); Adam Lebor, *A Heart Turned East: Among the Muslims of Europe and America* (London: Little, Brown, 1997); Philip Lewis, *Islamic Britain: Religion, Politics and Identity among British Muslims* (London: I. B. Tauris, 1994). On interfaith initiatives, see Akbar S. Ahmed, "Salman Rushdie: A New Chapter" (London) *Guardian: Review*, January 17, 1991; Ahmed, "Islam Is a Religion of Tolerance," Podium: From a Lecture Given by the Fellow of Selwyn College at London's Liberal Jewish Synagogue, (London) *Independent*, January 13, 1999; Shahed Sadullah, "Akbar Ahmed's Away Win against Salman Rushdie," (London) *News International*, January 24, 1996; Sadullah, "Akbar Ahmed's Unique First in Interfaith Dialogue," (London) *News International*, May 21, 1996; Sadullah, "Lord's Book Launch Marks New Point in Search for Lasting Relationship between Islam and the West," (London) *News International*, February 19, 1999. For the recommendations of the Runnymede Trust highlighting the prejudice against Muslims see *Islamophobia: A Challenge for Us All* (London, 1997).

42. See, for example, "Condemnations of the Luxor Massacre," reported on *The World at One*, BBC Radio 4, November 18, 1997; also Malise Ruthven, "Islam in the Media," in *Interpreting Islam*, edited by Hastings Donnan (London: Sage Publications, 2002), p. 55.

43. The pejorative term "Paki," broadly used by racists for all Asians, nonetheless derived from "Pakistani."

44. See also Pew Global Attitudes Project, July 14, 2005 (pewglobal.org).

45. The lines, he said, came from M. Fethullah Gülen, *Criteria or Lights of the Way* (London: True Star, 1998), p. 19.

46. M. Fetullah Gülen, *Sufism: Emerald Hills of the Heart* (Rutherford, N.J.: The Light, 2004), p. v.

47. Grant Slater, "Speaker: Education Key to Curbing Extremism: Experts on Islam, Other Religions Sound Off," *Oklahoma Daily*, November 6, 2006.

48. Yusuf al-Qaradawi, *The Lawful and the Prohibited in Islam*, edited by Ahmad Zaki Hammad and translated by Kamal El-Helbawy, M. Moinuddin Siddiqui, and Sayed Shukry (Islamic Book Service 1982; originally published 1960).

49. For revealing insights into Arab media, see Emirates Center for Strategic Studies and Research, Abu Dhabi, *Arab Media in the Information Age* (London: I. B. Tauris, 2006).

50. "Arab Satellite Television: The World through Their Eyes," Special Report, *Economist,* February 24, 2005.

51. See, for example, Samantha Shapiro, "Ministering to the Upwardly Mobile Muslim," *New York Times Magazine,* April 26, 2006.

52. St. Augustine, *The City of God* (New York: Random House Inc., 1950), p. 113.

53. Pervez Musharraf, *In the Line of Fire: A Memoir* (New York: Simon & Schuster, 2006).

54. For more insight into the president's struggles, see ibid.

55. Nina Shea, "On the Line: Textbook Intolerance in Saudi Arabia," Voice of America interview, June 3, 2006.

56. See the interesting discussion on the Arab world by the distinguished Indian diplomat Talmiz Ahmad, *Reform in the Arab World: External Influences and Regional Debates* (New Delhi: India Research Press, 2005).

57. For a full explanation from bin Laden himself, see "Bin Laden's Letter to America," *London Observer,* November 24, 2002.

58. Ibid.

59. For Ibrahim's worldview when he was in office, see Anwar Ibrahim, *The Asian Renaissance* (Singapore: Times Books International, 1996).

60. Akbar S. Ahmed, *Pukhtun Economy and Society: Traditional Structure and Economic Development in a Tribal Society* (London: Routledge and Kegan Paul, 1980).

61. The following themes were also presented by Ibrahim during his lecture at the Berkley Center, Georgetown University, October 19, 2006. Ibrahim cites Iqbal frequently in *The Asian Renaissance.*

62. Ibrahim, *The Asian Renaissance.*

63. For his own ideas, see Nuh Ha Mim Keller, *Becoming Muslim* (Amman: Wakeel Books, 2001).

64. For Anwar's ideas, see M. Syafi'i Anwar, "The Development of Progressive-Liberal Islam in Indonesia: Challenges and Opportunities," paper presented at the International Seminar on Progressive Islam and the State in Contemporary Societies, Institute of Defence and Strategic Studies, Singapore, March 7–8, 2006.

65. See Indonesian Survey Institute, "Support for Radical Religious Attitudes and Behavior" (Jakarta, 2006).

66. Amineh Ahmed Hoti, "A Journey to Understanding: Reflections from Indonesia" (www.pakistanlink.com [May 26, 2006]).

67. Akbar S. Ahmed, *Jinnah, Pakistan and Islamic Identity: The Search for Saladin* (London: Routledge, 1997).

68. Philip Woodruff, *The Men Who Ruled India: The Guardians* and *The Founders* (New York: St. Martin's Press, 1954).

69. Anthony Kirk-Greene, *On Crown Service: A History of HM Colonial and Overseas Civil Service, 1837–1997* (London: I. B. Tauris, 1999); Kirk-Greene, *Symbol of Authority: The British District Officer in Africa* (London: I. B. Tauris, 2005).

70. Akbar S. Ahmed, *Resistance and Control in Pakistan*, rev. ed. (London: Routledge, 2004; originally published 1991), p. 35.

71. Supporting facts and figures in the discussion about the *Jinnah* film will be found in the detailed audit report of the entire project prepared in 2000 by Brown, McLeod and Berrie, the accountancy firm based in Cambridge, and published in the press. For the professional opinion of the lead actor Christopher Lee about the director of *Jinnah*, see Christopher Lee, *Tall, Dark and Gruesome* (London: Midnight Marquee Press, 1997); Christopher Lee, *Lord of Misrule: The Autobiography of Christopher Lee* (London: Orion, 2003). For an authoritative overview of the controversies of the time, see Masood Haider, "Pakistan's Treatment of Intellectuals," *Pakistan Link*, January 25, 2002.

72. Lebor, *A Heart Turned East*, pp. 142–45.

Chapter Five

1. Samuel P. Huntington, "The Clash of Civilizations?" *Foreign Affairs* 72 (Summer 1993).

2. See Thomas L. Friedman, *The Lexus and the Olive Tree: Understanding Globalization* (New York: Farrar, Straus and Giroux, 1999), p. xix.

3. For a recent analysis of new trends in reality television and its capacity to re-create aspects of social identity and consumer lifestyle, as well as to change ordinary people into celebrities and celebrities into ordinary people, see Dana Heller, *Makeover Television: Realities Remodelled* (London: I. B. Tauris, 2006).

4. Jonathan Sacks, *The Dignity of Difference: How to Avoid the Clash of Civilizations* (London: Continuum 2002), pp. 106–07.

5. See Paul Vallely, "UN Hits Back at U.S. in Report Saying Parts of America Are as Poor as Third World," (London) *Independent*, September 8, 2005.

6. See Alkman Granitsas, "Americans Are Tuning Out the World," *YaleGlobal*, November 24, 2005.

7. Brook Noel with Art Klein, *The Single Parent Resource* (Los Angeles, Calif.: Champion Press, 1998).

8. For a vivid account of the vapid mind-set and behavior of the "me" globalization generation, see Tom Wolfe, *I Am Charlotte Simmons* (New York: Farrar, Straus and Giroux, 2004).

9. See the game's website, LeftBehindGames.com.

10. Jose Antonio Vargas, "Way Radical, Dude: Now Playing: Video Games with an Islamist Twist," *Washington Post*, October 9, 2006.

11. See Steven Peacock, ed., *Reading 24: TV against the Clock* (London: I. B. Tauris, 2006).

12. Paul Farhi, "Calling on Hollywood's Terrorism 'Experts,' Homeland Security Chief Compares Reality and '24,'" *Washington Post*, June 24, 2006.

13. Khalid Hasan, "Fox Show Demonises Muslims," (Lahore) *Daily Times*, January 19, 2007.

14. Dave Gilson, "Michael Savage: America's Laziest Fascist" (Salon.Com [May 20, 2004]).

15. Deborah Tate, "U.S. Senator: 'Outraged by the Outrage' over Iraqi Prisoner Abuse, Capitol Hill" (VOAnews.com. [May 12, 2004]).

16. Bob Drogin, "Most 'Arrested by Mistake': Coalition Intelligence Put Numbers at 70% to 90% of Iraq Prisoners, Says a February Red Cross Report, Which Details Further Abuses," *Los Angeles Times,* May 11, 2004.

17. Max Blumenthal, "Conservative Ann Coulter Describes Muslims as Ragheads; Senate Leader Ducks Comment" (http://rawstory.com/news/2005 [February 10, 2006]).

18. Ellison replied that his constituents "know that I have a deep love and affection for my country. There's no one who's more patriotic than I am, and so you know, I don't need to . . . prove my patriotic stripes" (cnn.com transcript, November 14, 2006). To illustrate America's long history of religious tolerance when he joined the U.S. Congress, Ellison took the oath of office on Thomas Jefferson's Quran.

19. Jimmy Carter, *Palestine: Peace Not Apartheid* (New York: Simon & Schuster, 2006).

20. See Robert Greenwald, *Outfoxed: Rupert Murdoch's War on Journalism,* a documentary film produced in 2004 that shows media empires have been running a "race to the bottom" in television news.

21. Andrew J. Bacevich, "What's an Iraqi Life Worth?" *Washington Post,* July 9, 2006.

22. Hanna Rossin, "Younger Graham Diverges from Father's Image; Ministry's Patriarch Accepted Islam, but His Son Condemns the Religion," *Washington Post,* September 2, 2002, p. A3.

23. Alan Cooperman, "Anti-Muslim Remarks Stir Tempest; Leading Evangelicals Back Baptist Preacher," *Washington Post,* June 20, 2002, p. A3.

24. Richard N. Ostling, "Jerry Falwell Calls Islam's Prophet a 'Terrorist' in Television Interview," Associated Press, October 3, 2002.

25. Richard Leiby, "Christian Soldier: Lt. Gen. William Boykin Is Inspiring Faith in Some and Doubt in Others," *Washington Post,* November 6, 2003, p. C1.

26. For incidents quoted, see Council on American-Islamic Relations website.

27. "Distrust of Muslims Runs Deep in U.S.," Reuters report, (Lahore) *Daily Times,* December 3, 2006.

28. Richard Saunders, *Poor Richard, 1734. An Almanack for the Year of Christ 1734* (Philadelphia: Yale University Library), p. 349.

29. David Hackett Fischer, *Washington's Crossing* (New York: Oxford University Press, 2004) p. 379.

30. See www.quoteland.com/author.asp?AUTHOR_ID=288.

31. Sean Loughlin, "Rumsfeld on Looting in Iraq: 'Stuff Happens,'" CNN (www.cnn.com/2003/US/04/11/sprj.irq.pentagon/ [Saturday, April 12, 2003]).

32. Bob Woodward, *State of Denial: Bush at War, Part III* (New York: Simon & Schuster, 2006), p. 134.

33. "Putin Jabs Bush: 'We Certainly Would not Want . . . the Same Kind of Democracy as They Have in Iraq,'" in *Think Progress* (http://thinkprogress.org/2006/07/15/putin-jab/[July 15, 2007]).

34. Ryan Lenz, "Soldier Pleads in Iraq Rape, Murder Case," Associated Press, November 15, 2006.

35. Robert H. Reid, "Videotape Alleges Three U.S. Soldiers Killed in Revenge for Rape-Murder," Associated Press Worldstream News, July 11, 2006.

36. Jason Tedjasukmana, "Indonesia's Skin Wars," *Time*, April 10, 2006.

37. Philip Hitti, *History of the Arabs* (New York: St. Martin's, 1970), p. 363.

38. Indeed, Woodward, *State of Denial*, revealed Kissinger to be one of President Bush's top foreign policy advisers.

39. Ayaz Amir, "Unintended Consequences," (Karachi) *Dawn*, August 4, 2006.

40. Saad Eddin Ibrahim, "The 'New Middle East' Bush Is Resisting," *Washington Post*, August 23, 2006.

41. Clayton E. Swisher, *The Truth about Camp David: The Untold Story about the Collapse of the Middle East Peace Process* (New York: Nation Books, 2004), pp. xxi–xxii.

42. John Mearsheimer and Stephen Walt, "The Israel Lobby: Does It Have Too Much Influence on U.S. Foreign Policy?" *Foreign Policy* 28, no. 6 (2006); Scott Ritter, *Target Iran: The Truth about the White House's Plans for Regime Change* (Emeryville, Calif.: Nation Books, 2006).

43. David Wallechinsky, "The World's Ten Worst Dictators," *Washington Post*, January 22, 2006.

44. Ibid.

45. Kenneth Pollack, *The Persian Puzzle: The Conflict between Iran and America* (New York: Random House, 2004), p. 83.

46. Elton L. Daniel, *The History of Iran* (Westport, Conn.: Greenwood Press, 2000), p. 160.

47. Dafna Linzer, "Past Arguments Don't Square with Current Iran Policy," *Washington Post*, March 27, 2005.

48. Karen Armstrong, *The Battle for God: Fundamentalism in Judaism, Christianity and Islam* (London: HarperCollins, 2000), p. 249.

49. Ibid., p. 251.

50. Pollack, *The Persian Puzzle*, pp. 93–94.

51. Armstrong, *The Battle for God*, p. 251.

52. Ibid., p. 256.

53. Pollack, *The Persian Puzzle*, p. 127.

54. Since then Carter has developed as a sensitive world-class statesman, as is evident in Jimmy Carter, *Our Endangered Values: America's Moral Crisis* (New York: Simon & Schuster, 2005).

55. Pollack, *The Persian Puzzle*, p. 183.

56. Efraim Karsh, *The Iran-Iraq War 1980–1988* (Oxford: Osprey, 2002), p. 44.

57. Pollack, *The Persian Puzzle*, p. 198.

58. Karsh, *The Iran-Iraq War*, p. 57.

59. Michael Dobbs, "U.S. Had Key Role in Iraq Buildup," *Washington Post*, December 30, 2002.

60. Ibid.

61. See Seyed Mohammed Khatami, "Dialogue among Civilizations and Cultures," in *After Terror: Promoting Dialogue among Civilizations*, edited by Akbar S. Ahmed and Brian Forst (Cambridge: Polity Press, 2005).

62. See the idea and practice of "the Karbala paradigm," which predisposes the Shia to fighting injustice and tyranny through personal sacrifice, in M. J. M. Fischer, *Iran: From Religious Dispute to Revolution* (Harvard University Press, 1980).

63. Robert H. Reid, "For Iran, Defiance So Far Has Had Little Cost," Associated Press Worldstream News, September 19, 2006.

Chapter Six

1. Akbar S. Ahmed, *Discovering Islam: Making Sense of Muslim History and Society* (London: Routledge, 2002; originally published 1988).

2. For the rest of the poem, see Akbar S. Ahmed, *More Lines: Selected Poems* (Karachi: Royal Book Company for Pakistan Academy of Letters, 1980), pp. 37–40.

3. In a rare display of editorial candor, *Washington Post* devoted its lead editorial of October 26, 2005, to Vice President Dick Cheney under the banner headline, "Vice President for Torture." The conclusion of the hard-hitting editorial was: "In other words, the vice president has become an open advocate of torture."

4. Akbar S. Ahmed, *Jinnah, Pakistan and Islamic Identity: The Search for Saladin* (London: Routledge, 1997); Stanley Wolpert, *Shameful Flight: The Last Years of the British Empire in India* (Oxford University Press, 2006).

5. Rajmohan Gandhi, *Eight Lives: A Study of the Hindu-Muslim Encounter* (State University of New York Press, 1986), p. 178.

6. Anthony Giddens, *Runaway World: How Globalization Is Reshaping Our Lives* (New York: Routledge, 2000), p. 34.

7. Jonathan Sacks, *To Heal a Fractured World* (London: Continuum, 2005).

8. United Nations Population Division, *World Population "Prospects": The 2004 Revision* (http://esa.un.org/unpp.index.asp [January 22, 2007]).

Epilogue

1. On January 2, 2007, Nafees and I found ourselves at the National Cathedral as part of the funeral service for President Gerald Ford. Senior Rabbi Bruce Lustig and I were officially listed as "Representatives of Faiths," and we joined

the procession to escort President Ford's casket as it entered the cathedral (www. cathedral.org/cathedral/pdfs/FordFuneral.pdf). Nafees and I were seated alongside the choir and, as it happened, I was seated three to four feet behind the pulpit from where the eulogies were delivered by both President George H. W. Bush and his son, President George W. Bush. "Remember this extraordinary day, my child," I said after the ceremony to Nafees, who was now active in the interfaith movement and had opened the first ever Abrahamic society at Walt Whitman High School in Bethesda. "Thanks to our friend Bishop John Chane, we took part in American history, and as he wished to honor us we were seated within a few yards of five American Presidents—and several future ones." The spirit of healing, forgiveness, and compassion that suffused President Ford's service would, I knew, stand Nafees, a teenager facing a long and troubled century, in good stead.

INDEX

Abacha, Sani (president of Nigeria), 107

Abbasid Empire, 220

Abduh, Muhammad, 36, 41, 224

Abdullah (king of Jordan), 70, 93–94

Abdullah (king of Saudi Arabia), 230

Abu Bakr (friend of Muhammad; first caliph), 44, 97, 98, 141, 209. *See also* Muslims—role models

Abu Ghraib (Iraq prison), 3, 41, 128, 195, 201, 203. *See also* England, Lynndie

Abyssinia, 106–07

Adalet ve Kalkinma Partisi (AK Party; Justice and Development Party; Turkey), 155, 229

AEI. *See* American Enterprise Institute

Afghanistan: anarchy in, 5, 91, 109, 128; bin Laden, Osama, and, 89–90, 176; deaths in, 162; globalization and, 86; Islamic models in, 39–40; meaning of, 85; Muslim views of, 3, 10; Operation Mountain Storm and, 87; Our Voices Together and, 260; Pakistan and,

174; solutions for, 225; Soviet Union and, 153, 168; Taliban in, 89, 91, 109, 176–77; television in, 91–92; tribes in, 91, 93, 95, 177; U.S. and, 4, 10, 88, 95, 137, 168, 258–59. *See also* Al-Qaeda; Taliban

Africa, 10, 106–16

Aga Khan University (Karachi, Pakistan), 167

Agence France-Presse, 113

Ahmadinejad, Mahmoud (president of Iran): Israel and, 9, 226–27; media presentation of, 240; as president of Iran, 240; religious beliefs of, 242; speech before the UN, 241; U.S. and, 171, 194, 226–27, 261, 239; worldview of, 240. *See also* Muslims—role models

Ahmed, Abdullahi Yusuf, 112, 114

Ahmed, Akbar: definition and views of Islam, 187–92, 248–51; family of, *ix–x*, 154, 248–49; "Jinnah Quartet" and, 190–92; September *11, 2001,* and, 6–8; in the U.K., 152, 153; views of, 3, 21, 46–47, 81, 128–29, 130–39, 159, 187, 196–97;